The Dyslexia Empowerment Plan

The
DYSLEXIA
Empowerment
PLAN

A Blueprint for Renewing
Your Child's Confidence and
Love of Learning

Ben Foss

Ballantine Books 🏠 New York

The Dyslexia Empowerment Plan is a guide to helping children understand their dyslexia, gain confidence in themselves, and figure out what they need to thrive in the world. Although it includes a number of specific suggestions, The Dyslexia Empowerment Plan is not a one-size-fits-all program and must be read with your child's individual situation in mind. In particular, neither this nor any other book can replace the advice you may receive from an attorney who is knowledgeable about applicable law and familiar with your school-age child's background.

As of press time, the URLs displayed in this book link or refer to existing websites on the Internet. Random House, Inc., is not responsible for, and should not be deemed to endorse or recommend, any website other than its own or any content available on the Internet (including without limitation at any website, blog page, information page) that is not created by Random House. The author, similarly, is not responsible for third party material.

Published in the United States by Ballantine Books,
an imprint of The Random House Publishing Group,
a division of Random House LLC, a Penguin Random Company.

BALLANTINE and the HOUSE colophon are
registered trademarks of Random House LLC

The National Center for Learning Disabilities Checklist is excerpted from
The Dyslexia Toolkit. Copyright © 2013 by National Center for Learning
Disabilities, Inc. All rights reserved. Reprinted with permission.
For more information, visit www.LD.org.

HEADSTRONG NATION is a registered trademark of Ben Foss.

Intel® Reader is a registered trademark of Intel Corporation.

LIBRARY OF CONGRESS CATALOGING-IN-PUBLICATION DATA
Foss, Ben.
The dyslexia empowerment plan : a blueprint for renewing your child's
confidence and love of learning / Ben Foss. — First edition.
pages   cm
Includes bibliographical references and index.
ISBN 978-0-345-54123-9 (hardback)—ISBN 978-0-345-54124-6 (ebook)
1. Dyslexia. 2. Dyslexic children—Rehabilitation. 3. Parents of
children with disabilities. I. Title.
RJ496.A5F67 2013
618.92'8553—dc23   2013023931

Printed in the United States of America on acid-free paper

www.ballantinebooks.com

2 4 6 8 9 7 5 3 1

First Edition

For Joe Stutts, the father of the movement

CONTENTS

INTRODUCTION

Some people think being successful when you are dyslexic means "overcoming" dyslexia. Nothing could be further from the truth. By many measures, I have achieved success: I have worked in the White House; I've got a combined JD/MBA from Stanford University; I directed a research group at Intel; I started Headstrong Nation, a not-for-profit organization dedicated to serving the dyslexic community; and now, in the ultimate irony for a dyslexic person, I've written a book.

I know that I've been able to accomplish my goals because I have integrated dyslexia into my life, not because I overcame it. It is part of who I am, just as I am a man and I am from New Hampshire. Indeed, I have found that my greatest strengths are directly tied to my most severe weaknesses. It is the process of recognizing my weaknesses and strengths—and connecting them in my life—that has made me successful and, more important, happy.

What I've learned can provide a path to independence for anyone who is dyslexic. It took me almost twenty-five years to fully embrace my dyslexia, and throughout the book you'll follow my journey. My goal is to give you the tools to empower your child so that you can let go of your own fears, opening the door to a successful future for both of you. If I had had these tools when I was growing up, I would have started the integration process much earlier and skipped years of debilitating shame.

This book is not like anything else you have read about dyslexia or specific learning disabilities, the legal category under which services for us dyslexics are provided. Whereas most other books or "experts" will promise a cure for your child, I'm here to say that the real truth is that there is no disease. In the mainstream dyslexics are the minority, but that doesn't make us less valuable. We just do things a little differently. To use a commercial metaphor, it's like we're Macs, whereas the majority of people are PCs. This book—and your mission as a parent—is about moving the model for your child from dyslexia as disease to dyslexia as identity, an identity we can all be proud of.

WELCOME TO DYSLEXIA

Whether your child is on the cusp of being identified or you've known about his dyslexia for quite some time, I say welcome to the club! It's safe here, and you can let go of your fear and anxiety about this identification. Believe me, I know how you feel. I was there and so were my parents, and I can tell you with 100 percent certainty that it will get better. Indeed, you're going to have fun. That may seem overly optimistic, but I am confident that if you work through the steps in this book, your child will reclaim her joy of learning and you will both thrive.

There are countless accomplished people who are already in this club today. They are successful academics, win Nobel Prizes, make major contributions to the arts, and are at the top of the medical, legal, and business worlds. They are cops and firefighters and pilots. They are teachers and authors, entrepreneurs and filmmakers. In short, they are able to do whatever they want once they master a few simple rules of success. Whether you are dyslexic yourself, the parent of a dyslexic child, or both, know that you are not alone. This book will show you the path to figuring all of these rules out for yourself, your child, and your family.

Regardless of cultural or economic differences, I feel a great sense of community with everyone who is dyslexic. It's like we grew up in the same place, the same country—the Nation of Dyslexia. We have a shared experience, a connectedness, and it's palpable when we are together. Many of us have the same strengths (exceptional auditory or verbal skills, or the ability to think strategically) and the same weaknesses (such as reading poorly). Dyslexia is part of more than 30 million Americans—one in ten of us. Every time your child gets on the school bus and there are fifty people on that bus, there are likely five other kids who are dyslexic.

In the Nation of Dyslexia, nobody spells well. There's no good handwriting. But we're great listeners and often good public speakers. I like to think we are fun at parties. We work harder than many of our mainstream peers. Yet my emigration into mainstream culture does not mean I have to divorce myself from my dyslexic attributes. If you're from another country and immigrate to the United States, you will likely want to adopt some American customs. But you won't completely leave your homeland culture—the food, the dance, the work ethic, the holidays—behind.

Everyone in Dyslexia carries a passport that allows easy entry into a number of bordering countries, including the nations of Dyscalculia, Dysgraphia, and ADHD, to name some of the major ones. In my view, we are all "in the club"—my catchphrase for the broad family of people who experience the non-obvious disabilities generally housed under the umbrella term of "specific learning disabilities." Your child may hold dual citizenship with one of these. For example, 40 percent of people from ADHD are also from Dyslexia, though the opposite is not the case, as there are more dyslexic people than ADHD folks. All of us share a common bond, a common history. When I hang out with ADHD people I get them, I understand their profile, and I may even have some of their characteristics. I have used the term *dyslexia* throughout this book, but the lessons are for people from all these nations and I consider them all kindred spirits based on our overlapping experiences.

I've also learned through my dyslexia that every one of us—including mainstream readers—lives on a spectrum of strengths and weaknesses. Some people can run a marathon in three hours (few), some can walk a mile (most), some can't make it out of a chair (few again). Depending on your context, those facts can matter more or less. Franklin D. Roosevelt could not walk a mile yet became president of the United States, so no single weakness tells the full story. Not every child who has difficulty reading or spelling is dyslexic, but there are a set of characteristics that unite this profile. For example, I'm ambidextrous: I play sports lefty, and I do everything else righty. That is a characteristic that you could predict as likely based on my dyslexia. When I meet someone from Dyslexia, dollars to donuts they have some form of cross laterality or are left-handed. And that's just one of dozens of characteristics that are associated with this profile, ranging from an ability to see patterns fast to a lack of ability to associate a sound with a letter symbol.

One of the most important characteristics associated with dyslexia is entrepreneurial thinking. Indeed, 35 percent of American entrepreneurs are dyslexic. I have found that discussing dyslexia and the path to independence in terms of this unique characteristic invites people from all economic and academic backgrounds to realize the strengths that come with their profile. All dyslexics can connect with their inner entrepreneur, regardless of their field of interest, so that they can capture that spirit of making change and use it to fulfill their dreams.

Your child is already a part of this world. Yet in order for your child to get the most out of his or her profile, you'll need a handbook that helps you get around. This is particularly true if you are not a resident of Dyslexia yourself. This book is that guide.

THE GOOD NEWS: THERE IS NO CURE, BECAUSE THERE IS NO DISEASE

Most schools and reading programs designed for remediation of dyslexia are based on the idea that dyslexia equals brokenness. Their aim is to transform the child into a person who can read without problems. But I'm here to tell you that's just wrongheaded. I've learned that if you make your primary goal teaching your child to read or spell just like every other child, you're going to decrease your child's chances of achieving success. It's like telling a person in a wheelchair that she needs to put in more time to learn how to walk.

Even the most well-intentioned parents will be tempted to look for signs that their child is "cured" and no longer dyslexic. I can imagine that it's your dearest hope that your child won't have to spend a lifetime contending with a world not built for him. Some parents will even deny that their child's school has accurately identified the problem. "My kid loves books, so dyslexia can't be the issue," they often argue. The truth, however, is that the dyslexic kids who "love" books do so because they associate books with intelligence and as a way to demonstrate their love of learning. The dyslexic child who claims to love books is smart; he's looking for camouflage in the only intellectual context he knows.

There are three types of reading: eye reading, ear reading, and finger reading. A child with dyslexia will never eye-read as well as his peers, and that, I hope to reassure you, is fine. Yet all children need to be exposed to vocabulary and ideas to be successful in school. If your child was blind, providing text as audiobooks or Braille would allow her to read with her ears or with her fingers. No one would ever claim that a blind person was lazy or stupid for not reading text with her eyes. When I listen to audio, that's ear reading. When I speed it up to four hundred words a minute, four times the pace of standard speech—a skill you can learn about in this book—I am leveling the playing field for me. It's not what the mainstream conceives of as reading. But it's ear reading. It's learning. It's literacy.

I am introducing these terms to address an underlying bias in our schools: that eye reading is the only form of reading. You can help move the needle on this limited assumption by using the terms *eye reading*, *ear reading*, and *finger reading* yourself and explaining them to your child. We need to celebrate a child's love of ideas and quest for knowledge and give her permission to not like standard books at the same time! When we give kids opportunities to gather information and explore ideas in other ways, they will thrive.

Eye reading is what children are taught in school, but it is no better than ear or finger reading in terms of information absorption or comprehension. In fact, each reading approach has both benefits and challenges. Whether you walk on two feet or use a wheelchair to get around, the goal is to get from one place to another. No matter if you roll or walk, you will still get there; indeed, you can get there faster in a chair if you know what you are doing and the landscape is conducive to it. Focusing on eye reading overlooks the real goals of education, which are learning, independent thinking, and mastering the ability to make new connections in the world of ideas.

I will concede that eye reading is a valuable skill, and given it is the default for most education, it has a built-in benefit that ear and finger reading do not, but that is a social choice we make. Just as being able to walk up stairs is useful because many buildings do not have ramps, eye reading is useful because it is the standard way into printed material. If we got rid of all stairs, then being in a wheelchair could be a benefit, e.g., allowing you to roll through a marathon is easier than running it. However, the key point is that none of these choices is inherently better, but we choose to make one more favored. The trick is then to learn how to avoid putting a moral judgment on a social choice.

A dyslexic person may be able to get through one page of text in six minutes of eye reading, while mainstream people do it in one, but if they can access the information in one minute with their ears, that is a better path.

A central theme in this book is that we must question what we are taught is the "normal" way to do things, and instead integrate multiple ways for our children to access information. *The Dyslexia Empowerment Plan* redirects the drive to fit in toward learning in the best way possible. As a parent, you can confidently embrace the notion that while your child may not love eye-reading books, he is going to love learning just as much as you do, if you can match his educational needs with the skills he has.

DON'T FORGET TO HAVE SOME FUN

Parents can easily become fixated on the long-term goal for their child: receiving an appropriate education. Yet it's equally important to take a step back and remember that your child is still a kid, and he should be able to enjoy all that childhood entails. Don't turn every weekday into a long series of tutoring sessions and every weekend into catch-up time for homework. Make sure that your child is developing hobbies that he enjoys and not merely as a way to prove that he is competent. What's more, take time for yourself. You are doing exactly what you are supposed to be doing just by thinking through these issues carefully and doing research. Knowing this should give you the space to put aside some of your anxieties and perhaps even take in a movie or go camping now and again. The worst thing you can do is try to deal with dyslexia by forfeiting the rest of your life.

NEW TOOLS, SAME CHALLENGES

In many ways it's easier to be dyslexic in today's world than ever before, mostly because of advances in computers and speech technology. In 2013, there's more computer power packed into the cell phones in students' backpacks than there is sitting on teachers' desks. The acceleration of microprocessor power is making things such as optical character recognition and speech recognition ubiquitous. We see it with Siri, the speech application used in Apple's iPhone, or the speech functions on Android smart phones. These fancy new devices allow you to talk into your phone and have your speech converted into text or read back to you. They aren't presented as "assistive technology." They're just cool. And, more important, they are helpful. If you are a dyslexic person or the parent of a dyslexic child, I recommend that you allow technology to become your new best friend.

My motto has always been that necessity is motivating, but frustration is the real mother of invention. When I got to graduate school, it took three weeks for my university to convert my textbooks to digital text so I could listen to the assignments (ear reading) using a computerized voice. This frustration led me to invent the Intel Reader, a handheld electronic device that can take a photo of any text and read it aloud on the spot, a device CNN called "too groundbreaking to ignore." As of this writing the Reader is still shipping and costs about $550, though technology moves fast and it may soon be replaced with new and even better tools. Again, this device doesn't help me or anyone else overcome dyslexia, but it does let dyslexics into the world of books and other printed materials. More important, it gives me independence. When I use it, I don't have to rely on any institution or individual to help me do my job. It also gives me on-the-go access to very fast speech technology. Later in this book I'll explain why and how your child should learn this skill, but for you to understand how different my reading world is from that of a mainstream eye reader, it's worth checking out a demonstration of me using super-fast speech. The website for the nonprofit I started (www .headstrongnation.org) has a demonstration. You'll hear how differently a dyslexic brain can process audio, and it will give you context for the rest of the book. For me, reading a book in the traditional way is like listening to a bad cell phone connection, but speech technology is like a landline: the transmission of information is clear and crisp.

Yet even with access to the most advanced technology, it is still as hard as ever to be dyslexic. Larger class sizes are making it difficult for teachers to individuate instruction and work with children one-on-one. School systems are becoming more test-driven, and budget cuts make them more rigid in the way they approach teaching. This is partly due to the No Child Left Behind Act of 2001, which specifies that in order to receive federal funding, schools must prove that their students are meeting educational standards. Because of mandates, both public and private schools are forcing kids into narrower categories of acceptable behavior, and teachers respond by focusing on fewer ways to teach, which ultimately gives students fewer learning options.

When I was eight, the terms *dyslexia* and *specific learning disabilities* were relatively new to the educational landscape, and dedicated "special ed" classes were not common. My dad, who is not dyslexic, remembers going to a meeting with my teachers and, because he had never heard the word, asking, ironically, "Dyslexia? Can you spell it?" My school had recently received government funding for special ed classes, and the administration offered this option to my parents, who agreed to the school's suggestion that I join special ed. Being sent to a different classroom for special help was sometimes uncomfortable for me, but my parents were all for it if it might help me.

Today, being in the special ed classroom or working with its curriculum often carries a tremendous stigma. Some parents would rather not place their child in an alternative classroom, preferring to avoid the label, even if their child isn't succeeding in a mainstream setting. The sign on the classroom door isn't the relevant issue. What's most important is that you and your child can ask for the tools she'll need to succeed.

WHAT DYSLEXIA LOOKS LIKE

I love being dyslexic because I like my brain. If your bright, engaged, and engaging second grader starts receiving D's and begins getting into fights and acting out to distract the teacher, it may be that, like me, he has an identifiable specific learning disability.

Brain science has proven that dyslexia is not the result of bad parenting, poor schooling, or any sort of social or psychological shortcoming. It is a distinct physiological characteristic relating to brain function. It's only recently that neuroscience can show us through imaging exactly how different the dyslexic brain is, as you can see on the scans on page xx. Dyslexia manifests in the temporal parietal region of the brain, shown in those images, as well as in the angular gyrus, which is deep inside the brain and not shown here. These areas, among others, are where research suggests automatic language processing happens.

In *The Dyslexic Advantage,* authors Brock and Fernette Eide propose that dyslexia is also rooted in different brain activity patterns. The Eides cite research indicating that dyslexics rely more heavily on the right brain, the side that excels at seeing the big picture rather than the details. Interestingly, in research conducted in 2003, Guinevere Eden and colleagues determined that all readers begin using both sides of the brain when learning to read, but that most (i.e., those who are not dyslexic) eventually shift that activity to the left side of the brain, while dyslexics do not.

Dr. Manuel Casanova at the University of Louisville School of Medicine, a researcher the Eides interviewed, found that in the dyslexic brain, the cortices—the layers of cells that form the outer part of the brain—are of a different character compared to the cortices of non-dyslexics. In dyslexics, mini-columns—conglomerates of neurons that are arranged vertically—found in various parts of the cortices are connected by longer axons than they are in non-dyslexic brains. And length of axons is generally predictive of certain abilities: shorter axons usually correlate to a better ability to process fine detail and distinguish nuance in the specifics of symbols and sounds. By contrast, longer axons correlate with a better ability to see large connections and concepts at play. Casanova argues that this means that dyslexic brains are inclined to be stronger at big-picture thinking and weaker at processing fine details.

The Eides explain this complicated science in terms of the classic metaphor that dyslexics can see forests with ease (the big picture) but struggle with trees (the details), and this fits with my personal experience. The first activities in which children are intellectually evaluated at school are "tree" activities: spelling, reading, doing math. "Forest" learning—putting these skills to use to think through larger concepts—comes later for most kids (and certainly later in most school curriculums). But brain research now suggests that dyslexics are apt to see forests first and are going to struggle with mastering tree-level learning. Yet seeing the whole picture all at once can be a very powerful form of conceptualization. When I came up with the idea for the Intel Reader, I was sitting in my office playing with my flatbed scanner and laptop when it occurred to me that the cell phone sitting on my desk had all the elements—a camera, a microprocessor, and a speaker—that I would need to point the device at some text, have the text recognized and processed, and listen to the text converted to speech. In about three seconds, I just saw the whole thing: a general design involving an ultra-mobile motherboard, optical character recognition, and text-to-speech software. I also understood the impact of thermal dynamics (the device could not be too hot to hold) and the ergonomic design (it had to feel friendly in your hand) on user interaction. But if you asked me how to create any specific component of the design—for example, how to write a particular line of code, or how to route a trace on the motherboard—I'd be at a loss. Still, I could see the whole and could articulate the big picture, and today I am named on five U.S. patents for the invention of the underlying new technologies for the Intel Reader. This forest-seeing vision is a common way of thinking among entrepreneurs, and one central to their success.

Eye reading, for me, is like washing clothes with a scrub board and a bar of homemade soap, whereas most people own the latest model of washer. However, if you want to talk about a different activity, say speaking in public, then the metaphor shifts: I have a top-of-the-line sewing machine, while most others are getting by with a needle and thread. I also have an exceptional language capability. I can be pithy or loquacious, and I have an elaborate—at times downright baroque—vocabulary. At the same time, I can't spell any of these words. Heck, I might misspell *spell*.

I wish I could have seen and understood these elements of the brain when I was young and struggling to fit in, because the brain images clearly show what I've found out to be true: that no matter how hard you try, you can't change who you are. Seeing the picture of my dyslexic brain was incredibly powerful for me. The key to my happiness occurred when I stopped trying to change my brain, and started changing the context around me.

DISPELLING THE SHAME OF DYSLEXIA

When we launched the Intel Reader it was considered an incredible piece of technology. It was a handheld computer that had one of the smallest PC motherboards possible and ran on the latest Intel microprocessor. It had optical character recognition, text-to-speech, a

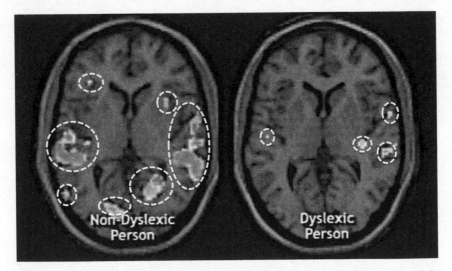

In the functional magnetic resonance images (fMRI) above, brain activity while reading is shown in the areas highlighted with dashed circles. The brain of a typical reader is on the left, and my brain is on the right. As you can see in these images taken at Stanford Medical School, when I'm reading, my brain shows low activity in the language areas, including the temporal parietal lobes, which sit on both the left and right sides of the brain.

high-resolution screen, and eight hours of battery life, as well as an Intel brand to make it familiar. Yet there was still a problem: the major barrier to adoption was that people didn't want to admit that they couldn't read the way everyone else did. While we sold many to schools and to institutions, individual sales were less strong. Dyslexic people were nervous about being seen as different just by using it. John Chambers, the CEO of Cisco Systems, Inc., offered them for free to all 100,000 employees. One would expect that there were at least 10,000 dyslexic people in the company, based on the national percentage of occurrence. To my knowledge, no dyslexic took him up on it. That was when I realized that the only way to address the underlying caution about identifying publicly as dyslexic was to remove the shame we were all carrying.

Shame is a feeling that you are unworthy because of something you are. It is different from guilt, which is feeling bad about something you did, such as stealing or cheating. Even today, my ability to read is in the bottom 15 percent compared to the rest of the population. I'm also in the bottom 1 percent when you ask me to identify any letter that you put in front of me. When I was little, the school staff's overall response to my reading issues was, "Try harder; try this reading method, or this one." When I didn't get the results they were looking for, I concluded it must be because I was lazy or stupid. I desperately wanted to be seen as competent, so I accepted their model and tried to fit in. Privately, I thought I was a bad person, that I was the only one who could not read or spell well. To say that it took me years to unwind those shameful feelings is a gross understatement. The goal of this book is to help your child avoid this experience.

As you begin to unpack the story of your child's dyslexia, it's very likely that you're going to encounter some unexpected surprises. This is deep emotional water and you should proceed cautiously. I'll do my best to give you signposts and help you find the right path for you and your family. Given that dyslexia is genetic, it's highly likely that other members of your family may have a similar profile. Perhaps you yourself or your sisters or brothers might fit this profile. I've seen many instances in which people who were never given this identification find themselves resetting their concept of who they are, as well as examining their fundamental relationships in their family (e.g., who was the smart brother or the pretty but not academic sister). Just by reading this book you may be unlocking powerful feelings in the process, including potential anger, resentment, or fear, which is why it is so important not to rush through this material.

The shame surrounding the term *specific learning disabilities* or *dyslexia* is deeply rooted. My friend Giano attended an elementary school in San Francisco where the teachers placed top readers in the Eagle group, the next best in the Hawks, after that the Crows, the Sparrows, and finally the group for the poorest readers: the Chickens. If a kid was hardworking, the assumption went, he would read faster and be promoted to the next-better bird group. But this ladder is based solely on one skill. I can't imagine that there was one child who was placed in the Chicken group who didn't find it insulting to be associated with a flightless bird. It also overlooks the larger reality that every child has strengths and weaknesses, and by choosing only one standard of measurement, it limits all learning and forces kids to judge each other.

Many people have great difficulty during their childhood. Some people have experiences that are awful: child abuse, alcoholic parents, and on and on. Gershen Kaufman, PhD, a leading psychological expert on the general topic of shame, believes that the level of shame associated with reading disabilities "often matches, in intensity, the shame experienced over incest." I was floored when I read this, but it was the first description that got to the core of the experience I see within the community. One dyslexic friend of mine described his shame as "slow-drip trauma." He felt unworthy and "not normal" every day. As an adult, he was treated for Post Traumatic Stress Syndrome that was caused by his experiences in school. You can get your child on the path to avoiding this just by working through this book.

But what is normal? I avoid the word in all contexts, as it carries a lot of hidden values and moral judgments, made-up ideas about how the world should work. When someone is presented as "not normal" in the context of eye reading, that turns into "not normal" in the larger context of school. Eye reading is seen as an innate skill necessary for schoolwork. When a child's life is centered on the school day, being seen as a failure in this one skill can be the defining experience of a young person's life. If you are terrible at a core life activity, in this case reading in school, you begin to assume you must be the problem, and you hide it. That is shame.

Children absorb the models of who they should be from three primary sources: their parents, their peers, and their teachers. For the majority of dyslexic children, the odds are that peers will mock and teachers will not understand, thus it is critical that a parent is strongly supportive and seen as taking the child's side if he is to avoid the shame associated with this profile. Moreover, if a person feels shame in one area deeply, it can spread to other, non-related areas. For example, if a woman thinks her body is not attractive, she may decide that she is also not good at conversations, or feel shame about having a loud laugh. The same is true for a dyslexic child. If he is unhappy with his eye reading, he may decide, wrongly, that he should feel shame over his athletic ability, or his ability to tell a joke. Ironically, those skills may be strong and could be a bridge out of shame, but if the root cause is not addressed, the whole child can be affected.

What's more troubling is the fact that there is a correlation between self-loathing and self-injury. I know firsthand; I did some terrible things to my body when I was growing up. I developed a series of ways of embracing risk in order to make myself successful. I was a soccer goalie. I was a public-speaking champion. I was a downhill ski racer. I picked high-pressure hobbies, and subconsciously I taught myself how to handle risk. I achieved a lot: MVP in the state championships in soccer and captain of the state-championship-winning downhill racing team in high school, among others. These were markers of success that I desperately needed to buoy my confidence. But at such a cost! In the process of achieving these successes I did a lot of damage to myself physically. I've broken my knees; I've broken

my spine, twice; I've broken my hands. I had five concussions my senior year in high school and punctured a lung. But all this damage is
even more interesting when I mapped it to the rest of my life. Ninety
percent of my injuries happened when I was in school and before I
was talking about my dyslexia publicly. This may seem a jarring contrast with the successes I've mentioned, but sadly, the self-damage
phenomenon is real for many children. When I talk with my peers in
the dyslexia movement, a majority of them had a specific plan for
suicide when they were teenagers. I am fine today, but the hiding left
scars, figurative and literal, for many of us.

Shame is also incredibly time-consuming, a luxury even the most
facile readers don't often have. When I got to college, I hid my disability by faxing my term papers home to my mom to have her read
them to me over the phone so I could find my spelling errors. I was
unwilling to let my classmates know that I was having difficulty with
tests. This hiding took extraordinary effort: it sucked up huge
amounts of energy, emotion, and money, both for me and for my parents. If I had had the tools presented later in this book, I could have
saved many hours every day and, more important, done this work on
my own. But twenty years ago, shame kept me from looking for community or telling the world what was really going on with me.

So I know full well that if I could change one single thing about
dyslexia right now, I would alleviate shame and make everyone who
is dyslexic feel positive about him- or herself. I would do that long
before I would change your child's ability to eye-read. That's because
she could think for the rest of her life, "I can read well now, but I hate
myself over the fact that I was called lazy and stupid." And that's not
healthy. I'd much prefer your child to say, "I like myself. It's going to
be fine. I just need a different path to learning." Since I "came out"
and started talking about my profile openly, I have been much
healthier—not to mention saving a lot of money on medical bills!

Your child will be happier and healthier if she integrates her dyslexia into her self-concept, and this book will help you help her do

that. You'll learn how to bypass shame altogether so that your child can thrive, now and for years to come.

HOW THIS BOOK WORKS

Just by starting this book, you've shown that you're someone who cares. Your child is already in a better situation than most kids with disabilities, particularly kids with dyslexia, because you are taking the time to read this. It's not that this book is a magic bullet. It's because you are putting in the effort to learn and support your child.

Part I of the book shows you how to identify your child's profile and help her understand who she is. This will involve getting a formal identification, one that schools and testing agencies will honor. You will also learn to map your child's strengths and weaknesses, and to play to her strengths while supporting her weaker areas. You will also be taught to identify the attitudes that most often lead to success in the long term, and help your child develop them. We will explode some of the myths of dyslexia and get you the real facts on what the science and research tell us about this profile. The underlying goal is to set you up to take on the central challenge of dyslexia in the context of the mainstream world: shame.

Part II focuses on teaching your child how to tell others about dyslexia so that he can get the help he needs to succeed, first at school and then in other areas of life. Your role is to teach your child that he has a voice and, while he is small, to support that voice by speaking up for him when necessary. As soon as possible, you want your child to learn to advocate for himself. Every moment that he is speaking for himself with knowledge and ease, he is greatly increasing the chances that he will have a better life. You will teach your child to develop resiliency, and equip him with metaphors and stories that will help him get the resources he needs. You will learn that your child is not broken, and recognize that if the educational system she is currently in is set up in a way that allows her to fail, it is very possible that the system itself needs an overhaul.

In Part III of the book, you'll learn how to change the system that you're working with, especially if your child is not getting the help she needs. You will also meet some role models you can look to when it comes to forming community and thinking entrepreneurially.

Along with this book, you can go to my nonprofit's website, www.headstrongnation.org, to take advantage of the interactive features. On the website you'll find two distinct types of references. The first are a handful of links, mentioned right in the text of the book, that will enhance your understanding of an example or key point—for example, the demo of fast speech I mentioned earlier (you really should go see it before starting the next chapter). The second are the resources that you can use to develop your own plan and set of accommodations for your child. Many of these have demo videos as well, but they can be viewed after you are done with a section of the book. The website also contains additional content, not found in this book, to help you find community, the most important antidote to shame.

Dyslexia is a non-obvious attribute, invisible not only to outsiders (no one looks dyslexic) but also to the person him- or herself. We dyslexics do not know what we are missing out on because we do not have access to the mainstream ways of doing things. In order to correct for this, we have to rewrite the script for learning and make dyslexia obvious to the world and to ourselves. It is that rewriting of your child's history and, thereby, your child's future that is our project together. Let's get started!

A NOTE ON MY DYSLEXIA AND WRITING

I have found that people have a hard time believing my dyslexia when they see only the final product of my written work. These days, I generally speak to a computer and use Dragon Naturally Speaking to have it transcribed, greatly increasing my speed and accuracy when writing. For this book, that material went through four rounds of edits, including structural, copy and proofing, further polishing the material. Below is the first few paragraphs of this book written as I would write it in raw format. In this case, I listened to the text and transcribed it without the benefit of spell check or word correction now standard in most word processors. I publish it to let you see "behind the curtain." Yes, I am dyslexic for life and proud. Consider this my native tongue.

INTRODUCTION

some people thisn being successful means overcoming dyslexia. Nothing could be further from the truth, By many measures I have achieved success. I have worked in the white house. I ve got a combined JD/MBA from standorf university. I directed a research group at Intel. I started Headstrong Nation, a not for profit dedicated to helping the dyslexic community. An now, in the ultimate irony I have written a book. I know that I have been able to accomplish my goals because el have integrated dyslexia, not because I overcame it. It is is part of whi OI am. Just as I am a man and I from New Hampshire. Indeed I have found that my my greated strengths are directly tied to my most sever weakenesses. It is the process of of recognixing my weaknesses and strengths and connecting them in my life, that has made me successful. And more important happy.

What I have leanred can provide a path to independence for anyone who is dyslexic. It too me almore almost twenty five years to full emplrace my dyslexia. My goal is to give you the tool to empower you to eplower you child so that you can let go of your own fears, openning the door to a successful future for both of you. I f have day the tools when I was growing up, I would have started the integration process nd skipped years of shame.

This book is not like any other book you have read about dyslexia or specific learning disabilities or the legal catagoy under service which dyslexia are provides. Whereas most other book or experts will promise a cure for your child. I ma here to say that the real turht is that ther eis no disease. In the mainstream dyslexix are the minoroty. But that does not make use less falauable. We just do things a littel differently. To use a commercial metaphor, where as the majority of people are PCs. This books, and your mission as a parent is about moveing the model for you child from dyslexia as disease to dyslexia as identifty. An identity we can all be proud of.

PART I

KNOW *the* FACTS

CHAPTER ONE

Embrace Your Child's Profile

My friend Steve Walker, a very successful dyslexic entrepreneur, tells me all the time that you could not pay him enough money to go back to any type of school setting. He even says that he would sooner kill himself than go back to school. Yet in the same breath he will also say that you could not give him enough money to take away his dyslexia, because it is a part of who he is. Many times when I was in school or taking a standardized test, I rejected an accommodation because I was embarrassed and ashamed: I did not want to stand out, or I was frustrated that it would take too much effort to get permission to have my exam read aloud to me. Sometimes the shame runs so deep that a child wants to get away from it all entirely. In 2010, an eight-year-old boy in Texas who was having trouble reading jumped out a second-floor window of his school to get away from the teasing he endured for being "different." He survived relatively unscathed (a bush cushioned his fall), but his story illustrates the lengths some of us will go to escape the shame and embarrassment we feel about being "not normal." If you can help your child learn to embrace himself for who he is at a young age, you will avoid much of the pain Steve, the boy in Texas, and I endured. For these reasons, it's crucial that everyone in your family embrace the child's learning profile.

These stories illustrate the dark side of how some schools handle dyslexia. The majority of teachers and administrators are well-intentioned and look for ways to help your child. However, they often miss the most important point, which is that the goal is not to fix your child—your child is not broken. The goal is, instead, to play to your child's strengths, support his weaknesses, and give him access to information.

Throughout this book I've tried to provide you with a realistic picture of how school officials are likely to behave. My hope is that you'll have great teachers and a wonderfully cooperative administration, but I also want you to be prepared in case you have to deal with schools that are not cooperative, or even downright hostile to the idea that your child has a right to a free and appropriate education.

Once you've moved past the idea of brokenness, dyslexia remains difficult to define. Oddly, there is no clear agreement among experts as to what constitutes dyslexia. Here is my definition, based on the latest science and my personal experience with the community:

> Dyslexia is a genetic, brain-based characteristic that results in difficulty connecting the sounds of spoken language to written words. It can result in errors in reading or spelling as well as in a number of areas not considered major life activities, such as determining right and left. Individuals who are dyslexic can be highly independent and intelligent. Dyslexia is also characterized by a set of strengths that typically come with this profile in one or more of the following areas: verbal, social, narrative, spatial, kinesthetic, visual, mathematical, or musical skills. Overall, it is characterized by an increased ability to perceive broad patterns and a reduced ability to perceive fine detail in systems.

Throughout this book I use the word *dyslexia* to describe a range of specific learning disabilities (SLDs) that include dysgraphia (difficulty with handwriting and written communication), dyscalculia (difficulty with mathematical formulas), dyspraxia (kinesthetic and motor impairments), and central auditory processing disorder (difficulty interpreting speech). The underlying experience of shame and being an outsider is quite uniform across the populations of people with SLDs, as well as for children who have been identified as having attention deficit/hyperactivity disorder, either on its own or accompanying any of these other profiles. Even within the specific family of dyslexia, there is a tremendous range of what this profile can look like. This is true for our weaknesses as well as our strengths. If your child does not fit exactly into any of these definitions, it is still possible that his school would consider him to have an SLD (often referred to as "learning disorder not otherwise specified"). The fundamental challenge is that if you look up *dyslexia* or any of these other terms in the *Diagnostic and Statistical Manual of Mental Disorders*, you will find a definition for a host of disorders that make people "not normal"—but there is no clinical definition of "normal."

The definition of dyslexia I give above is most useful when interpreted in light of your child's specific context. At different ages or in different social contexts, people will have different expectations of your child's skills. For example, when he is three years old, no one is checking on his reading skills, and therefore no disability is perceived. Similarly, when he is a teenager and singing the lead in the school musical, the disability is not apparent. But on a third-grade spelling test or on the SAT, it is a major issue.

The most important factor to consider is your child's age. Below I've outlined four age groups and listed the consequent contextual factors that you need to consider. Keep in mind that this is a broadstrokes analysis; the more-detailed work you'll do in Chapter Three and the formal identification you will seek after working through Chapter Seven will tell you more about how you should proceed. For example, an eight-year-old who was only recently identified as dyslexic but who exhibits high levels of resiliency will require a different set of strategies than a twelve-year-old who was identified as dyslexic at the age of seven but has a mind-set that orients her toward thinking she is broken.

Ages 8 and younger: Children in this age range are still considered by mainstream standards to be learning how to read. On the positive side, this means that your school will be interested in improving standard eye reading and may be willing to make resources available. On the other hand, the school may delay providing accommodations or interventions, claiming that it is unclear that your child has a disability.

Ages 9 to 12: In this age range, most mainstream schools will assume that your child has mastered reading, and they will expect her to begin using that skill to learn other subjects. If she is two or three grade levels behind in reading, this will put her at a significant disadvantage relative to her mainstream peers. It is likely that she has internalized that she is a bad reader (and is therefore carrying the shame that she is a bad person), and you'll need to put extra attention into rewriting the scripts that she plays in her own head about her competency and worth.

Ages 13 to 17: Dyslexia can often be discovered later in a child's academic career if he has become particularly adept at avoiding detection, or if his schools have not put in the time and attention to identify his learning profile.

Ages 18 or older: It is surprisingly common for students to be identified as dyslexic for the first time when they make the transition to college or to a work environment. Coping strategies that they have built in order to hide their dyslexia or to help them catch up in a weak area may no longer work when the bar for academic achievement or professional output is raised.

There is no cookie-cutter formula for approaching your dyslexic child's success. Strategies will shift based on many factors, including how your school is responding, the attitude your child has, what strengths your child has, and what goals you and your child have. We will map these factors in the next few chapters to help you tailor the general rules to your child.

Different experts in this field will use less holistic definitions of dyslexia than the one I offered above. In legal terms, and for the purposes of receiving accommodations in a public school, dyslexia falls under the category of "specific learning disabilities" as laid out in the Individuals with Disabilities Education Act (IDEA) of 1990. This is the law that established funding for special education in the United States. You'll learn more about this law in Chapter Seven. An updated version of the definition of SLD was inserted into the law in 1997 and reads as follows:

(A) IN GENERAL.—The term "specific learning disability" means a disorder in one or more of the basic psychological processes involved in understanding or in using language, spoken or written, which disorder may manifest itself in imperfect ability to listen, think, speak, read, write, spell, or do mathematical calculations.

(B) DISORDERS INCLUDED.—Such term includes such conditions as perceptual disabilities, brain injury, minimal brain dysfunction, dyslexia, and developmental aphasia.

(C) DISORDERS NOT INCLUDED.—Such term does not include a learning problem that is primarily the result of visual, hearing, or motor disabilities, of mental retardation, of emotional disturbance, or of environmental, cultural, or economic disadvantage.

If you find yourself a little perplexed by this language, you're not alone. The definition has the sound of something designed by committee. It first appeared in law as part of the Children with Specific Learning Disabilities Act, which was part of the Elementary and Secondary Education Amendments of 1969. The same definition has been tweaked slightly since then and folded into IDEA. It does not give us a specific definition of dyslexia per se, instead associating it with a very broad range of other learning phenomena. The category of "brain injury" has nothing to do with the experience of being dyslexic, but was thrown in there in order to try to preserve a right to inclusion for a broad range of children. In this definition, dyslexia is characterized as a "disorder," as opposed to a characteristic. The word *disorder* suggests that something is "wrong" or that the person is broken. However, disability can be defined only in a particular context, which is to say if there was no such thing as written text, there would be no disability related to reading. Finally, the law tacks on a list of things that are *not* specific learning disabilities, a clunky artifact of the legislative process that is analogous to explaining that an apple is "a fruit that is not an orange, a banana, a kumquat, a watermelon, a strawberry . . ."

A somewhat better definition is offered by the International Dyslexia Association:

> [Dyslexia] is characterized by difficulties with accurate and/ or fluent word recognition and by poor spelling and decoding abilities. These difficulties typically result from a deficit in the phonological component of language that is often unexpected in relation to other cognitive abilities. . . . Secondary consequences may include problems in reading comprehension and reduced reading experience that can impede growth of vocabulary and background knowledge.

This definition is still less than perfect. It focuses only on the weaknesses and relies on a lot of jargon, such as "decoding abilities." In this context, that term refers to a specific skill set associated with eye reading.

Regardless of how you technically define dyslexia, the fears and the myths that often accompany it remain largely the same. Let's look at some of the most common fears.

IDENTIFYING FEARS

Now that you have a better idea about what dyslexia is—and is not— the best way to dissolve the shame that can surround it is by identifying the fears both children and parents have that are related to it. You might not even have the right language to express your fears yet, but as you read through those I have collected and listed here, some (or all) may speak to you. Articulating or owning up to a fear is the first step toward eliminating it.

I Fear That My Child Is Less Than Perfect

Often people discuss dyslexia in terms of it having been *diagnosed*, but that word reinforces the notion that dyslexia is a disease, a scourge, an imperfection, and that someday we can find a cure. As I said in the introduction, there will be no cure because there is no disease! Dyslexia is a characteristic, like being male or female, or from a certain state, or a graduate of a certain university. There's nothing less than perfect inherent in any of those descriptions, is there? You can start changing this practice in your own house today, replacing the phrase "*diagnosed* with dyslexia" with "*identified* with dyslexia."

Semantics aside, this worry over imperfection runs deep. Parents often are afraid to formally identify their child as dyslexic because they don't want to confront the idea that they did not notice the issue themselves. They feel they have been imperfect protectors for their child. If your child's identification as dyslexic has been surprising for you, seeming to come out of left field, you are not alone. The typical four- or five-year-old dyslexic child has been humming along, nailing developmental milestones (walking, talking, drawing) and generally doing fine. He or she may be athletic and sociable and even show an aptitude for learning. Yet once reading or writing is introduced, you seem to have another child entirely; dyslexia sends the entire household into whiplash as all family members go from expecting normalcy to bracing for disappointment.

When the news arrives in first or second grade that your otherwise perfect child is "slow to read," you may have initially heard that as just "slow," that is, not as good as the other children or, worse, stupid. This identification *should* sound like "Your child needs glasses," but instead, because we are so invested in "normal," you may have heard it as "Your child is broken and will never be like you." She is not broken and will learn to love learning if you arm her with the right information and tools.

The other component to this fear is the worry about what other people will think. In one recent national survey by Roper Worldwide, a national polling company, 51 percent of people in the United States agreed "that sometimes what people call specific learning disabilities are really just the result of laziness and are not disabilities." As a result, many parents will hide any suspicion they have about problems their child might be having because they want to avoid the stigma of the label "special ed" or "specific learning disability."

Another common reaction is to not even tell the child about her dyslexia as a way to protect her from the negative associations this terminology can have in the classroom and from the negative feelings this can stir up. Some parents tell teachers not to mention it, or even home-school their kids to get them out of a system based on labels. If this describes you, I understand where you are coming from, but at the same time you need to understand that you are doing your child a disservice. Labels are useful to the degree that they describe a cluster of characteristics that allow you to predict the future. Accurately defining a child as dyslexic is a useful piece of information. Letting a child know only that he is a poor reader, or a "special person" with "differences," can be much more damaging.

Think of it this way: if you are going on a hike, knowing the destination and the conditions you'll face will help you prepare for the trip. If you are going hiking in monsoon season in India, that's a very different hike than if your itinerary was in the desert, and you need different equipment for each locale. Ignoring the conditions will make everyone's life harder. So, just as it's important to identify where you'll be hiking, it's important to identify what challenges your child is facing, so that you can get the right tools to make the journey smoother. Moreover, children are smart. They know when there is a problem, and if you can talk to them directly about it using some of the techniques outlined in this book, you will be able to remove the shame associated with the label, rather than avoid the label and leave the shame.

I Fear That My Child Isn't Smart

I see this particular fear with parents all the time. Often, this is a fear that parents can't quite admit to having, even to themselves, but it's evident in their body language and attitude. The truth is, dyslexia is not about intellect. Dyslexia is a physiological characteristic. We dyslexics have a specific issue with interpreting text, and that is not synonymous with a lack of intelligence.

If your child was blind, would you consider him stupid? Of course not. The entire concept of "smart" is vague and comes from society; it's a word we use to describe a whole bunch of characteristics and to which we all bring our own particular biases. Although it includes academic performance, this is not the only factor. Later in this book you'll learn how to determine your child's strengths and weaknesses, and ultimately how to reject concepts that schools or the society around you wants to impose.

I guarantee that dyslexics such as General George S. Patton and molecular biologist Carol Greider, who won a Nobel Prize in Physiology or Medicine, were told at some point in their lives that they weren't smart, and look how they turned out. I'm not saying that your child is destined to become the next great general or revolutionize science, but your child does have the potential to live up to your hopes and dreams, and come up with a few of his own.

I Fear That My Child's Intellectual Development Will Be Stunted

Many parents worry that without the ability to read with ease, their child will not be able to grow intellectually. This fear stems from the logic that eye reading is the only or the best doorway to a world of imagination, knowledge, and the capacity to make connections that will allow a child to be happy and productive. If you learned through printed material, it's understandable that you might think your dyslexic child will not get the same exposure to ideas and knowledge.

But you can expose people to literacy through any kind of media. Learning and literacy are about ideas, not words on a page, and ideas can be integrated and understood whether the child is hearing them with her ears, feeling them in Braille with her fingers, or reading them with her eyes.

Research tells us that exposing children to language is much more important to their development than forcing them to read with their eyes, and introducing new words is more important to their intellectual development than teaching them how to get those words off the page. That's one of the reasons educators want parents to continue to read to children well past the point where they can usually read on their own.

Children who are dyslexic will often understand and learn information when it is read to them, even if it is at a higher intellectual level. This is the case for all children. The difference is that for dyslexics you need to shift the format to get it into their brain. Their brain is ready to learn; you just have to choose the right path. They will grasp the nuances of imaginative fiction whether it is on the movie screen, through an audiobook, or any other way you choose to share it. Blind people do not read the way that the rest of the world reads, yet we still believe that they are learning when they run their fingers over a Braille version of Shakespeare's poems. In the same way, I am still reading when I listen to audio with my ears.

As a non-standard reader, I am able to have all the same experiences of embracing literature. In addition to audiobooks, I also have those experiences through film or by listening to audio content. Too many parents fixate on the form rather than the experience: "But I want my child to know what it is like to curl up in bed with a great book." He can; it will just be with an audiobook or with a film. And your child will come to enjoy pleasures you do not know, such as the joy of humming through audio at super-fast speeds while getting chores done, or speaking to an audience of hundreds without notes. The written word is not the important part; it's just another vehicle.

I Fear That My Child Will Never Learn to Read

Focusing on learning to read is a necessary part of schooling, and there are some helpful instructional eye-reading programs being used to good effect in schools; you'll learn about them later in this book. Eye reading is a useful skill, and even small improvements will help increase your child's overall independence. However, for a dyslexic child there will be a time when this remediation will no longer be effective. This is when you can focus more on other avenues of learning.

Think of a dyslexic as you might a person who has injured her spine and now needs to use a wheelchair to get around. That person may spend about a year focusing on rehabilitation, getting the most she can out of her body. Then the focus will necessarily shift to accommodation efforts and environmental modifications—putting in wheelchair-accessible ramps and lowering the sinks. In the world of dyslexia, the common practice is to focus indefinitely on reading as the goal even when the focus should clearly move on to other things.

Case in point: Not too long ago I was the honored guest at the president's dinner for the International Dyslexia Association. One attendee approached me and suggested I should come to her summer eye-reading program. "I'll get you reading in no time, Ben," she said. Her heart, like that of so many teachers, was very much in the right place—she wanted independence for me. What she missed was that it was my turning away from eye reading and toward ear reading that had given me that much-needed independence.

Let me put it plainly: I do not eye-read well. Legendary financial investor and businessman Charles Schwab does not read well with his eyes either. There are Nobel Prize winners and Harvard professors who do not read well because of dyslexia. And yet every one of them is successful, thoughtful, and engaged in the world of ideas. Yes, you can get someone to read a little better, but by definition, a dyslexic person will always be at a reading level well behind that of his peers. I might get to the point where I can compete with a fifth grader in terms of eye reading, but I will never match the people who went to law school. The way I was able to show them that I belonged there, and match them intellectually, was to abandon eye reading and embrace *learning*.

Reading is an intensely private, internal experience. As a result, most dyslexics do not know how far behind their reading skills are relative to their peers. For example, I participated in a clinical study of adult dyslexics a few years back and know from this formal testing that I read at one-fifth the speed of a typical college-level reader. So if on average my classmates in law school spent five hours a night reading, I would have had to spend twenty-five hours to cover the same ground if I hadn't used audiobooks. Before I figured this out, I thought I was doing okay, when in fact I just could not see how badly I was lagging. Worse, I thought I should simply try harder, that the problem was me, not the book. This is important to remember when coaching children. Even if they think they are keeping up with their peers, they may not have an idea how far behind they are and will miss that the gap is getting wider as their peers get better at eye reading. It wasn't until I taught myself how to use fast speech technology that I could finally match the reading speed most non-dyslexics achieve. And that is when everything for me changed for the better. I realized right then that I didn't need to read the way everyone else does in order to be successful.

I Fear That My Child Will Not Be Like Me

I once met a woman named Emily who told me that more than anything, she wanted her dyslexic daughter to love books. From our conversation I could see that Emily loved her child very much, and she also placed a high value on reading and education. Emily was an elementary school teacher and was in charge of the English as a Second Language program in her school. Books were a very powerful symbol of knowledge and creativity for her. She wanted to share the joy of reading with her child, and at a deeper level, she wanted her daughter to be successful. But what came through clearly in our conversation was that Emily was hoping for a future of common ground with her daughter through her daughter's mastery of the things Emily loved to do. Once I brought this to her attention, Emily agreed with my theory and was able to focus on her daughter's strengths instead of dwelling on her weaknesses.

The universal truth is that your child is not going to be just like you. He is not going to like all the same music you like, he is not going to like the same food, and, as he gets older, anything that you tell him that you do like, he may go out of his way to reject, for a while, just because you like it! Finding your own path is what growing up is all about. Sure, there'll be periods of mimicking when your child will seem your spitting image. And there will certainly be times of rebellion. But in either case, don't make the mistake of confusing eye-reading skill with intelligence, with work ethic, or with family tradition. Instead, focus on what your child is learning that you are also interested in (not the other way around), and work to find ways that help him continue to learn about what interests him.

I Fear That My Child's Experience Will Mirror My Own

I often hear from parents who fear emerging similarities, rather than differences, between themselves and their child. Dyslexia is a hereditary trait. Parents who had a bad special ed experience are often reluctant to have their child formally identified. The classic scenario is the dad who is dyslexic and the mom who is not. The mother tries to nurture the child, and the father pushes the child to fit in, to be "normal." I have heard of extremes in some households, where the dyslexic parent physically or emotionally reprimands the child for getting bad grades, perhaps playing out his own issues by telling the child she is worthless or stupid. This has a doubly negative effect: not only do the child's grades not improve, but the home becomes a hostile environment, instead of the one place the child might hope to get support. If you or your spouse was in special education or was never identified but felt trauma in school over your own challenges, you can also work with the lessons of this book, breaking down your own shame so that you can form community with your kids.

The fact is that with today's identifications, the special education experience of the past does not have to be repeated. There are wonderful new tools and pathways for your child, and this book will lay them out. Years ago, my mother could not have been admitted to an Ivy League school because they did not accept women. These days, 50 percent of the Ivy League schools have a woman as their president. The lesson is to put the past behind you and focus on your child's future.

I Fear That My Child Will Never Be Independent

When you equate reading with intelligence, it's not a big leap to also equate reading with independence. But of course, the key to independence is not reading but developing resiliency and emotional skills. And resiliency and emotional skills are what's needed to understand that not being able to read well in the traditional sense is not the end of the world. Filmmaker Steven Spielberg, singer Cher, and business executive Richard Branson are all dyslexic. No one could ever say that they are also not independent!

I Fear That My Child Will Never Fit In

Parents intrinsically want what's best for their children, and they often think that means being accepted by the mainstream. No child wants to be perceived as different from her peers either. In order to fit in, dyslexic kids have to work twice as hard just to keep up with the minimum that is expected. They are like ducks moving across a body of water: seemingly relaxed and poised above the waterline, but furiously kicking below. With that metaphor in mind, it never surprises me to hear the great lengths dyslexics go to in order to mask their inability to read or write.

I know a dyslexic man who would go on job interviews wearing a fake cast on his right hand in order to make sure that he didn't have to fill out paperwork, and therefore would not have to disclose his dyslexia. My own defensive technique was to go to interviews for the basic service jobs you get when you are a teenager—parking cars or running a cash register—with a pre-printed resume that I created with my mom. I knew that the prospective employer would hand me a form to fill in and expect me to enter my name, street, social security number, and so on by hand. I knew that I would definitely get some of this information wrong and worried that no boss would hire someone who could not spell his street name or recall the name of his last employer. My gamble was that most employers would see the pre-printed resume and assume that I was "professional." But what I was really doing was masking my disability—and keeping my shame alive by trying to hide who I was.

From birth, society has fitted us each with a kind of suit. I come from a highly educated family and therefore I got handed—figuratively—a tailored suit, a pressed cotton shirt, and Italian shoes, as well as a stack of business cards to hand out. My dyslexic friend Joe Stutts is from rural Alabama and is twenty-five years older than me: he got a set of coveralls and a shovel. Joe went on to fight and win a federal court case that established dyslexia as a disability. I was able to go to law school not because of my suit, but because of what Joe Stutts did for dyslexics. Indeed, I value his contribution so much that I have dedicated this book to him. You will learn more about him in Chapter Nine.

No one fits easily into predetermined roles, but people with dyslexia have an even harder time with their fit. Returning to the suit metaphor, we spend all this time trying to cram ourselves into a pair of too-tight pants. Now, some people will tell you that if you just lost enough weight or had smaller thighs, the pants would fit. But that is a colossal waste of time: instead, just find a different set of pants that are comfortable and functional. Better yet, turn the ones you have into cutoffs, or a flight suit, or even a kilt you can wear proudly!

I Fear That People Are Judging Me

Parents also have a desire to fit into their own peer group. If your friends are casually boasting about their second graders who can read chapter books, it can be hard to say, "My son made great progress naming letters this week!" School administrators have told me about parents ending friendships with other parents who kept trumpeting their kids' success or, worse, parents who put undue pressure on their kids to succeed just so that the parents would not be embarrassed in social situations.

In a perfect world, we would celebrate all children for their strengths, and early chapter book reading would be valued equally with your son's singing ability or your daughter's facility with big puzzles. Unfortunately, when you're talking school, people care more about standard reading proficiency. Through this book you will learn how to recognize all of your child's amazing strengths: verbal wizardry, champion interpersonal dynamics, spatial memory, or, most important, the resiliency that fuels entrepreneurship and the expansion of human potential.

Understanding that you and your child are not alone is the first important step to take on your journey. In fact, internalizing that you are part of a larger community is essential to your child's success in becoming a fully integrated, happy, and independent person. Given that your child is a citizen of the Nation of Dyslexia, you are going to meet many parents just like yourself, and you won't feel so alone.

INTEGRATING DYSLEXIA BEGINS WITH CREATING A SENSE OF COMMUNITY

If you or your spouse is dyslexic, showing that you can embrace that aspect of yourselves and integrate it into your daily activities is immensely empowering for your dyslexic child. Creating this kind of small community in your own family is the single most important thing you can do to help your child. The feelings of shame associated with dyslexia start with the relationships with parents. When a child is young, she believes her parents are infallible. If one of the parents cannot read well and is comfortable with this, he can then say to the child, "We're going to read a book together. I have a hard time with sounding out words, so I have an audio version of tonight's book. We're going to sit and listen to the audio while we read the paper book too." You can start this narrative with your child when she is as young as three or four years old, and certainly introduce it at later ages if it is a new concept to you now. These simple statements and actions can help tremendously with the stigma associated with dyslexia.

If a child is struggling in school, being bullied on the playground, and thinking that she is a bad person for not trying hard enough to read, she needs her home to be a safe space. Coming home to a parent who criticizes her for not trying harder is going to cause her to hide from you and from herself; it is in these lonely times that the worst emotional damage occurs.

I do not take lightly the work that is involved in talking about your dyslexia with your child. I spent the first thirty years of my life hiding my dyslexia, so I know well the urge to do so! It's hard for many people. A good friend who is a national public advocate for specific learning disabilities recently called me in tears when he learned that his own child was dyslexic: he was terrified that the boy would be put through the same harassment he had endured, and even more scared to admit to his son that he was dyslexic as well. Yet he was able to fully face his truth, and now they have a family community around this issue and a tradition of story time with audiobooks that are read aloud to father and son together at home.

If you don't have dyslexia in your immediate family, you may find it just a few steps outside the nuclear group. Again, what's important is to find a community of role models for your child, and these can be dyslexic relatives who are managing life well, or unrelated adults who are dyslexic. One boy I know talked to his grandmother, who said, "Welcome to the club!" and it made him feel better. Visit the website www.headstrongnation.org and you can watch videos of adults and kids talking about their dyslexia, as well as find out about community-building networks.

One of my favorite organizations is called Eye to Eye, a national mentoring program pairing college students who have a specific learning disability (SLD) with younger kids who have SLDs. They partner not only in a community but across communities, developing pen pal programs between mentee groups in different cities, creating a community of students like them all over the world. I have more on their work in Chapter Nine. One of the program coordinators told me that when an elementary school kid in an Eye to Eye program heard about the pen pal program, the child said, "Wait a second . . . You're telling me that there are other kids like us? I thought we were the only ones." I can assure you that even if your child has not verbalized this thought, it is likely how she feels. Kids will not know that special ed exists in every school, or that 35 percent of entrepreneurs are dyslexic, or that someone in the family also has difficulty reading—unless we talk about it with them.

PARENTS SET THE STAGE FOR FUTURE SUCCESS

As parents, your primary goal is to constantly remind your child that everything is going to work out fine, because with your help, it will. I know that sending this message will not always be easy. I come from a highly literate, book-oriented family: my father is a college professor, and my mother has published academic articles. While I have since identified other relatives in my extended family who were dyslexic, the inherited nature of this profile was not well understood when I was growing up, so my parents were not looking for it in me.

One experience my parents had that prepared them for dealing with a "nontraditional learner" was that they had been Peace Corps volunteers and lived in Nigeria for a number of years before I came along. They had enough world experience to know there's more than one way to do almost anything. This philosophy is a major factor in my success, because I have abandoned what people thought was standard. My parents' experience in a different culture allowed them to see my world from my point of view, and for that I will forever be grateful.

My parents always had a concept of me as a worthwhile person. They recognized that dyslexia was not an excuse for bad behavior, and they had standards I had to follow. But when I acted out, hitting another kid in class or yelling at him, they knew to look deeper and see what was happening, rather than assume I was a difficult child with an attitude problem. They knew that I was thoughtful and had ideas to express. They could see that the experience of being dyslexic and being ostracized at school was tearing me apart. They did not believe that I needed to fit into a mold, and that gave them permission to love me for who I was. My mother once told me, "It was very important to me that you come through this whole."

My parents demonstrated this in a number of different ways, both within and outside the context of reading. Their strategy was to support my independence generally and to allow me to be my own person. It showed up even at my first haircut. When I was between three and four years old, my mom took me down to our small-town barber shop, with a striped barber pole out front, worn leather seats, and combs stored in blue liquid. The owner sat me in the chair atop a phonebook, put a cape on me, then turned to my mom and said, "How shall I cut his hair?" My mom, in turn, asked me, "Ben, how do you want your hair cut?" I replied, "I don't want my hair cut." She confirmed with me that I was not interested in a haircut, then offered to pay the owner and suggested we were going to be on our way. Surprised, he said, "You're going to let a three-year-old tell you what to do?" Mom looked at him and replied, "It's *his* hair."

When I was older and increasingly frustrated by my weaknesses at school, my parents thought that getting physical seemed like a good way to deal with it. They took me to all kinds of sports tryouts or activities: volleyball, soccer, lacrosse, and even West African dance festivals. Their strategy was to keep looking for opportunities until I found my passions.

When it was discovered that I was not the fastest kid on the block, they explained that this was something you couldn't change but that you could work with. Instead of giving up soccer altogether, my mom suggested that I should try playing in goal. She noticed that I could move in three-dimensional space well, and we found I excelled in that position. Years later in high school, as a goalie, I would be the most valuable player in the state championship playoffs. But I would have quit soccer because I wasn't fast if my parents hadn't helped me see an alternative path. They realized the importance of being a part of a team, as well as the need for everyone to find something he or she is good at.

Soccer was still not a mainstream sport in the United States when I was growing up, but in Hanover, New Hampshire, the coach had thirteen state titles to his name, and the biggest rivalry for the school was a soccer match with the next town over. Winning that match earned you an above-the-fold photo on the sports section for a paper that covered the surrounding ten towns. And winning the state championships could get you on the front page. Being part of those teams gave me status in high school and made it easier to walk in the doors every morning even though I knew I was going to have the lowest SAT scores in my peer group.

Whenever I found something that was interesting, my parents supported that interest, even if they didn't particularly share it. At one point I got very interested in medieval stuff: warfare, Dungeons and Dragons, the Crusades. I built little model towns and catapults. My dad got down in the trenches, as it were, with me, playing medieval-themed computer games or helping me glue together balsa wood to make a moat spanner that could conquer any miniature fortress.

They also made an effort to examine my learning style, which was incredibly important. When I was in second grade, they hired a private learning specialist to evaluate me after the school had picked up that I was having difficulty with text. The specialist discovered that I was an auditory learner, one who learns through hearing, and my parents made use of that information. Though my father initially frowned on my watching TV, my mother defended it as a key learning tool for me, since hearing and seeing content was easier for me than following words on a page.

I watched lots of Discovery Channel, PBS *Masterpiece Theatre*, and the news. Yes, I watched some *G.I. Joe* and *Transformers* too, but my mother understood that everyone needs a guilty pleasure and she could see that for the most part I was using television to learn. She recognized that I wanted knowledge and saw I could get that from TV. My dad came around to this view and eventually celebrated using alternative ways to learn, even listening to *The Hitchhiker's Guide to the Galaxy* with me in its original radio broadcast form on vinyl record.

Today the debate in many homes will be over time spent playing video games. Like my dad, parents might worry that their child could lose ground to other students because he is gaming all the time. But as my parents learned, it is the nature of the content, not the form, that matters. There are kids' games for the computer that are wonderful learning spaces. Look carefully at what your child is playing. Learn how to play it with him if he will allow you. I am not talking about educational software games that teach spelling, nor am I talking about first-person shooter games. I am talking about games kids like and ones that require learning skills. Are they picking up three-dimensional thinking skills when they play *Minecraft*? Are they working on how to create a budget to delay gratification by investing in digital infrastructure, like in *Roller Coaster Tycoon*? As the years go by, the games will keep changing; in order to understand the gamer in your child, you need to put in the time to learn why he is gaming.

Like me, your child will want to spend some time relaxing with games too. Maybe you read a trashy novel or watch baseball on TV— we all need that kind of relaxation time. But neither you nor I am doing this all the time. Balance will help your child thrive. Most important, if you feel the need to talk to him about making a change— limiting the time he plays those games, for instance—discuss it with him and work together on a change of behavior. A harsh home environment will isolate your child further and lead to the damage to his learning you are trying to avoid. If he feels attacked, he will react, and you will not get the best out of him at home or school.

I feel that my parents did a phenomenal job helping me find ways to be successful and advocating for me. The only area where my mother has regrets about my childhood is that she hung on to the dream of me reading books much longer than she should have. She continued to give me books for my birthday well into my twenties. She was right to help me focus on the skill of reading when I was little. But by fourth grade, most students have moved from learning to read to reading to learn. She was fixated on books as the only form of learning, or at least blind to the degree to which the form was painful for me. It was not until I was twenty-five that I got angry one Christmas morning and set an absolute rule: "No books for Ben. No photography books, no books on travel. I hate books and want them away from me!"

If you are a mainstream reader, you are likely cringing when you read this, subconsciously thinking, "But he will lose out!" Did I? I had a 3.9 GPA in college, was a national finalist for the Rhodes Scholarship, and was invited to Buckingham Palace by the royal family for winning the British Isles Debating Championship. I am hardworking and thoughtful, but I hated books then because I did not have access to them: they were a symbol of everything I could not do. Today my mom realizes that encouraging me to love books was at absolute odds with helping me learn. You shouldn't strive for perfection—no parent is perfect—but understanding fundamental truths about your kids and learning is best for the whole family.

CREATE COMMUNITY WITH YOUR SCHOOL

When I was young, my parents worked in partnership with my school, not only to find accommodations for my classroom learning but also to ensure that the school took my dyslexia into account in helping me grow as a person.

In sixth grade, a new boy moved to our town. He was from Australia, and for whatever reason, I hated this kid. One day in gym class, I threw a ball right in his face in a way that was clear that I was intentionally punching him. My mom got a call from the vice principal and had to come to the school to pick me up. Later, she was stern when she talked to me about it. I acknowledged I should not have done it. I apologized to the kid.

Two weeks later, I did it again.

This time, the principal punished me by keeping me out of class, making me sit in her office for the afternoon. My mother, of course, knew that this respite from reading and doing written work wasn't the right approach. "Ben will enjoy being out of class, and he'll hit the kid again," she explained. Instead, they agreed that I would not be able to attend an upcoming field trip to the science museum, which was by far a worse consequence for me.

What I see in this anecdote is that my mom believed that good behavior was important, and I needed to learn that it is not okay to hit people. She explained to school administrators how I worked and found collaborative ways to get that message through to me. I never hit the kid again and generally acted out a lot less, as I now knew that the adults in my life had my number.

This is especially important to remember when thinking about your dyslexic child's behavior patterns. Making trouble, cracking jokes in class, and even getting in fistfights are often strategies to get out of reading. It is so important to understand your child's motivation for acting out and address the root cause as well as the actions. If you can get your dyslexic child access to learning in a way other than text, while still setting high standards for behavior, you are likely to get much better results.

My parents did have antagonistic relationships with one or two specific teachers along the way who put up barriers to my learning. One teacher they had a hard time with was my high school French teacher. This woman was emphatic that I needed to master French spelling in my second year of taking the language. I had excelled in my first year of French because entry-level language classes are taught in an auditory context.

My mother was called in after I flubbed my second test, and told the teacher that because of my dyslexia the teacher couldn't require me to spell vocabulary words. The teacher was insistent that she was not going to relax her high standards: all students learned to spell in second-year French, she said. My mother couldn't make her understand that I couldn't spell in English, let alone in French! I ended up quitting French at the end of that year and starting Spanish the next (since the first year of study would again be all verbal). But I quit foreign languages altogether after that. Along the way, I failed to get what the French teacher wanted me to have—a solid foundation in her favorite tongue, let alone a love of it. If the teacher would have accepted me for the skill set I had, my experience with French class might have been entirely different.

LETTING GO OF FEAR AND SHAME

A few years back I was asked to give a speech at an important convention on dyslexia and education, but on the night of the event, I was not feeling well. Before I went onstage I took a couple of Tylenols, but instead of feeling better, I felt worse. So after the speech I took more Tylenol. The next morning I couldn't pull my head off the pillow. Four days later, after taking the pills all week, I looked at the bottle for the tenth time and noticed that I was taking Tylenol PM. This version contains an antihistamine that acts like a mild sedative. Missing those two letters made a big difference!

In my college years I would have been seething. My internal monologue would have been, "How could I have been so stupid? I would have nailed the speech if I had read that label. Stupid, stupid Ben." More important, I would have told no one about it. But this time I thought it was funny. Walking out of the hotel, I ran into a senior researcher in the field and one of the board members of the organization. I told them the story in full with a bemused sense of self-mockery, and they thought it was hilarious: The night's poster boy for dyslexia was so dyslexic that he doped himself before telling everyone about dyslexia!

Little mistakes are going to happen all the time. I've booked a plane flight out of the wrong city or showed up at the wrong terminal because I read the information incorrectly on my printed itinerary. While there can be major risks here, such as taking the wrong medicine, most of the time I have systems in place that reduce this risk. My computer reads text aloud to me, or I will ask my assistant for help. You can help when your child is young by double-checking text with her and then by helping her work with systems for independence with text, as outlined in Chapter Six. But these systems are not flawless. I am not promising that you or your child will not make mistakes after reading this book. In fact, I guarantee that people who are dyslexic will continue to screw up when it comes to spelling and reading, no matter what training they've received. Anyone who tells you otherwise has a bridge to sell you too. But I will promise you that you and your child will bounce back faster and become more connected to others if you open yourself to self-acceptance and community. The resiliency these things breed will open doors you and your child never could have imagined.

CHAPTER TWO

Discard the Myths

Many people think dyslexia equals stupid or lazy. I knew this from my own school experience, but when we launched the Intel Reader this fact came barreling down toward us directly from the press. While we got tons of positive media coverage, including great reviews in the *Wall Street Journal* and the *New York Times,* one major technology blog, Engadget.com, began their review of the product with the headline: "Intel Reader Reads Books to the Lazy and Infirm."

When I first saw this in print I was stunned. For the record, dyslexics are certainly not sick, as the word *infirm* would suggest. The authors meant that one for the blind folks who could also use the device (and, by the way, blind people are not sick either). But the idea of dyslexics being lazy struck me as the most damaging part of the headline. To call someone lazy is an attack on his character, implying that he could stand to try harder. This is equivalent to saying it is not worth society's time to help such a person, and that it is his own fault that he is failing. We would confront anyone who said this about a veteran in a wheelchair or a grandmother who is losing her sight. Yet because we cannot see dyslexia, this vicious lie gets repeated and believed.

After a little reflection, and the realization that they planned to leave it up on their site (as of this writing, it is still there), I published a blog post saying "thank you" and laying out the odd upside to them putting this in the headline: they were providing proof that some people actually believe this junk. The headline was something tangible I could use to underscore how real this myth is.

In addition to the pain associated with being insulted, the myth of laziness is most corrosive because it is the one that is the least true. Most people who are dyslexic are working three times as hard as a non-dyslexic just to get a B-minus putting in hours that, without the barrier of text or spelling, could well earn them an A. When someone says a dyslexic child is "just not trying," it's a nasty surprise attack because the critic has undermined the quality of the effort the dyslexic is putting in. I can guarantee that your child is working harder than most kids in her class, especially when you consider all the effort that is likely going into hiding the fact that she is having trouble.

No matter how integrated your thinking is regarding dyslexia, you will still have to deal with a lot of people who are misinformed about dyslexia, most of whom will not have read this book. The institutions that you will come across and the people whom you meet have created a set of expectations to define dyslexia in their own minds. Many of them are untrue. Here's a list of the most common myths I've come across, and why they are false and, when left unchecked, harmful.

MYTH #1: INCLUDING DYSLEXIC PEOPLE LOWERS CLASSROOM STANDARDS

Many people in positions of authority see their role as maintaining high standards for an institution or a profession. The teacher who chooses to drill her students on spelling every week might see herself as the person responsible for preparing kids—in terms of both skills and studying technique—to get good grades in years ahead, even in college. She'll stick to her techniques because it's what she believes has always worked. The creators of the SAT may see their role as helping colleges or universities assess applicants for admission, and the colleges and universities that require SAT test scores are reinforcing the idea that high test scores equal intelligence. When you tell the teacher or those test makers that a spelling quiz or timed multiple choice test is not a good measure of a person's potential for doing great work, they can become very rigid about their respective missions. While they might nod while you talk about accommodating dyslexia, they don't have any vested interest in changing their approach. It's not "the right way," according to them, and they likely will only pay lip service to change.

Unfortunately, defenders of high academic standards are often measuring the wrong things. A useful analogy here is baseball. For many years, a major way of judging a hitter was his batting average— the chance he would get a hit each time he came up to bat. However, getting a hit is only one way to get on base; getting walked or getting hit with a pitch will also do it. All those factors, which involve being able to read pitches and work an at-bat, go into another measure of a hitter's ability, on-base percentage. As was outlined in the book *Moneyball* (and the movie of the same name), when the Oakland Athletics and then the Boston Red Sox began using these more comprehensive statistics to pick players in the 1990s and early 2000s, they began winning like never before.

Getting back to schools, the SAT has an extremely poor track record in predicting who will do well in college. One study from the University of Pennsylvania concluded that the SAT predicts less than 4 percent of a student's cumulative GPA at the school. Put another way, the SAT misses 96 percent of the factors that truly matter when predicting a person's success in college. Indeed, there is a growing trend to dump the SAT as a measure of aptitude for college applicants. In 2012, the University of California dropped the SAT Subject Test from its admission requirements. Bates College made the SAT optional in 1984 and, after a five-year study of the effects, dropped it altogether in 1990. Over the course of the study, those who submitted their SAT scores with their application were only 0.1 percent more likely to graduate, and on average had a GPA that was only 0.05 points higher than their peers who didn't submit SAT scores. Keep in mind that at Bates, admissions officers still rely on a variety of measures to assess how likely it is that a student will do well in college; it's just that they have found that high school grades, recommendations, and essays are better predictors of future college performance than a static test.

Similarly, the teacher who insists that giving five hours of homework a night to seventh graders works because 25 percent of her students go on to great colleges is the equivalent of a medieval doctor who bleeds people to cure them. Yes, some children will get into college, and some of those patients got better, but the long hours of homework and the bleeding did not cause the successful outcomes.

If you measure students on their resiliency or their proactivity, rather than their spelling, you would be much more likely to pick true winners. So if anyone ever suggests to you that having your dyslexic child in a mainstream classroom means that the school's standards are being lowered, you can point out that you are trying to find better ways to predict outcomes for everyone and that the current standards are often the problem. Instead, we want to make everyone in the classroom a better learner, and we want to figure out how to measure the qualities that matter to long-term performance.

MYTH #2: YOUR CHILD CAN BE FIXED

Many adults will distance themselves from dyslexia by saying, "I used to be dyslexic." A common variation is, "I am still a little bit dyslexic." The first statement implies they found a cure. The second person admits they are still a little flawed. The implication in both cases is that this is a medical condition or a bug in the system that can be fixed.

It is true that some people who have difficulty with text because of dyslexia do improve their reading over time. But they will never be in the top half of eye-reading ability compared to the mainstream.

Right now I could keep up with fifth-grade eye readers when it comes to getting words off a page. But I am not in fifth grade. I can think and communicate with the best of my class from graduate school; I just cannot spell *graduate* half the time. The key challenge here is that people who feel the need to distance themselves from dyslexia are still wrestling with shame. They want to hide from the label, and saying "I used to be dyslexic" is a way to dodge the assumptions that come with the label.

Another reason some people don't embrace the term *dyslexic* is how long ago they were born. If you went through elementary school before 1975, screening for dyslexia was uncommon because dyslexia was not a well-understood learning issue. In that era, teachers told kids to stop being lazy or to stop faking their problem with reading to get out of hard work. Adults now, these people internalized that they did not have an identifiable problem (and may think they were lazy or stupid), so they had better not claim the label. And this may be why they are uncomfortable with the label for their own children now.

A slight variation on this can occur with younger people. Given that dyslexia is non-obvious, people rarely have concrete proof that they have dyslexia and doubt their own membership in the club. Counterintuitively, some will resist being called dyslexic because they feel like a fraud using the term to describe themselves and do not want to overreach into the world of accommodations. All these people would do well to get a formal identification, as discussed in Chapter Three, and integrate their own strengths and weaknesses. But again, shame is generally at the core of this resistance to embracing the profile of dyslexia.

Because of technological advances, including books as MP3s; voice commands, such as Siri, on smart phones; and dedicated audio devices such as the Intel Reader or the Victor Reader by HumanWare, problems with eye reading or spelling perfectly are no longer a major barrier to success. Fixing or curing dyslexia is all that much more absurd a notion in an age when the line between accessing data via text and accessing it via spoken word has virtually disappeared. The *written* word is irrelevant. What is relevant is the *word*, be it spoken, rendered in Braille, or synthesized into speech by a computer. For me, and for your dyslexic child, access to knowledge is like turning on the radio. I know—and they need to know—which station to tune to. If your child is dyslexic, at some point he or she will find that attempting to read the way non-dyslexics do is grossly ineffective. However, with the right classroom accommodations your child is going to learn; how she does it may just look different from what everyone else in the class is doing. If your child tries to learn the mainstream way—by insisting on eye reading—he'll fall behind badly.

MYTH #3: READING IS THE BEST WAY TO LEARN

A central contributor to a dyslexic's sense of shame is the fixation on eye reading as the best way to learn. Humans are naturals at language and have been for tens of thousands of years. A baby will develop speech in roughly a year of living; some speak before they can walk. Yet text as a representation of language and as a learning system is only about five thousand years old; furthermore, most text was handwritten until the last thousand years, and only with Johannes Gutenberg's invention of the printing press around 1450 did printed text become widespread. Just in the last hundred years have we had an expectation that there would be a free public school system for even a majority of children, and it is really only in the last sixty years, since the landmark Supreme Court case *Brown v. Board of Education*, that we have had a belief that all children should be given an equal chance at education.

When I come across someone invested (emotionally or traditionally) in books as the best way to learn, I usually like to point to the blind as an example of where their logic drops off. If someone lost her vision at eighteen, would we automatically tell her she is not going to college because the blind can't learn at that level? No, we would get her access to the needed materials through Braille or audiobooks.

Would it be easier if she could read with her eyes? Definitely. But that is a result of a context. Stairs are no better a way to get into a building than a ramp, but for centuries, we made stairs the mainstream way. We all agree we must have ramps for public buildings and businesses. We need to extend this flexibility to other areas of life as well.

Once we let go of eye reading as the only way to learn, we can embrace other options. Students generally put four to five years into mastering eye reading. We teach the alphabet starting in kindergarten, and by fourth grade the assumption is that students are now reading to learn rather than learning to read. I fully believe that all dyslexic children should try to learn to read and should be given world-class instruction in doing that, including the Orton-Gillingham system of teaching reading (you'll learn more about this in Chapter Six). But it is also important to introduce ear reading and other forms of learning at the same time.

My dad remembers a number of instances where he saw me take to ear reading rather than eye reading when I was young, even though I couldn't articulate it as such. After school I used to come home, plop down on the couch, and put on one of my prized records of Basil Rathbone reading a piece of classic literature, such as *Treasure Island* or *Peter and the Wolf.* As my dad describes it, he would see tension wash out of my face and my eyes drift off into a focused but calm gaze. He also recalled how enthusiastic I was whenever he read to me. I still remember learning about mitochondria—the energy powerhouse of cells—from his reading of the classic novel *A Wrinkle in Time.*

As an adult, I adapted to a faster way of listening. I put as much time into learning to read with my ears as most put into eye reading. This means I can now listen faster and for longer than most people can read with their eyes, leveling the playing field.

The critical point is that there is damage being done to a dyslexic student's psyche if you frame reading as learning and learning as reading. Imagine if we focused all of school on singing. Some students would take to this and thrive. Others would struggle. If we kept telling all children that they had to be good singers, we would be slowly traumatizing the poor singers into thinking they were bad people.

MYTH #4: YOUR CHILD ISN'T MATURING AT THE SAME RATE AS OTHER CHILDREN

One of the most frequent retorts that people who are either unfamiliar with dyslexia or intentionally trying to delay access to services will use to rebuff your request for help is to tell you that your child is simply maturing slowly: "He'll learn to read just like everybody else; just give it a few months." While it is true that children develop the skill of reading at different ages, dyslexia is a response to a biological difference in his brain, which has nothing to do with maturity. The assessment of dyslexia in Chapter Three as well as a formal identification performed by an expert will be able to distinguish between a standard learning curve for reading and the specific phenomenon that is dyslexia.

MYTH #5: IT'S BEST TO KEEP THESE PROBLEMS HIDDEN

Even though my parents were supportive, I was properly identified, and I took advantage of accommodations, for most of my life I was still hiding my dyslexia in a deep dark box. When I went to my law school reunion recently and told people I was writing this book, even my close friends had no idea why I was so interested in dyslexia.

Until I learned to integrate my dyslexia into the rest of my life, I was constantly lying to the world and to myself, doing damage as a result. I was angry at school and at myself for every failure because I knew I could think big thoughts but I could not spell or read them with my eyes. Early on, I developed elaborate methods of camouflage to hide who I was. The first I can remember was in third grade. I desperately wanted to be seen as a smart person. I went to the library every day after school, but I would go straight down to the basement where they kept the vinyl records of BBC radio broadcasts. It was the only content I could get into my head easily.

One day I saw a poster at the library for a bookmark design contest. It explained that the top designers would get their picture in the paper and posted on the wall in the library. The winning bookmark design would also be reproduced and handed out to patrons who came into the building that year. I had dreams of people thinking: "That Ben Foss, he loves books! He must be so smart!" This was my chance to blend in.

I drew a bookmark featuring nutcrackers and walnuts and the words "loosing my place drives me nuts." Here is a picture of what was the proudest moment of my young life:

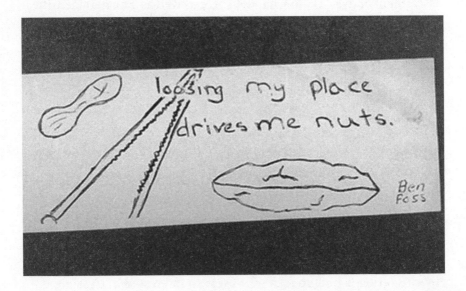

In a testament to my dyslexia, I wasn't even aware I'd misspelled *losing* on the bookmark until 2012, when I proudly showed it to a friend who noticed. I now wonder if the judges thought it was some sort of joke on my part. Regardless, I won an award and got my picture taken and placed on the library wall and in the local paper. Yet I had literally never read a book. I wanted to win that contest so I would have something to prove that I was bookish. That seemed like a critical way to protect myself at the time.

From the vantage point of thirty years later, I can see that I was telling the truth: it did drive me nuts to lose my place, an experience every dyslexic has with every sentence she reads. But it was seen as cute kid wordplay: "Ben must be so literate." And of course I made sure my name was clearly written out in block letters, not script. There was no value to an artist's illegible scrawl when you are trying to advertise yourself as fully part of the "book world."

Fast-forward to when I was fifteen. I was trying to make the varsity soccer team because I knew it would gain me the kind of praise I wasn't regularly getting in the classroom. During a tryout scrimmage, I got caught too far off my line, and a striker lofted a soft kick up over my head and into the goal. I was furious with myself. While the play moved back down to the other end of the pitch, I stood there so angry I could scream. Being a cool kid—gone. Getting my name in the paper—gone. Never being bullied—gone. Getting out of class early for games—gone. I could feel the earth crumbling beneath my feet and me falling into an abyss. Once no one was looking at me, I turned around and punched my hand full force into the goalpost. The impact snapped the knucklebone on the ring finger on my right hand. I pulled my glove off and inspected the situation: the bone was pushing up, stretching the skin. I put the glove back on. This was a way out of the shame I felt. I walked down the field and said, quite calmly, "Hey, Coach, I think I hurt myself on the last play." As I was whisked off to the emergency room, even though I lied to my parents about the source of the injury, I knew what I was doing: I had found a physical reason to explain why I was not good at something. I knew my classmates would tell stories of how tough I was, instead of focusing on the play I missed. As wildly misplaced as my strategy was, at the time I was proud I had hurt myself to protect my high school reputation.

I hear stories all the time like this from people who inhabit the

Nation of Dyslexia. The teenage boy who raced a motorcycle into on-coming traffic to prove to his friends that he was tough. The teenage girl who earned a triple black belt in jujitsu, breaking four bones on other people in competition to prove she was the best. Your children will be inclined to do things like this, taking risks small and large that allow them to feel powerful or included, because for them it feels like life or death. They will hide what they are doing from you if you have not helped them digest the mountain of criticism that they are experiencing around their work ethic and their intelligence—essentially about their worth—or if you have projected the attitude that hiding these things about ourselves is the healthy approach. It's not!

You and your child will be much happier if you can get over the notion that dyslexia is best kept secret and instead tell people what is really going on with your child and looking for ways to rely on his or her strengths.

MYTH #6: DYSLEXIA IS THE FAULT OF BAD PARENTING

Another common myth that parents too often buy into is that their child's dyslexia is somehow a result of their mistakes. Dyslexia does not happen to your child because you are a bad person or because your Maker either hates or loves you. It is not traced to eating the wrong things during pregnancy, or waiting until nursery school to familiarize your child with the alphabet. However, if you are asking yourself whether you or your spouse/partner have the same dyslexia-predisposing genes as your kids, the answer is yes, unless of course your child was adopted. There are rare cases where a brain injury can cause difficulty with reading, but this is not the case for the vast majority of dyslexic kids. As someone once said to me, "You don't get dyslexia from drinking the water."

It is a certainty that you or members of your family are carrying these genes, if only in a recessive capacity. For example, my mother is an outstanding reader who earns her living editing books. My father might have trouble spelling a word once in a while, but he is not considered dyslexic and reads in a standard way. My brother is a mainstream reader and loves to joke about my dyslexia, once giving me a T-shirt that said "I Dyslexia ♥." But my grandmother—my father's mother—fit the profile to a T. I still cherish her letters, misspelled and with her scrawl wandering all over the page. She was from an era when women of her background were expected to throw parties and raise children, so no one ever thought of her as dyslexic or even broken when she did not excel in school. Relatives on my mother's side are dyslexic as well, so despite her being a professional book editor, she could easily be the source of these genes.

The key word in this myth is *fault*. Dyslexia is like your child's height. Yes, your genes played a large role in it, but your actions did not do anything to cause it. And if you can find the sources of those dyslexia genes in the family, you can begin to create a community that will make your child feel less alone. The other element of the word *fault* that you need to get over is the notion that there is a problem in your child. There is not. There is a problem in the environment your child lives in. Reading is one way to learn, but making it the only way is where the fault really lies.

MYTH #7: BOYS ARE MORE LIKELY TO BE DYSLEXIC THAN GIRLS

There are a number of studies that show that the incidence of dyslexia in boys is the same as that in girls. One longitudinal study from Yale tracked more than four hundred students in Connecticut, demonstrating an equivalent incidence between the sexes. In another study in North Carolina, researchers tested children in the first and third grades with the same result. There was even a study of two hundred identical and two hundred fraternal twins in Colorado; again, no gender skew was found.

It is true that there are more boys in special ed for dyslexia and other specific learning disabilities, but this is because boys who are frustrated by their difficulty in school tend to act out, and girls tend to clam up. Negative behavior increases the odds that a child is going to get identified, because the child is causing a problem that has to be addressed. For girls, because they tend to behave better, the teacher may think, "Jane keeps to herself, but that's fine." You will want your child to get the support he or she needs, so ignore this common misperception and find out what is really going on with your son or daughter.

MYTH #8: DYSLEXIA IS A DIFFERENCE, NOT A DISABILITY

Many people will resist using the word *disability* to describe dyslexia. Some people don't like the word, believing that it implies that something is broken or seriously amiss, and will choose the word *difference* instead. Others will use a different euphemism, such as *special* or *uniquely skilled*. This behavior is similar to real estate agents renaming an up-and-coming neighborhood in order to sell more homes: suddenly the sketchy south side of town is called SOMA for "South of Main" in an attempt to distance it from the tough reputation of the old name. It is still the same neighborhood, though, and if you live there, you are less interested in what it is called than in how you will be treated there. The same thing is true of teachers or professionals who want to soften the blow on children by limiting the use of the word *disability*. It would be much more effective to call it what it is and make the person feel comfortable about that reality rather than trying to sugarcoat it in the gauze of "specialness."

In a legal context it's critical to understand that dyslexia and specific learning disabilities are categorically included under the term *disability*. It is important for your child to maintain this designation when communicating with a school administration or with a testing agency because of the legal rights and protections that come with the term. Separately, it's key to understand that the word *disability* is one that generations of people have fought to create. The Americans with Disabilities Act is not called the Americans with Differences Act. Under that law, the process of learning (and, with recent amendments, reading specifically) is part of the definition of "major life activities" that can be affected by a disability. Dunking a basketball would not be considered a major life activity, so the inability to dunk is not a disability. But if you have difficulty doing something that everyone expects mainstream people to be able to do, you have a disability. The key here is to get over any stigma you feel about the word *disability* itself.

We all have weaknesses, and you should be comfortable discussing them. Being able to say that you are a person who has weaknesses shows humility. Similarly, saying that you are a person with a disability should not convey that you are incapable, but merely that there's a specific life area where you're not part of the mainstream.

I will grant that the term *learning disability* is not particularly attractive. To me, the difficulty is the use of the word *learning*. I do have a disability, but it is related to reading text. We already know that people who are dyslexic can learn quite well, thank you very much.

Some people fail to embrace the concept of disability, or the word, because they don't understand the nuances within this profile. To really think through the nature of a person's disability, you need to understand two subcomponents of her profile. The first is whether a disability is an innate disability or an acquired disability. Dyslexia is an innate disability, meaning that it is in us from the day we are born and it only reveals itself when we are asked to do certain text-based activities. The man who has an innate disability never has an experience of the world in which he did not have that component of his profile. As a result he rarely wants to change that element of himself. On the other hand, a person who incurs a spinal cord injury in her twenties and uses a wheelchair for the rest of her life has an acquired disability.

My friend Mark was born without hands, and didn't really understand that he was different from other children until he went to school. Within his own family no one really made a big deal of the fact and expected him to play just like all the other kids. These days when you ask him if he would prefer to change himself, he's the first to say that he is happy how he is. The same is true of me. There's no amount of money you could give me that would entice me to give up my dyslexic brain. This is in part because I like the way it thinks but it's also because I love the ways in which I can connect with other people in the community based on our shared experience.

Hopefully, your child will come to love all aspects of himself including the disabilities and strengths.

The second issue is whether the disability is obvious or non-obvious. Note that I don't use the term "invisible." My dyslexia is not invisible. If you do an fMRI brain scan you can see pronounced physical markers of it.

A person who has an obvious disability such as a missing limb has no choice but to be open about her disability profile. As a result she can often carry less shame than people with non-obvious disabilities. This is not an absolute rule, but in the case of a non-obvious disability, people have the option to and often choose to hide their disability. As a result, shame encroaches and the cycle of self-loathing and further hiding begins.

A person with an innate disability that is also non-obvious has a highly specific character: these people are likely to hide a part of themselves for much of their lives. No wonder there can be such a river of shame flowing under the surface. My experience is that the way to deal with this is to make all disabilities obvious by talking openly about it. This draws people toward you and you then have an opportunity to create community.

MYTH #9: BEING DYSLEXIC MEANS YOU ARE STUPID, RETARDED, OR LAZY

As ignorant as this statement may sound, 80 percent of teachers associate the term *learning disability* with mental retardation. Even though the term *mental retardation* itself is now outdated, and the waters have been muddied with a recent law that changed the official federal designation for developmental delay to "intellectual disabilities," this misperception is just not true of the typical dyslexic.

The most malicious manifestation of this myth often occurs on the playground, where other kids will use the slur *retard* to describe children who are dyslexic. I'm in the camp that says once you get to know people and you hear them use *retard* or *retarded* to describe something, it's worth pointing out to them that term comes from *mentally retarded*, that that term is outdated even for people with developmental disabilities, and that in the context of dyslexia it is being used as an insult. Imagine if someone were to say, "What are you, a dumb Polack?" when another person made a mistake. In both cases, the slur should be dropped. One very effective approach is to offer an alternative. As one friend of mine suggested, replacing *retard* with *ridiculous* is a good technique. "That coat is retarded" becomes "That coat is ridiculous!"

The other variation on this myth is that your child is lazy. When disability is non-obvious and you can't point to a specific physical issue that causes a problem, many people will assume that it's simply a matter of drive. Ironically, the student who is dyslexic is often working two or three times harder just to keep up with her peers. The double whammy is that the child arrives home exhausted from the day at school and has zero reserves left to do homework or participate in family activities. As a result, the child can be seen as lazy because he comes home and doesn't want to do anything. If you can provide your child with the accommodations and supports he needs in school, he'll have the energy to participate like any other kid.

MYTH #10: DYSLEXIA IS A GIFT

The inverse of "dyslexia means you're stupid" is that dyslexia is a gift. Many people point to the fact that people who are dyslexic are highly creative. The reasoning goes that if you can help children understand that their dyslexia is a magic and special thing, they will embrace it. This does not work.

This argument is both condescending and undermining to self-esteem. People become accepted when we no longer notice a particular minority status and instead attribute their success to their individual capabilities. When you think of Serena or Venus Williams, their African American heritage is not the fact that makes them outstanding athletes, nor is the fact that they are women. They accomplish so much on the tennis court because they work incredibly hard and outperform everyone else in the field, not because of some "gift" related to their race or gender. They are gifted tennis players, but that is not a euphemism for black or female.

I will grant you that people who are dyslexic do often approach the world differently. But it is hard to determine whether that's in the nature of our brains or whether it's a response to the environment. Many people who are dyslexic do demonstrate a high degree of creativity. Keep in mind, however, that if you were to strap a cinder block to the leg of every child in second grade, a certain number of those children would end up being extremely creative. Does this mean that we should strap cinder blocks to the legs of all children?

When talking to your child, don't try to gloss over the challenges that come with dyslexia. Not being able to eye-read well is a real problem in mainstream society. The dyslexia itself is neither a curse nor a gift. It is just a trait.

A variation on the concept of being gifted is the notion that a child is "twice exceptional" (sometimes abbreviated as 2E). This term is intended to identify a child who is both dyslexic and gifted. I agree that it is possible for a student to have a specific learning disability and have exceptional strengths. Indeed, that is the entire premise of this book. But this 2E label doesn't describe a specific set of attributes, such as visual skill or being a good athlete. What's more, there's such a huge range of what the exceptionality can be at either end of the spectrum that the label doesn't tell you very much about who your child is. This means it is largely a title to make parents and children feel better rather than to change how we teach children. Worse, it places the concept of "normal" firmly in between these two extreme points. By accepting the 2E label, we are digging the hole deeper by cementing "normal" into place and validating the notion that we can categorize children into a hierarchy based on their skills. This leads to the final and perhaps largest problem with this categorization: parents will often use this term as a way to distinguish their child from other students with specific learning disabilities. This buys into the notion that we should rank our children against each other and that we should be interested in what the school system or other parents think of our own child. The 2E label is essentially used as a weapon: "Yes, my child does have a weakness, but she is better than those other children." Families who don't have a child who gets the label of "gifted" separate from her "special education" label get left holding only the negative side of this identification. We would all do much better to address all children as individuals and to create learning profiles for them that allow their strengths and weaknesses to be recognized and understood.

MYTH #11: USING NON-TEXT-BASED WAYS TO LEARN IS JUST A CRUTCH

Frequently parents will be concerned that if their child uses audio or kinesthetic learning at a young age, he will not learn to read because he has become reliant on a crutch. These alternative ways of accessing information, which will be detailed much more extensively in Chapter Six, are not a crutch; they are a ramp. Referring to alternative ways of learning as a "crutch" connotes that the person using those alternative strategies is broken; without the crutch, the logic goes, he would heal on his own and return to standard ways of doing things.

To repeat: dyslexia is not a short-term situation or an injury to be healed. It is a trait that will last a lifetime and needs to be incorporated into people's entire way of being. The best way to do this is to discover what their strengths are in terms of learning, which is exactly what we'll do in the next chapter. However, having strengths does not make you a "super-crip," as some of the disability literature warns. While it's true that some people can compensate by being able to do exceptional things, this is not the rule and you should not put your child in this position, making him find one area of success to make up for other weaknesses. For example, not all blind people can scale Mount Everest; not all one-legged teenagers will become captain of the high school swim team. And while your child will be able to determine his best learning style, I'm not asking him to perform extra-amazing feats of awesomeness such as memorizing the name, date, and winner of every battle in the Civil War in order to demonstrate that he has "overcome" a disability. The key is that having dyslexia is really not a flaw, and accommodations that play to his strengths are certainly not a crutch.

MYTH #12: DYSLEXIA HAPPENS ONLY IN THE UNITED STATES

Dyslexia is present in every country in the world. Interestingly, dyslexia can manifest in different parts of the brain depending on whether the native language is character- or letter-based, yet the overall occurrence of dyslexia is about the same. It's important to understand this because difficulty with written text is not simply about letters and words; it's about symbols (e.g., Japanese kanji) and concepts, and keeping them in order.

In my travels I have enjoyed getting to know leaders in the dyslexia community in places as far away as Ireland and Brazil. While much of the information in this book focuses on a U.S.-specific context—the American school system and legal framework—a lot of it can be applied in other countries as well. In particular, shame and the negative, harmful emotional state that results are international phenomena. As a parent of a dyslexic child, you're part of something larger than just your child, so don't let people convince you that this is some American invention that is the result of stressed-out parents or our particular school system.

MYTH #13: IT'S BETTER THAT I DON'T TELL MY CHILD THAT HE IS DYSLEXIC

Frequently parents or teachers will choose to hide the fact that a child is dyslexic from the child. Sometimes the child figures it out for himself in some way, assuming that because it is being kept secret, he should be embarrassed about it. Worse, the child might jump to the conclusion that he is stupid and that he will always be that way.

When dealing with a young person, I always think that it is best to be honest as well as give your child the full context of his dyslexia: both the social and scientific aspects that we've been discussing. It's also important to go over the testing with him before it occurs and to explain at each step that he is smart and intelligent and cared for.

A friend of mine read an early draft of this book which made him realize that he may be dyslexic. He spoke with his brother about it, and found out that his parents had tested him as a child; he just didn't remember. The brother was even able to pull the testing records out of storage. It turned out that he was in fact extremely dyslexic and his parents had made a choice not to reveal this to him in an attempt to prevent him from feeling stigma. The revelation left him shaken, although now he is very glad to have the more accurate information. As Steven Spielberg put it after he was identified as dyslexic, "it was the missing puzzle piece." He had to spend significant energy thinking through what it all meant to him, and even now it is still unfolding, a process that can take years.

One of my favorite stories in relation to this is that of a member of the Random House team I encountered during this book's publication process. During our time working together, she let me know about her son's dyslexia. She was told by an expert when he was first identified that she should withhold this information from him. After touring a school that supports students who are dyslexic, her son announced that he really liked the school and hoped that he would go there. She decided to reject the advice she had been given and say, "You know why you like the school so much? It's because all of those students are dyslexic just like you." He got quiet and looked at her and nodded. Later that night while he was brushing his teeth he suddenly announced, "So you finally decided to tell me that I have that thing!" She said, "Yes, and what is that thing?" "That I have arthritis!"

This was a word swap gem that only a dyslexic mind would make. The key to the story is that the child was actually quite happy to know that he was dyslexic. For myself, the more proof and context I have gotten on dyslexia, the happier I have become.

LEARNING TO INTEGRATE DYSLEXIA

Integrating dyslexia is the polar opposite of "overcoming dyslexia." I measure how well someone has integrated dyslexia into her life by how in control of the message she is—and, more specifically, by how likely someone is to know that she's dyslexic because *she wants them to know*. The last part is critical. I was known as dyslexic for much of my school years, but not by my choice. The odds that anyone knew I was dyslexic were about 70 percent throughout elementary school because I was in special ed and I had to leave class to get services, which in and of itself made public my learning issues. In middle school, I was mainstreamed and the likelihood that others knew of my dyslexia dropped to about 10 percent because I hid it as much as I could.

By the time I got to high school, my metaphorical camouflage let me sneak by with less than a 5 percent chance of someone knowing.

My least integrated time was in college. I had a new group of friends, and I put huge amounts of energy into faking that I was mainstream. I'd estimate that maybe 1 percent of my peers knew I was struggling with the mainstream way of learning. To use the analogy again, I was the duck on the pond, moving fiercely under the water to stay afloat but calm and poised on the surface. After college, it was clear that there were people in my life who needed to know about my dyslexia. For instance, I needed to tell my boss: "I'm not going to be able to be the person who does the final proofread on this, and I need to talk with you about why." But I didn't disclose my dyslexia unless I had to.

When I got to law school, I still held my secret identity fairly close. I didn't tell my classmates, but I did tell the administration because they provided me accommodations. I told one or two professors. Perhaps about 10 percent of people I knew understood what I was dealing with. When I got to business school, a school administrator took me aside and said, "Why don't you just go talk to your professor about this?" One of my professors turned out to be dyslexic, and I realized, "Wow! Talking about this can give me a chance to connect." I became more open. By the end of business school, I'd estimate that half of my peers and social circle knew that I was dyslexic, and I brought it up with most of my professors.

After graduate school, when I was working at Intel, I didn't make any effort to disguise the fact that I am dyslexic, and I often offered the information to people at work. When I got to leading the team on the Intel Reader, almost nobody *didn't* know that I am dyslexic. Today you have to work hard to keep the information at bay. Try the old Google test: enter the name Ben Foss and all you will see is me and dyslexia! My friends now joke with me that I should have a T-shirt that says: "Have I told you that I am dyslexic . . . *today*?"

My most critical moment of integration came the day I met Joe Stutts, a man I consider to be the father of the dyslexia movement and

someone you'll get to know better in Chapter Nine. I first met Joe
when I was in law school and learned how his civil rights case was the
reason a person with dyslexia was seen as having a right to be included in the workplace. I felt this sense of pride about how gutsy he
was. I looked up to him and took what he said seriously. I decided to
make a film, *Headstrong,* about him, and I flew to Alabama to meet
him. Fighting back the tears, I told him how long I had spent trying
to get over the fact that I couldn't read. He just looked me dead in the
eye and said, "Well, get over it." I loved that answer! To me, Joe's response showed full integration. He simply does not have a problem
with the fact that he's dyslexic.

You will be able to measure your progress toward full integration
by how well you and your child are moving toward full disclosure.
However, this should be a partnership: if your child does not want
others to know, you telling all her friends in school is about the worst
thing that could happen. It is best to start with your immediate family and work your way out into the broader community from there,
focusing on teaching your child how to tell the story herself and getting her buy-in for each additional disclosure. We will discuss this
more in Chapter Five.

I wish my own integration of dyslexia hadn't taken so long. There
are plenty of examples that show it doesn't have to be as it was for me.
The key to integration in younger kids is community. Twenty years
ago, a group of parents in the San Francisco Bay area set up the Parents Education Network (PEN) to give them a community in which
to talk about what their children needed. Ten years later, their children were growing up and, good self-advocates that they were, suggested they start their own group: Students Advisors for Education
(SAFE). SAFE members speak on panels at schools in front of teachers and their non-dyslexic peers in order to establish positive images
of kids who are dyslexic or ADHD. The panels have been so successful that in 2010 SAFE began holding an annual conference called
Education Revolution, or EdRev, which now draws more than three
thousand kids, parents, and educators each year to fun activities held

in Giants Stadium. Unlike other dyslexia conferences, this one bursts with youthful, dyslexic energy. I regularly tell parents of kids who are dyslexic or ADHD that they need to bring their child to this event to see young kids advocate for themselves while having fun. My hope is that other student groups will build on the SAFE model and start similar events around the country to help build community, the best single ingredient to address shame and integrate dyslexia.

The shining example of this is an exercise I saw at EdRev last year. The organizers put together an event for teens and kids the day before the main conference and brought in a facilitator: Alexandra Cantle, a Los Angeles–based dyslexic artist. All the children were given a literal soapbox to paint and cover with images that they felt represented them. They were then given an opportunity (no one was required) to stand on their soapbox in the center of a large and very supportive circle and tell the world what they wanted others to know about them. I saw more than a hundred young people get up and talk—some for two or three minutes to tell stories of how they wished teachers understood them, others for as little as ten seconds just to say, "I am smart." The capper was that at the conference the next day, the children carried their soapbox around with them, and whenever they felt the urge, they would stop in a hall, get on the soapbox, and tell their story to whoever was willing to listen. Advocacy has never looked so wonderful!

In the next chapter you'll begin to see what it's like to have a clean slate, one free of shame and ready for learning and success: no fears, no myths, just the facts, starting with determining your child's strengths and weaknesses. We will begin with identifying his weaknesses and the path to finding out if he can be formally identified as dyslexic. Then I'll begin to show you how to find his strengths and how to use them to make the most of his educational experience. Finally, we will look at the attitudes that will make all this work for everyone.

CHAPTER THREE

Identify Your Child's Strengths

As part of the process of assessing what was giving me trouble in school, I was given an intelligence test when I was young. My mother didn't tell me how I scored because she didn't believe the numbers accurately reflected who I was. Though I think I could have handled the information—especially since I know my parents would have been careful to explain the intent of the test and the meaning of my score—I urge you to take the same skeptical attitude when it comes to the various testing that has to happen in order to establish your child's profile. Tests are important only up to a point. Above all, it is important to underscore that your child is not broken, and that often these tests reflect parts of our culture that are themselves flawed. I have designed measures that are very different from the majority of the testing you will encounter. You'll learn how to identify your child's strengths and focus on the attributes that will lead to his or her success. Before I lay them out, however, let me give you some history on the origins of the more typical testing you will be asked to provide by your school.

Through most of the nineteenth century and the first half of the twentieth, eugenicists—scientists interested in manipulating the genetic composition of a human population—had a prominent voice in the scientific community. People often focus on race or religion when they think of this movement, but people with disabilities were a major target as well. Many of us know about the extreme examples of this thinking: the Nazis attempted to cleanse the German population of people with disabilities in a program known as T4, and estimates suggest that they killed more than 200,000 people with various disabilities. Many people do not realize that eugenicist thinking was also prominent in the United States. By 1925, twenty U.S. states had forced-sterilization programs for people with disabilities. In 1942, Dr. Foster Kennedy, professor of neurology at Cornell Medical Center and director of the department of neurology at Bellevue Hospital in New York City, proposed in the *American Journal of Psychiatry* that the United States undertake a program of killing children with disabilities at the age of five in order to relieve them of "the burden of living." In each of the examples above, the disabilities were those that were easy to detect—obvious physical ones or mental health issues that presented in dramatic fashion. The practice, however, spoke of a larger norm that disability and variation was unacceptable. At this time people who were dyslexic were being segregated and pushed out of schools, and while this is in no way equivalent to killing or sterilizing people, it was all part of a larger culture of demonizing unacceptable characteristics.

This effort to define disability as unacceptable and a form of eugenicist thinking can also be linked to the development of the Stanford-Binet Intelligence Scales and the notion of intelligence quotient, or IQ. In 1904, psychologists Alfred Binet and Theodore Simon, at the request of the French government, created a test to identify developmentally delayed children and established the very first system of special education. To his credit, Binet immediately saw that categorizing intelligence ran highly negative risks, including teachers lowering expectations for "labeled" kids and excluding them from the mainstream. He advocated for individual case studies but found that a universal scale was needed to provide mass screenings. His work was later adapted and became the foundation of the modern

Stanford-Binet Intelligence Scales, which is still widely used today. In this process of adapting Binet and Simon's work, eugenicists put their mark on the test, what we now think of as the measure for IQ.

In 1917, Robert Yerkes, a eugenicist and the head of the American Psychological Association, proposed using a variation on the Stanford-Binet scale to evaluate American recruits for the First World War. He developed the army's Alpha and Beta tests, overseeing their administration to more than a million recruits. In many cases, recent immigrants were tested in English even if they did not speak the language, and people of color were sometimes not given pencils to take the exam. The seriously dubious results of this study were used to support racist immigration policies and led to the exclusion of people from entry into the United States based on their having been assessed as potentially "defective." The bogus results were also used to build elaborate screening tests that were applied to other aspects of life in the United States. For example, Carl C. Brigham, who worked for Yerkes, went on to develop the SAT based on the Alpha and Beta tests.

Though these tests are no longer being so unfairly administered, I think it's important to understand their checkered history.

As a first step in the process of identifying your child's learning profile, he or she may need to take the Stanford-Binet IQ test or other tests in the same vein. These tests will help experts identify your child's weakness and determine if he or she fits the standard definition of dyslexia and therefore qualifies for extra help or services. (I offer more information on these tests below.) The next step involves taking an inventory of your child's *strengths*. I will outline below the eight major strengths that often come with dyslexia so that you can determine which of these your child exhibits. Understanding your child's strengths will inform the accommodations plan you will design and likely serve as a guide all along his or her path in school and life.

Finally, you will want to look at the attitudes, habits, and approaches that have been shown to lead to long-term success for dyslexic people (and, really, all people). While your child is unlikely to exhibit a majority of these attitude characteristics right now, given how early we are in the process, considering where your child sits on the continuum of possibilities will give you a benchmark. This starting point will help you monitor progress and help your child understand how to be more in control of her life.

DOES YOUR CHILD QUALIFY FOR EXTRA HELP OR SERVICES?

Most testing related to dyslexia focuses on a person's difficulty with spelling, reading, and connecting sounds with a series of letters. This narrow focus on a limited set of skills greatly skews the conversation, blocking us from seeing a full picture of any person. Yet if you are going to ask for supplemental educational services for your child, request that she be placed in special education, or be granted accommodations in the classroom and academic testing environments, you will have to work within this narrow skills focus.

I cannot emphasize strongly enough that defining your child solely in the context of his ability to spell or read the standard way is a terrible idea. The more detailed screeners that appear later in the chapter, which focuses on other skills and attitudes, provide a much more complete picture of your child, and will form the primary basis of the work you do with this book. A formal assessment, however, is the only way that you can get certification of your child's status.

Your interest in this book suggests you have reason to believe your child is dyslexic or has some related specific learning disability. The checklist I have developed below will give you a general indication of whether or not they need detailed testing. The National Center for Learning Disabilities (NCLD) has developed a much more comprehensive checklist for the full range of specific learning disability profiles. They have graciously agreed to allow me to reprint it for this book. It is in Appendix D.

The Dyslexia Indication Checklist

PART 1: ANSWER THE FOLLOWING QUESTIONS AS HONESTLY AS YOU CAN BY CIRCLING YES OR NO. FOR EACH YES ANSWER, AWARD ONE POINT. *Does your child:*

1) Show mixed handedness, doing some activities righty and others lefty?   Yes/No
2) Mispronounce unfamiliar words when reading them?   Yes/No
3) Come up with reasons not to read something, especially aloud?   Yes/No
4) Tend to learn by talking to people or watching media rather than by reading with his eyes?   Yes/No
5) Have problems memorizing a series of numbers?   Yes/No
6) Have any of your extended family members been identified as dyslexic or having a specific learning disability?   Yes/No
7) Frequently lose his or her place or skip lines when eye-reading?   Yes/No
8) Sometimes forget how to spell short words she knows how to use?   Yes/No
9) Confuse words that sound similar such as *magnets* and *maggots*?   Yes/No
10) Use and understand complex words that he would be unable to spell?   Yes/No

0-3 points: Consult NCLD checklist (Appendix D) to explore other pro-files
4-10 points: Dyslexia possible; consult NCLD checklist and then discuss with teacher as outlined in Chapter 5 and Chapter 7.

For the record, today, with all my degrees and accomplishments, I score a 9 out of 10 on this list. If your child scored in the "Dyslexia possible" category based on the Dyslexia Indication Checklist above you may want to approach your child's school about a formal identi- fication. It is a good idea to complete the NCLD checklist before re- questing this meeting.

It's important to reiterate that your child's weaknesses in the areas highlighted above have nothing to do with her overall intelli- gence. Indeed, you may receive results from testing that show your child to be very intelligent in some ways. When I was in third grade I remember a test about analogies. The woman administering the test quizzed me verbally, asking questions such as *"Hat* is to *head* as . . . A) *bark* is to *dog*; B) *glove* is to *hand*; C) *axle* is to *car*; or D) *sun* is to *moon."* I quickly answered "B, glove is to hand," and I correctly an- swered her other questions as well. For analogies, they told my par- ents, I could master twelfth-grade-level work even though I was just eight years old, yet I couldn't spell *glove*, let alone *analogy*! If you see such a pattern, it remains important that you get accommodations and supplemental services for your child, as emphasized in Chapters Six and Seven. If, say, your child has a sophisticated verbal vocabu- lary but struggles with reading, he may be given reading material that is not as challenging as he can handle—*See Spot Run* is intellectually thin gruel. A formal identification will help you get him access to material that challenges his mind.

STANDARD TESTING OPTIONS

I've made clear my skepticism of testing as a useful measure, but agencies such as the Educational Testing Service (which administers the SAT) require you to get your child professional administration of one or more of the following to help determine if he is entitled to an accommodation during the test: effectively, you are getting testing done just so you can pay them to take the test! The most common as- sessments for securing accommodations on the SAT are listed below, along with the publisher's online description of each one. I agree that people do have differing levels of skill, but the notion that a ninety-minute written test can pinpoint someone's abilities in a few numbers is shortsighted at best and moronic at worst. Indeed, I get angry when I read the descriptions, as they are such a profound example of the use of numbers to create shame. I have also listed the current cost for each test (to a professional buying them, as listed on the respective publishers' sales pages). Note that schools are obligated to cover these costs under certain circumstances, though these costs are generally a one-time fee for a practitioner until the instrument is revised. That cost is, in part, why a school might resist identifying your child.

- *Kaufman Adolescent and Adult Intelligence Test (KAIT).* Measures problem-solving skills using fluid and crystallized abilities. Age range: 11 to 85+ years. Cost: $1,733.00.
- *Reynolds Intellectual Assessment Scales (RIAS).* Measures verbal and nonverbal intelligence and memory. Age range: 3 to 94 years. Cost: $440.00.
- *Stanford-Binet Intelligence Scales (SB5).* Measures fluid reasoning, knowledge, quantitative reasoning, visual-spatial processing, working memory. Age range: 2 to 85+ years. Cost: $1,087.00.
- *Test of Nonverbal Intelligence, Third Edition (TONI-3).* A language-free assessment of nonverbal intelligence and reasoning abilities. Age range: 6 to 89 years. Cost: $376.00.
- *Wechsler Adult Intelligence Scale—Fourth Edition (WAIS-IV).* Measure of cognitive ability. Age range: 16 to 90 years. Cost: $1,145.00.
- *Woodcock-Johnson III Normative Update (NU).* Measures general intellectual ability and specific cognitive abilities. Age range: 2 to 90+ years. Cost: $1,036.50.

You are not responsible for these costs if your school is doing the screening, but a portion of the costs will hit the school; for example, the school has to buy the new version of the test every time it is up-dated. Even the scoring sheets are extra, as much as four dollars a pop! Then there is the cost of having experts administer the tests and interpret the results. Training to do them is expensive and a provider will charge one hundred and fifty dollars an hour to conduct ten hours of testing, so you are looking at a minimum of fifteen hundred dollars before they even write up the results. Like it or not, when you add it all up, you start to see that a lot of people are making a pretty penny on the testing process; the involved parties have a vested inter-est in making sure that intelligence testing remains a key part of the disability assessment process. More galling to me, though, is that many of these tests don't give credit for creative answers. Consider the sample question from the WAIS-IV test below. My dyslexic brain approaches these problems with little regard for convention, often finding two or more solutions.

WHICH 3 OF THESE PIECES GO TOGETHER TO MAKE THIS PUZZLE?

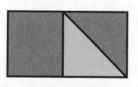

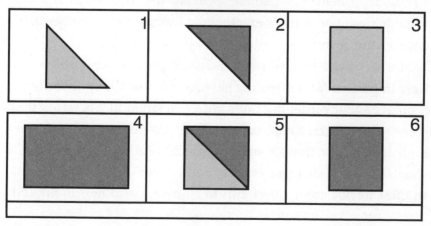

The "correct" answer is blocks 6, 1, and 2. However, what if you allow for stacking? In that case, 6, 1, and 5 would work. So would 6, 3, and 2, or 4, 1, and 2!

But if I gave three of these options as my answer, I would get it wrong, and my score would say I was less intelligent. In this model, coming up with creative solutions equals being *less* intelligent. My dyslexic peers often rant to me about these sorts of problems in standardized tests, where they have often out-thought the test writers. Again, you will have to deal with this system and these tests to get services, but do not believe for a moment that the score tells you anything about the potential or creativity of your child.

DEFINING STRENGTHS

As I've mentioned before, many dyslexics have an ability to follow audio with ease and at a faster rate than non-dyslexics, which is what the Intel Reader is, in part, designed to capitalize on. Interestingly, I once played the Intel Reader for a non-dyslexic friend at a faster-than-normal rate (remember to check out the demo online). His response: "When I listen this way I have to concentrate so intensely and filter everything else out. If I miss just one syllable, then I've lost the word, then the sentence, then the entire concept, and then I am lost. It is strenuous. It demands absolute focus all the time to get it done." Wouldn't you know, that's exactly how I would describe my experience reading print?

In my case I read terribly and spell poorly—weaknesses that were important for me and my parents to know about—but my vocabulary and my listening skills are a real strength. So, rather than read with my eyes, I read with my ears, listening to text at a very high speed (four times standard speech). Rather than write in a standard way, I talk to a computer and it writes down my thoughts. In these ways, I use my strengths to address a weakness in my ability to work with systems that schools and offices have chosen as the standard.

Learning where your child's strengths lie will allow you to determine where your child will thrive. By giving her a pathway to learning that she'll enjoy, you'll quickly see that she will relish learning and do well with it. Identifying your child's strengths will help you find an effective path for her to manage her own gaps *and* her school's weaknesses. I've developed an exercise that will help you do this.

Rather than provide you with one or two scores analogous to an IQ or SAT score, this exercise, "The Strengths Star," maps your child's skills in a visual way. It revolves around the eight major categories of strengths that I have found are most common in dyslexics. It is based, in part, on more than two hundred interviews with dyslexic individuals from my days at Intel, as well as on my own reading of the current research and the thousands of folks in the dyslexia community I've met during my travels.

From the eight categories of strengths, you'll be identifying your child's top three. If this assessment identified only your child's top strength, you'd be missing good complementary strengths. If you were to identify more than three skill strengths, you might dilute the effectiveness of understanding those top three.

This exercise will also help you map the best pathways into your child's head and the most effective pathways for him to express his thoughts. Think of your child's brain as a geographical location. You're trying to get information in, and you quickly learn that some paths are easier to follow than others. The reading path may turn out to be rocky and craggy, with terrible weather; it's just plain hard to get through. But the listening path might be a flat, flower-filled sunny meadow. So why would you continually choose the craggy, hard, cold route when you have this perfectly good, warm, easy-to-navigate path that you could be using on a regular basis?

My questionnaire asks you to rate things on a scale of "that's extremely accurate for my child" to "that's not at all accurate for my child." These questions will most likely uncover for you two or three areas where your child's score is under 15 points (that is, most answers at the "moderately" or "slightly accurate" level) and two or three where the score is over 15 points (with some answers in the "extremely accurate" or "very accurate" range); in rare cases you might have one area scoring at 25 points or one category at 5 points. Having as clear a picture as possible will help you see the path for your child better and will allow her to work with her strongest assets as you try to support her in school and beyond.

MAPPING YOUR CHILD'S STRENGTHS STAR

Before you complete this assessment, talk with your child about the goal of this exercise. Your child may have already noticed that you have started reading a book called *The Dyslexia Empowerment Plan*. Many children won't say something but may be wondering, "Is Mom reading about me?" If they're running some of the negative scripts about shame that we discussed, they may also wonder, "Is Dad angry at me? Does he want me to not be dyslexic?"

It's very important to engage this type of self-talk head-on. Have a discussion with your child about why you're reading the book. You might tell him about some of the myths and the facts that you've learned so far, underscoring that you love him and you're much more interested in what he can accomplish than in what he cannot.

Then complete this assessment once by yourself in order to determine your baseline of where you think your child's strengths lie. Next, go back through it with your child and ask her what *she* thinks. You may be surprised at the gaps that you find, including the possibility that you think your child has strengths in certain areas where she is unaware that she is particularly good. Emphasize that you're interested in supporting her and giving her opportunities to be independent, not in judging her likes or dislikes.

THE STRENGTHS STAR

How accurate is each of the following statements about your child?

5 Extremely accurate

4 Very accurate

3 Moderately accurate

2 Slightly accurate

1 Not at all accurate

VERBAL SKILLS
Your child:

1. Embraces opportunities to talk to adults or large groups of kids—
   e.g., wants to be in the school play, gets up onstage, or is comfortable speaking to a large group at a family reunion.

   1   2   3   4   5

2. Is at ease while talking to a group, smiling and appearing happy and
   very calm while talking.

   1   2   3   4   5

3. Has a large vocabulary, easily using in conversation new words she
   encounters.

   1   2   3   4   5

4. Seeks out and quotes dialogue from films or cartoons, repeating
   entire sections verbatim.

   1   2   3   4   5

5. Describes remembering events in terms of a verbal record of what
   happened, as though it was a radio program or a speech.

   1   2   3   4   5

Verbal Skills: Parent Perspective Score: _____

Verbal Skills: Parent and Child Score: _____

SOCIAL SKILLS
Your child:

1. Reads people's emotions and needs quickly and responds appropriately.

   1   2   3   4   5

2. Can talk to anyone, be it a close friend or new acquaintance, with ease.

   1   2   3   4   5

3. Is attuned to who has social power in a situation—who the cool kids are, which teachers are important, or how extended family members relate to each other.

   1   2   3   4   5

4. Likes complex social stories and can tell you about all the relationships between characters in a movie or story—for example, easily naming all of Harry Potter's friends and their houses at Hogwarts.

   1   2   3   4   5

5. Is excited to interact with new people and sees this as a chance to learn and make friends.

   1   2   3   4   5

Social Skills: Parent Perspective Score: _____

Social Skills: Parent and Child Score: _____

NARRATIVE SKILLS
Your child:

1. Tells, writes, or draws detailed stories with many characters and plot twists.

   1   2   3   4   5

2. Serves as a family historian, remembering who said what, when, and to whom, or where an event happened and what happened there.

   1   2   3   4   5

3. Loves biography, history, or fiction in film, plays, or TV, watching them constantly to learn about how and why things happened or to explore the world of imagination.

   1   2   3   4   5

4. Remembers everything as a story, including science or math, using elements from his own life to give context to abstract concepts—for example, "Grandpa served in the navy and used a compass; compasses tell you which way is north."

   1   2   3   4   5

5. Sees patterns and forecasts how systems might play out, based on recombined memories—for example, "Everyone in school picks a Halloween costume based on movies, so Batman will be popular this year."

   1   2   3   4   5

Narrative Skills: Parent Perspective Score: _____

Narrative Skills: Parent and Child Score: _____

SPATIAL SKILLS
Your child:

1. Wants to tinker with, take apart, and put back together toys or anything electronic or mechanical.

   1   2   3   4   5

2. Sets up experiments around the house with physical elements—for example, playing with mirrors, building large Lego creations, or becoming an expert in knot tying.

   1   2   3   4   5

3. Loves models and miniatures—for example, playing with dollhouses or toy dump trucks, or building his own from kits or from scratch.

   1   2   3   4   5

4. Wants to play with machines and tools in the house; talks about wanting to work in crafts or mechanical shops.

   1   2   3   4   5

5. Talks about being able to see three-dimensional objects in her mind, putting together toys or furniture without assembly instructions.

   1   2   3   4   5

Spatial Skills: Parent Perspective Score: ___

Spatial Skills: Parent and Child Score: ___

KINESTHETIC SKILLS
Your child:

1. Is a natural athlete who learns new sports or dances with ease, quickly mastering complex foot patterns or displaying good hand-eye coordination.

   1   2   3   4   5

2. Must move around to explain or learn, moving objects or himself to make a point or tell a story.

   1   2   3   4   5

3. Practices dance moves or sports moves around the house, repeating until she is satisfied she has them perfect.

   1   2   3   4   5

4. Always moving, climbing, running, jumping, or lifting things, rarely if ever sitting still for more than five minutes.

   1   2   3   4   5

5. Loves science experiments, field trips, or crafts, preferring to touch, smell, and manipulate objects instead of studying an abstraction of a process.

   1   2   3   4   5

Kinesthetic Skills: Parent Perspective Score: _____

Kinesthetic Skills: Parent and Child Score: _____

VISUAL SKILLS
Your child:

1. Is skilled at drawing and painting and takes time on her own to create visual art.

   1   2   3   4   5

2. Keenly focuses on hobbies in the visual arts, such as photography, video game making, graphic novels, or animation.

   1   2   3   4   5

3. Describes seeing things in pictures or talks about his thoughts as colors, maps, or drawings as a primary way to understand the world.

   1   2   3   4   5

4. Solves visual puzzles quickly, always finding Waldo in *Where's Waldo?* or seeing the quickest route to a location on a map with ease.

   1   2   3   4   5

5. Dresses in a visually distinctive way, picking colors and styles that communicate something specific about the wearer to others, regardless of whether it is a conventional or outlandish message.

   1   2   3   4   5

Visual Skills: Parent Perspective Score: ____

Visual Skills: Parent and Child Score: ____

MATHEMATICAL/SCIENTIFIC SKILLS
Your child:

1. Loves logic puzzles and computer games that involve math or science.

   1   2   3   4   5

2. Excels in explaining math concepts, talking about physical relationships or patterns in numbers long before his peers begin noticing these relationships.

   1   2   3   4   5

3. Relishes going to the science museum and doing experiments in school or at home, even if they are just pretend.

   1   2   3   4   5

4. Focuses on hobbies in the natural world—for example, learning about butterflies, dinosaurs, or astronomy—and shows an uncanny ability to explain these biological or physical systems.

   1   2   3   4   5

5. Enjoys math or science classes, especially when they are hands-on and involve visual or verbal presentations of math—for example, explaining a math problem rather than writing one.

   1   2   3   4   5

Mathematical/Scientific Skills: Parent Perspective Score: ____

Mathematical/Scientific Skills: Parent and Child Score: ____

MUSICAL SKILLS
Your child:

1. Relishes singing or playing music, making up his own songs and practicing his music skills with gusto.

   1   2   3   4   5

2. Idealizes DJs or musicians, listening to their work and discussing their styles in detail.

   1   2   3   4   5

3. Likes to put on shows or concerts featuring music or singing for siblings or friends.

   1   2   3   4   5

4. Skilled at using sounds for learning—for example, knows bird songs, animal calls, the fight songs of sports teams, or the sounds of specific engines or machines.

   1   2   3   4   5

5. Notices sounds in an environment before others and with greater skill, or notices rhythm in unusual places—for example, dancing to the rhythm of the washing machine, or naming a song before others can.

   1   2   3   4   5

Musical Skills: Parent Perspective Score: ____

Musical Skills: Parent and Child Score: ____

In the first column below, rank the eight areas with 1 being the highest score, in terms of which you think reflects your child best without thinking about the details of each category. It is possible that your gut will tell you that one should be higher than another even though the scores above suggest a different order. Then record the scores from the pass with your child. Recheck the questions, either adjusting your score within the subsection (that is, changing the 3 in one to a 4, or vice versa) to bring them into alignment or by realizing that the larger pattern is not what you thought it might be. Use the last column to create your final rank.

IMPORTANT: *If you have not talked the answers through with your child, be sure to do so on this second pass to get the most accurate information.*

	GUT RANK	SCORING RANK	FINAL RANK
Verbal	_____	_____	_____
Social	_____	_____	_____
Narrative	_____	_____	_____
Spatial	_____	_____	_____
Kinesthetic	_____	_____	_____
Visual	_____	_____	_____
Mathematical/Scientific	_____	_____	_____
Musical	_____	_____	_____

Mapping the Strengths onto a Star

To make your child's star, take the final numbers in each section and draw a point on the corresponding line. For example, if the verbal score is 18 and the social score is 12, put a point at 18 on the verbal line and 12 on the social line. Once you have marked each, draw a line connecting the point on the axis to the one to the right and left of it. Someone who has equal strengths in all eight categories would mark dots on the axis that would connect to form an evenly sided octagon. But no one—neither dyslexics nor people with strong eye-reading skills—has a completely even profile. We all have a shape that defines our strengths and shows clearly where we are less strong. You can print more of these axes from my website: it can be fun to use them for the entire family to see where everyone's strengths lie.

Many eye readers are often confused as to why we would map data in this form. However, people who are dyslexic are generally excited about the format. You'll see the stars elsewhere in the book in relation to me and other dyslexics. When you see the different shapes,

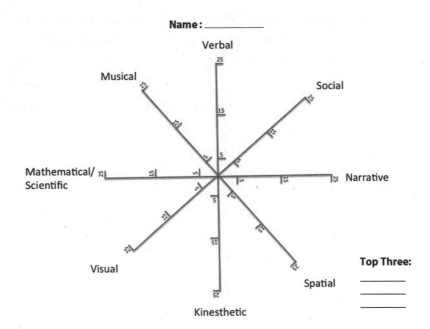

it will help you see the diversity in this community. So while the star may not mean much to you, my suspicion is that your child will find it illuminating.

Ben's Strengths Star

Now that you have mapped your child's profile, let me show you my star. I include this to underscore that everyone has some strengths, even if his or her weaknesses are also glaringly apparent.

	Q1	Q2	Q3	Q4	Q5	Total
Verbal	5	5	5	5	5	25
Social	4	5	5	3	5	22
Narrative	2	2	5	3	4	16
Spatial	3	3	2	1	1	10
Kinesthetic	3	1	1	2	3	10
Visual	1	4	1	3	4	13
Mathematical/Scientific	1	3	3	2	3	12
Musical	1	1	1	2	2	7

My map therefore looks like this:

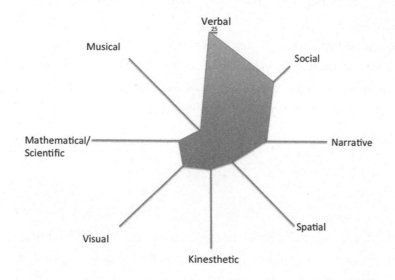

Notice that I am successful by many measures, but I am not strong across the board. The key is that I have figured out how to play to my top three skills: verbal, social, and narrative. In only one of these do I score 25. In my lowest, musical, I am at 7. In school I took to debate team and talked a lot in class. In the office I look for chances to present at meetings and to get to know members of the team well enough to support them in doing great work. When it comes to singing or drawing, I let someone else handle it. This willingness to focus on what I am good at and hand off when I am not strong allows me to channel my strengths to support my weaknesses. Because I am a terrible speller, I always make sure that I deliver something else useful, presenting to an investor or explaining our mission to a new member of the organization rather than creating the corresponding reading materials.

The shapes that result from this exercise will be unique, just like your child. Think about what you see here and ask yourself a few more questions:

- If you had to pick a job for your child when she grows up using only her top three skills, what job would you pick and why?
- Ignore a job's status or the income associated with it and make up three jobs your child might love. Keep in mind many world-changing jobs are not standard ones—such as a micro-sculptor or a robot prototyper.

WHAT YOU LEARN WHEN YOU DISCOVER STRENGTHS

Your child may be inclined to dismiss his own strengths as unimportant. For years I dismissed my ability to excel at public speaking; I thought that because it came easily to me it was really not a big deal. But I've learned that this skill is valuable and, in fact, is hard for most people. If I could have stood up in front of a class and submitted my exams orally instead of on paper, school would have been a walk in the park. It was not until I figured out that my friends were terrified of that prospect and couldn't organize their thoughts quickly enough for that type of format that I realized that my native capability was a skill I could leverage. Your child will likely want to have skills that she doesn't have (and will discount or belittle the ones this assessment identifies) for the simple reason that she—like any of us—wants to fit in. You will need to explain to your child, likely over and over, that the skills she has are valuable.

Consider this by-no-means-exhaustive list of well-known dyslexics who have capitalized on a skill strength area. Note that all of them, like me, are poor spellers and readers compared to their mainstream colleagues. While not everyone will turn out to be Cher or Charles Schwab, and many other factors contributed to these people's success, these folks demonstrate that playing to your strengths can place you on a very successful path. Also note that all of these dyslexics could fall on their faces in an area outside their strengths. I am guessing that it would not go well if Steven Spielberg tried to become a microbiologist or Carol Greider tried to take on film directing. Your role here is to emphasize to your child that he can use his given talents, be they spatial or social, to be effective. You can add non-dyslexic people who obviously have these skills as well. For instance, I have no evidence that Theodor Geisel, the man known to millions of children as Dr. Seuss, was dyslexic, but his narrative skill certainly made him successful. If one of your child's top three strengths is narrative, Dr. Seuss's prowess in that area will show him that a skill he might think is unimportant, could actually be the key to success and happiness.

Famously Strong Verbally

Whoopi Goldberg, Oscar-winning actress, co-host of *The View*

Anderson Cooper, host of CNN's *Anderson Cooper 360°*

Keira Knightley, actress

David Boies, attorney

Famously Strong Socially

Ari Emanuel, CEO, William Morris Agency

Dan Malloy, governor of Connecticut

Erin Brockovich, community advocate

Tom Kean, former governor of New Jersey

Famous Narrative Masters

Anne Rice, author, *Interview with the Vampire*

John Irving, author of *The Cider House Rules* and *The World According to Garp*

Steven Spielberg, film director, Oscar winner

Stephen J. Cannell, writer/producer, *The A-Team*, *21 Jump Street*, *The Rockford Files*

Famous Spatial Thinkers

Dean Kamen, inventor of the Segway

Steve Walker, founder, New England Wood Pellet

Willard Wigan, micro-sculptor

Béatrice Amblard, former Hermès artisan

Famously Kinesthetic People

Magic Johnson, NBA star, entrepreneur

Sir John Young "Jackie" Stewart, Formula One race car driver

Steve Redgrave, Olympic rower

Darcey Andrea Bussell, CBE, dancer, president of the Royal Academy of Dance

Famous Visual Thinkers

Chuck Close, painter, recipient of National Medal of Arts

Robert Rauschenberg, painter, recipient of National Medal of Arts

Richard Rogers, architect

P. Buckley Moss, painter

Famous Mathematical/Scientific Minds

Carol Greider, microbiologist, Nobel Prize winner

Diane Swonk, economist

Matt Schneps, Harvard astrophysicist

Nicholas Negroponte, started the MIT Media Lab

Famous Musical Stars
   Cher, singer, actress, Oscar winner
   Noel Gallagher, lead singer, Oasis
   Harry Belafonte, singer, actor
   Nanci Griffith, singer, songwriter

If you talk to any of the people on this list, I guarantee that some of them will explain that the strength associated with their success stems from their experience with dyslexia: they have fully connected their strengths to their weaknesses. A dyslexic filmmaker could have a particular knack for visualizing a scene or camera angle because she spent more time looking at the pictures in books than at the words. A dyslexic actor may have developed his ability to talk his way out of being in trouble in the principal's office by adopting five different personalities in the course of ten minutes. Above all, they all learned resilience and proactivity, as well as some of the other attitudes and approaches that we will review later in this chapter—worldviews that helped them throughout their careers.

SUPPORTING YOUR CHILD'S STRENGTHS

As a parent, you can show your child that you will love and accept him just the way he is by embracing his strengths. In other words, let him be what he is going to be. When you see his face light up with interest about something, follow his lead. If he tells you that he needs a drum kit or loves trains, see where the interest can take him and run with it. That specific interest may support a strength, which can put your child on the path to success. Every one of the people listed above was terrible at school in his or her early years, but eventually each of them found something that he or she was really good at and loved, and stuck with the thing. If we judged them based on their weaknesses, none of these people would be on our list.

One of the best ways to help your child develop resiliency and specific skills related to his strengths is by enrolling him in activities or classes that cater to or build on those strengths. That said, it is essential that you make sure the activity itself is taught in a manner that supports your child's strength. After all, what use is a visual-reasoning-related activity such as a class on graphic novels if it emphasizes a traditional textbook, or a kinesthetic-oriented dance class if it uses handwritten worksheets to teach the steps? Be sure to look for ways to incorporate the accommodations your child needs (outlined in Chapter Six) in activities that interest your child, giving her *full* access to the things she enjoys.

Your child can and should embrace his or her core skills. It might be seeing a new style of defense for the football team for a kid who's kinesthetic, or envisioning a support coalition that will get her elected to a school office for a kid who's got strong social skills. The key is to put your child in situations where his or her strengths can reinforce each other. Here is a list of activities that will likely build on your child's given strengths:

Verbal
>   Acting classes
>   Storytelling classes
>   Debate club

Social
>   Leadership in a local charity
>   Leadership in clubs
>   Sports team captain

Spatial
>   Inter-School Robotics Challenge (see Appendix C)
>   Metalworking and woodworking classes
>   Craft classes

Kinesthetic

> Sports programs (pick three to try)
>
> Dance classes
>
> Hiking, orienteering, and camping clubs

Visual

> Drawing and painting classes
>
> Video game graphics classes
>
> Mural painting at school

Narrative

> English and writing classes (accommodated with audiobooks
>   and speech-to-text software; see Chapter Six)
>
> Filmmaking classes
>
> Animation classes

Musical

> Expose your child to different musical instruments, sign up
>   for lessons in one that appeals
>
> Voice lessons
>
> Marching band

TAKE ADVANTAGE OF YOUR CHILD'S STRENGTHS

In addition to supporting your child through activities that appeal to her strengths, you will need to create space for your child to use her strengths *in the classroom*, validating them whenever you can. Based on my strengths profile, one of the things a learning specialist recommended to my mother was that I would have to find ways to do my schoolwork, specifically written reports, in a non-standard way. For instance, the specialist suggested that I hand in a tape recording of a book report instead of a written copy, and my mother thought that was a great idea. She went to the school and the school agreed. Then she brought me the good news, and I was not pleased. I was adamant that I was going to do a paper just like everyone else. I didn't want to have special accommodations because it made me feel like I was stupid. I was carrying shame about a weakness and therefore would not take advantage of a strength.

In this case, one way around my obstinacy might have been to develop a compromise. First I could have done an oral report leveraging my strength, and then I could have done it the way others did. The Jemicy School, a private school for kids with learning disabilities in Maryland, has developed a model that does just this. When a child is doing a term paper in high school, he masters the topic using a strength, be it audio, print, or visual learning. He is asked to give a report in any format he wants. This could include sculpture, video, or even cartoons. Then, once he has proven that he has mastered the content—say, the history of the Civil War—through a strength-based method, he is taught how to write a term paper on the same topic. Learning the content (e.g., who General Stonewall Jackson was) is separate from learning a form of expressing that knowledge (e.g., a term paper with good footnotes), with the understanding that the paper itself is not what has proved his knowledge of the subject. This staged method both takes advantage of students' strengths in learning and allows them to work on weaknesses.

ATTITUDE MATTERS

As you already know or will soon find out, the majority of people working in the area of learning disabilities focus on remediation as the ultimate goal. Your child is broken, the logic goes, and if you do the right things, the experts can fix him. As I've made clear, this is a deeply flawed theory, one with the power to create pathological self-loathing when it fails. It's missing a critical point: that there are specific attitudes and habits that will have a huge impact on whether your child will be able to apply her strengths at school and beyond.

Consider my own example and those of my successful dyslexic peers. Very few of us mastered reading with our eyes. None of us can spell well. But most of the important skills that we learned were in the emotional realm, leading to resiliency and good use of supports. This is not merely my opinion or even limited to the results of my systematic observations. Dr. Robert Brooks, a Harvard Medical School child psychologist, and his colleague Sam Goldstein, at the University of Utah, have spent their careers studying resilience in children, including those with SLDs and/or ADHD. They emphasize that fostering a child's strengths is a great way to begin the process of creating the ability to bounce back from adversity.

You now have a better picture of your child's strengths, and you should begin emphasizing them both in the tasks your child takes on and in praising her for what a good job she does using these skills. Brooks and Goldstein agree that one of the most important things you can do for your child to build resilience is to unconditionally accept him for both his strengths and his weaknesses. This means not attacking her when she makes mistakes and encouraging her to pursue activities in her areas of strength, as opposed to activities solely in *your* areas of interest.

Every child needs to have access to an adult who will coach her and accept her as she is. Besides a parent, children can turn to a sports coach, a minister, or a Scouting leader. Look for mentors in an area (based on your assessment of your child's strengths) that will help her flourish. If she is particularly musically gifted, it may be the person who teaches her how to play an instrument; if she has a love for kinesthetic learning, it could be a dance team choreographer.

It is also extremely important to develop a pattern of problem solving with your child. Brooks and Goldstein emphasize that it's important for children to have a sense of worth that comes from meaningful contributions to the world. A sense of his or her own competence and usefulness will help foster resiliency in your child over the long term. This involves giving him responsibilities in the household that are commensurate with his level of skill. This might range from putting the dishes away each night to helping you paint a room in the house. This could also be a volunteer activity (say, where your child helps deliver meals, or teaches a younger student how to play sports).

Brooks and Goldstein's work also points out the necessity of developing backup solutions when an initial plan doesn't work. Children are very capable of thinking through techniques that will help them stay on task or learn, so involve them in designing solutions and approaching mistakes as an opportunity to engage in problem solving. This mind-set can result in conversations that begin with "How can we do this better next time?" or "What accommodations would make this easier for you in the future?" rather than "You didn't try hard enough!" or "Why don't you focus more?"

The general principle that resiliency and other emotional skills drive success has been demonstrated specifically in the context of dyslexia and other specific learning disabilities as well. A study from the late 1990s conducted at the Frostig Center in Pasadena, California shows a striking result. The Center is affiliated with a school by the same name that specialized in teaching students with learning disabilities, including those with dyslexia. Researchers undertook a twenty-year longitudinal study looking to determine the factors related to positive adult outcomes for the school's graduates. The findings showed that "life success" depended much more heavily on a number of attitudes, behaviors, and characteristics than it did on any specific element of their academic achievement, IQ, or social background. The lead author was Marshall Raskind, who went on to become Director of Research at the Charles and Helen Schwab Foundation, which operated a program to disseminate information on learning and attention problems. The study demonstrated that the IQ scores or academic achievement of students while enrolled in school had between zero and 5 percent predictive power in explaining the variation in their long-term outcomes. At the same time, emotional and attitudinal success attributes (the authors named six: self-awareness, perseverance, proactivity, emotional stability, goal setting, and social support systems) explained 49 to 75 percent of the variance in the students' long-term outcomes. Put another way, academic achievement and IQ score predicted next to nothing about the future of these dyslexic students. What mattered most was their ability to bounce back, get help from others, and take action.

In this particular study, the highs and the lows were extreme. The researchers looked at measures of success: a good job, educational attainment, stable family lives. One graduate in the study was running his own software company in California at the age of thirty-five. Another, also thirty-five, was serving a life sentence in prison for murder. Either could have a high IQ, and indeed, they might both have strong verbal or narrative skills as well. But their ability to master emotional coping skills was what correlated best to their outcomes.

The general resiliency literature, as opposed to that focused on dyslexia, is also built on large data sets. In a longitudinal study started in 1955 on the Hawaiian island of Kauai, researchers tracked the lives of 698 babies born that year. Over the next thirty-two years they checked in on their progress at regular intervals. Roughly a third of the children were designated as living in high-risk circumstances, such as households with chronic mental illness, alcoholism, or major discord. Of these roughly two hundred students, a third would turn out to have successful long-term outcomes, equivalent to those of people who were raised in stable households. The researchers linked these children's success to their resiliency, showing that the right mind-set could change the course of people's lives, even when the deck was stacked against them. The findings in this study add empirical weight to Brooks and Goldstein's conclusion that unconditional love from an adult and giving a child responsibilities he can handle are important to developing resiliency. Overall, a hopeful attitude and a sense that you can beat the odds are the most important elements in building resiliency. As a parent, talking about dyslexia in the context of a hopeful future is a great way to begin this path.

The exercise that follows is intended to assess your child's attitudes and will set a baseline for your child from which he can improve. By having this insight now you greatly increase the odds that your child will be in the successful group rather than the challenged group. Almost all children who are dyslexic—indeed, most adults who are dyslexic—will score very poorly on this exercise the first time out. This is because without having had the support of the types of frameworks described in this book, they often see themselves as broken. Your role as a parent will be to help your child develop the underlying skills by discussing the stories and advice in this book and incorporating the messages into your daily routines. Six months from now you'll see improvement on these measures. And if all goes according to plan, two years from now your child will be knocking many of these out of the park. Think of this as a blueprint for the future rather than as a grade assessing how your child is doing today.

This assessment adapts measures that were outlined in the Frostig Center study as well as material from the general resiliency literature above. It is also built on my organizational behavior training at business school, and it incorporates my experience from more than four hundred interviews with people with disabilities while I was director of access technology at Intel. Finally, it is also based on interviews with members of the Headstrong Nation Fellows Network. This is a group of dyslexic leaders in their respective fields who gather once a year to talk about the future of our community. The Headstrong Nation Fellows Network includes astrophysicists, Oscar-winning filmmakers, and Emmy-winning actors as well as former prisoners who now advise about how to handle drug and gang problems in cities. Each Headstrong Nation Fellow exhibits strengths in these core areas:

- Resiliency
- Integration of specific learning disabilities
- Self-awareness

- Proactivity
- Emotional stability
- Goal setting
- Social supports
- Possibility thinking

The instrument below analyzes the same key attributes and attitudes and is a starting point for training your child to develop the approaches needed to be successful *and* dyslexic.

The Attitudes Star

How accurate is each of the following statements about your child?

5 Extremely accurate

4 Very accurate

3 Moderately accurate

2 Slightly accurate

1 Not at all accurate

RESILIENCY

1. Keeps going when there is adversity—for example, goes back out for a sport after not getting picked for a team the first time around.

   1   2   3   4   5

2. Talks about how difficulties are part of learning—for example, "Sometimes you don't get it right the first time."

   1   2   3   4   5

3. Describes himself as "someone who sticks with it," "not a quitter," or "a tough kid."

   1   2   3   4   5

4. Talks about how not everyone is perfect and can discuss mistakes made by someone who is a hero to him—for example, "LeBron's team lost to Dallas in the final in 2011, but he worked hard and won the next year."

    1   2   3   4   5

5. Talks about past mistakes with ease—for example, "Boy, I was terrible at drawing when I started, but now I am better."

    1   2   3   4   5

    Total Score for Resiliency ____

INTEGRATION OF SPECIFIC LEARNING DISABILITIES

1. Describes herself using *dyslexic*, *LD*, or the relevant profile term to a new friend or acquaintance with ease.

    1   2   3   4   5

2. Explains how her dyslexia or profile is relevant to events in school or life—for example, "I get audiobooks in English because I am not a good eye reader, but I am a good ear reader."

    1   2   3   4   5

3. Presents his strengths and weaknesses in a thoughtful way—for example, explaining to a teacher, "When I eye-read, it is like I have a bad cell phone connection to the page; a talking computer is much clearer, like a landline."

    1   2   3   4   5

4. Is at ease being associated with other students in special education or with disabilities (that is, displays an attitude opposite to something like "Those kids are retards").

    1   2   3   4   5

5. Praises people who try to help him—for example, "Ms. Jones is nice to spend time on this with me" (instead of something like "Ms. Jones is stupid and I hate her").

    1   2   3   4   5

    Total Score for Integration of SLDs _____

SELF-AWARENESS

1. Refers to her strengths and weaknesses related to dyslexia in a matter-of-fact way—for example, "I am pretty good at talking to people" or "I am not the best speller."

    1   2   3   4   5

2. Talks about habits and traits that are not related to his dyslexia—for example, "I am a fast runner" or "I sometimes forget to clean up my area."

    1   2   3   4   5

3. Is aware of and has ways to reduce or manage stress—for example, by drawing pictures or talking to a friend.

    1   2   3   4   5

4. Is interested in feedback that could help her improve her life.

    1   2   3   4   5

5. Notices when he has hurt someone's feelings or helped someone out and comments on it—for example, "I should have apologized after I said that" or "I helped Alex a lot when I offered to teach him how to play Risk."

    1   2   3   4   5

    Total Score for Self-Awareness _____

PROACTIVITY

1. Makes decisions in a timely manner, including both small ones (for example, "I want fish sticks for dinner") and large ones ("I want to join the Scouts this fall").

   1   2   3   4   5

2. Talks about her ability to make changes in her own life and in the world—for example, "I am going to learn to play the drums" or "I am interested in dinosaurs and am going to learn more about them."

   1   2   3   4   5

3. Participates in community, social, and family networks, engaging people in conversation and being part of the social scene.

   1   2   3   4   5

4. Can work on a project without coaxing or pressure from others—for example, enjoys a hobby that she can sustain on her own, such as drawing or rock collecting.

   1   2   3   4   5

5. Suggests that the family or a group of friends do new things—for example, "How about we try go-cart racing next week?"

   1   2   3   4   5

   Total Score for Proactivity _____

EMOTIONAL STABILITY

1. Shows balanced emotional states, reacting in proportion to the scale of events—for example, "I am frustrated that I got a C on this" rather than throwing a tantrum.

   1   2   3   4   5

2. Has rich and meaningful friendships with peers—that is, has two or more friends with whom she spends time and feels connected to.

    1   2   3   4   5

3. Takes part in social activities regularly—for example, going to birthday parties or being a part of school clubs.

    1   2   3   4   5

4. Expresses a positive and hopeful outlook—for example, "I think things will get better" or "I bet this time it will work out."

    1   2   3   4   5

5. Is open to feedback, listening when people want to tell him how he might do something better or that another person's feelings were hurt, and then changes his behavior in the future.

    1   2   3   4   5

Total Score for Emotional Stability ____

GOAL SETTING

1. Plans for the future—for example, "I want to save up for a new skateboard" or "Next year I want to join the glee club."

    1   2   3   4   5

2. Talks about goals he has currently—for example, "I am going to learn to play this entire piece of music" or "I want to go on the school trip to Washington, D.C., next year."

    1   2   3   4   5

3. Understands the step-by-step nature of goal setting—for example, "First I want to learn to use a yo-yo, then I want to work on some tricks."

    1   2   3   4   5

4. Sets goals that are attainable—for example, "I want to learn to play chopsticks on the piano" (instead of "I want to be Taylor Swift").

1   2   3   4   5

5. Has general goals that provide direction to his development overall—for example, "I like building things and I want to do more stuff where I get to build."

1   2   3   4   5

Total Score for Goal Setting ____

Social Supports

1. Actively seeks support from friends and family, getting guidance or encouragement—for example, "I want to become a good Boy Scout. Can you help me with knot tying this weekend?"

1   2   3   4   5

2. Has family and friends who set realistic goals for her—for example, "We want her to move up 10 percent this year in her grades" (instead of "If she does not make varsity, then she is not trying").

1   2   3   4   5

3. Explains on her own that she gets guidance and encouragement from people close to her.

1   2   3   4   5

4. Without embarrassment, uses help from family or mentors when offered—for example, "The drama teacher is going to help me learn my lines" (not "I don't want her to know I don't know the lines yet").

1   2   3   4   5

5. Maintains relationships with teachers and mentors—for example, "I told Ms. Jones, my teacher last year, that I got into science camp, and she was happy."

1   2   3   4   5

Total Score for Social Supports ____

POSSIBILITY THINKING

1. Enjoys trying new foods, meeting new people, or trying new hobbies.

1   2   3   4   5

2. Has a high propensity to prototype activities—for example, trying out a new way to get to school, a new way to dress, or a new way to train for a sport—in small steps, revising when it does not work.

1   2   3   4   5

3. Challenges people's sense of what is possible or what is appropriate, asking why we do it one way or whether we might do it another way in the future.

1   2   3   4   5

4. Willing to be exposed to criticism from peers or teachers when they do not agree with the way he is approaching a situation—for example, "Most people think cooking is not for boys, but I want to try it."

1   2   3   4   5

5. Interested in people who approach the world differently; open to learning lessons from new people and practices—for example, "Can we host an exchange student this summer? I want to learn about Japan."

1   2   3   4   5

Total Score for Possibility Thinking ____

As in the "Supporting Your Child's Strengths" section, take the scores in each section and draw a point on the corresponding axis. Once you have marked each, draw a line connecting the point on the axis to the one to the right and left of it. Remember that this will almost certainly be tight around the core of the star for now, but over time, as your child begins to develop these skills, the star will widen.

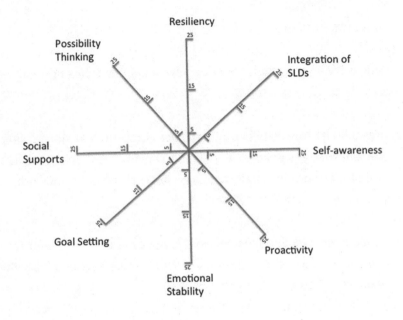

Now that you have this baseline, you can see where your child's relative attitudinal strengths lie. You will see the seeds of her long-term success. If she scored high in resiliency, you will want to coax that ember into a stronger flame, talking to her about how not everything works out the first time and how it is important to try things more than once. To be clear, there is no magic number that means success here. You should look for progress over time, rather than a definitive goalpost.

You will also be able to make substantial progress by taking small steps. If goal setting is a challenge today, build up this capability by starting with small goals that are unrelated to reading or dyslexia. You might focus on a hobby your son likes at first. If he is excited about dinosaurs, work with him on learning the names of ten of them and then promise him a trip to the museum or to rent the movie *Jurassic Park* and watch it with friends. Note here that I have not pointed to a goal such as "Correctly spell the names" or "Get an A on the quiz," instead suggesting that you teach the core skill of goal setting around something that is a strength and which your child enjoys. The goal setting or other skill can be applied to a tougher activity once he has the attitude mastered in an unthreatening context. Celebrating success when each small goal is met builds a positive association with goal setting, and will help your child develop along each vector.

As in other realms, shame can affect your child's attitude in each of the major categories. People who feel shame will be less resilient because they will internalize every small mistake as *entirely* their fault and more important to an outcome than it really was. They will be unwilling to own and integrate their dyslexia because they feel as though that flaw is in and of itself a moral failing. Those who are ashamed have highly limited self-awareness, as they see their characteristics as inherently bad, leaving them no room for a more balanced view. As a result, their proactivity is much lower because each forward step creates a risk of exposure and therefore increases feelings of shame. Their emotional stability will be uneven, with flare-ups of rage as a defense mechanism when it becomes clear that they are not succeeding, or deep bouts of depression when they find out that their disability may have an impact on fitting in with others. As a result, they're extremely unlikely to participate in rational goal setting, either because depression can interfere with their ability to plan for the future or because they will limit their goals for fear that they could be let down even more. Someone who feels shame about his dyslexia is extremely unlikely to take advantage of social supports, never seeking community. Ironically, community is the antidote to shame (I discuss this more in Chapter Nine). Finally, someone who feels ashamed is unlikely to see new possibilities and will be unwilling to try new things. But seeing new possibilities and being willing to try new things are essential attributes of success for a dyslexic person who cannot enter through the metaphorical front door and must always be looking for a creative or unexpected path that allows her to find a different way of learning.

HOW TO USE THE DATA

Everyone worries about failure for dyslexics. I am less interested in the failures than in the quality of the recovery. A person who fails but keeps trying and eventually gets it right can be successful. Indeed, we have a word for a person like that: *entrepreneur.*

You now have a list of what your child can do well, as well as a good sense of the emotional skills and attitudes she needs to develop to be effective in pursuing her dreams. You also have a framework that will allow you to find ways to build up his emotional skills and attitudes. With the exception of the category "integration of SLDs," all of these skills fit with the profile of an entrepreneurial thinker, regardless of whether she has dyslexia. People wonder why it is that 35 percent of entrepreneurs in the United States are dyslexic. I think it is because we all had to develop these core emotional skills just to get through grammar school. Our mainstream classmates may not have needed to become as resilient or self-aware; they may not have had to become proactive despite being frustrated and beaten down. They did not have to develop adaptive emotional stability or crisp goal setting. The dyslexic third grader who can talk a friend into telling him what was in the book is making good use of proactivity; the dyslexic teen who decides to take an English class about Shakespeare when she figures out she can get all the plays as video rentals is developing possibility-thinking skills.

USING THE DYSLEXIA HAMMER

Adopting entrepreneurial thinking will serve your child well, regardless of the career path he chooses. Jack Horner, Regents Professor of

Paleontology in the Honors College at Montana State University, is a winner of a MacArthur Foundation "genius" award and was the science advisor for *Jurassic Park*, even inspiring Steven Spielberg to model one of the film's characters on him. And he is dyslexic and does not have a college degree. When Jack Horner explains why he won the MacArthur, he points to his discovery of dinosaur embryos. Dinosaur eggs had been discovered more than one hundred years ago and a number of museums proudly count them in their collection. When he discovered a nest of dinosaur eggs at his Montana dig site, he decided to do what no other museum would have been willing to do. When he describes it, he frames it this way: "I had a tool that allowed me to discover dinosaur embryos: a hammer." I've seen the photograph of the egg when he initially hit it with his hammer. He held it together with a rubber band and then later glued the pieces back together. In his words "Glue is cheap." Seeing the possibility was genius, as was acting on it.

Similar "hammers" can be seen in many fields. Jack Laws, a naturalist who illustrates wildlife, developed a field guide that is like no other. Most guides divide animals or birds into genus or region or some other hierarchical categorization system. When he's out hiking and he wants to look up a bird, he first notices its color and its size, so he organized his categorizations by colors and sizes. If you want to look up a yellow bird that is small, flip to the yellow section and then look under small. Both these men illustrated that there seems to be an experiential nature to the discoveries that dyslexics make, using their ability to think outside of the system and seeing other possibilities.

Dyslexics are used to ignoring the conventional wisdom, because that way of thinking typically puts us at a disadvantage. Instead, we are constantly assessing how to use our personal strengths and available resources to develop goals on the fly, while creatively reacting to new contingencies. This works in business, as it does in school, the arts, or any other field your child may choose. Once again, your child will have to integrate his emotional experiences to do it well.

One of the most successful dyslexics of the twentieth century perfectly illustrates this point. General George S. Patton is arguably the single best field commander the U.S. Army has ever produced; some would say he was the best combat commander of the Second World War. And his challenges with text set him back terribly. It took him two tries to get into West Point because he didn't have the grades to get in the first time. Then he had to repeat his first year at West Point, as he failed math and ranked 139th in his class—in the bottom 10 percent that year—in English. His distraught letters home to his father sound much like the private fears and pain I have heard from countless dyslexic teens:

> I am nearly hopeless. I don't know what is the matter for I certainly work.... I hate to be so low ranking for I still think that I am smarter than more other men who rank me.... [I]t is exasperating to see a lot of fools who don't care beat you out when you work so hard.... I cant [sic] think of any thing but my own worthlessness so I will stop writing.
>
> *Your goaty son,*
> *George S. Patton Jr.*

Here is a man who became an expert fencer and then at age twenty-eight redesigned the sword that all military officers have to carry for formal events (now called, colloquially, the "Patton saber"). He went on to revolutionize tank warfare. In World War I tanks were lumbering, slow, big machines that were effectively fortresses. He turned them into fast-moving cavalry. As a result, he was responsible for taking more of the continent of Europe in a briefer time than anyone else in the history of the world. Finally, he would go on to liberate France from the Nazi regime, yet at the beginning of his career he thought of himself as "worthless." If his school ranked him so low, does this tell us that his school was broken or that Patton was? I see in his innovative mind an incredible mark of the strength of dyslexia. Once he got out of school and began using his resiliency, proactivity, and possibility thinking, he began to thrive. His ability to see the bigger picture—the strategic significance of speed over armor—and lead his forces by understanding what motivated them made him a great leader. Using entrepreneurial thinking and mastering the emotional skills I listed above are, I would argue, what made the difference for Patton. These skills can do the same for your child.

Your child should have big dreams and will be able to achieve them by focusing on his or her strengths. To do this she should learn from the parable of the giant sea turtle as told to me by Lou Salza, head of the Lawrence School in Cincinnati, Ohio:

Crossing the beach, the giant sea turtle looks awkward, kicking up sand and dragging itself slowly. But once it enters the water, that giant sea turtle dives deeper, swims more gracefully, and lives longer than most other animals in the ocean. If your child can make it through the difficulties inherent in the beach of school and make it to the water of life, she will be successful. And if you can change the nature of school to be more like life, where you can rely on your strengths and get help with your weaknesses, you will start seeing success that much sooner.

PART II

EMPOWERING
Your CHILD

CHAPTER FOUR

Allow Your Child to Dream Big

Every child needs to be challenged in order to grow and mature. It's important to help your child choose appropriate challenges that will make the most of both his aptitudes and his learning profile.

In the military, soldiers are taught to structure their thinking into objectives, strategies, and tactics. They learn to see the big picture and then figure out how to develop a careful and methodical plan to achieve the desired outcome. Substitute "dreams, educational goals, and tasks" for "objectives, strategies, and tactics," and you can apply this military thinking to helping dyslexic kids as well. Children's dreams may be achievements in or outside of school. In order to reach them, they need defined educational goals that can help support their dreams. These goals are then achieved by completing and mastering specific learning tasks and attitudes.

This process of defining dreams and goals is complicated for everyone, but for the dyslexic child, the conventions that other people use do not apply. While it is pretty hard to predict what might come our way, the majority of people use the school systems to help them find a path in life and shape their dreams for the future. Yet for the typical dyslexic person, school is an unwelcoming environment, and unfortunately, many people leave the system feeling hopeless about their future. Often the response to this anxiety is for the child to focus on fitting into a standard system that does not support her, which is a form of hiding, or the child tries to "fight back," which often leads to behavior issues and getting in trouble at school. Neither of these paths allows a child to figure out what she could become. Dyslexic children may not trust that they are as talented as other people, or they may not get to learn about an inspirational role model because eye reading is the only path offered to learning. And once they do find a passion in life, the conventional path is often blocked without the right accommodations. Your role as a parent is to unwind the script that is running in your child's head, removing the label of "lazy" or "stupid" and giving her every opportunity to dream big.

When you think about establishing dreams, goals, and tasks, consider every option, including nontraditional methods. Here's an example of something small: ordering a meal at a restaurant. There are certain tasks that occur when ordering a meal. We sit down. The waitperson approaches us and gives us menus. We read the menus, select something we like, order it, eat it, pay the bill, and leave. But this process has to operate differently for someone like me, who's dyslexic. I almost never order meals off a menu. Menus often have difficult words for me, particularly if they are in a foreign language, and I know that I can have trouble getting those difficult words off the page. Recently I was out with a friend who is also dyslexic and he explained to the waitress that he wanted the pizza that had oysters on it. "I've never heard of oysters on a pizza," he said. "Let's try it!" She looked at him in a somewhat dismissive way and said, "Those are oyster *mushrooms,* sir."

While he and I had a laugh over that, I like to bypass this scenario whenever possible. Like many dyslexics, I have developed a number of techniques so that I can more easily navigate menus. If I am with people who know me well, I may ask one of them to read the menu aloud. If I have a piece of technology with me, like the Intel Reader, I can just translate the menu into speech and ear-read it on the spot. Other times I will turn to the waiter and ask him what's good today. I often end up finding out what the chef is best at preparing by having this brief chat—perhaps the mussels are fresh, or the salmon is their signature dish and they are down to the last order. If all else fails, I'll wait to order last and see what everyone else is getting. In this case I can often cut a deal. If my dining partner has ordered something that I'm interested in, I can order something they might like to try and we can swap a taste. No matter which strategy I choose, most people never notice that my ordering-a-meal process is entirely different from what standard readers go through. What I really did was find my own path in order to accomplish my task. I generally make a point to reveal my dyslexia, as I find it brings me closer to people, but it is great to have options when that does not fit the situation.

If ordering the meal is a task, what was the goal? Heading out to a restaurant can simply be a way to get something to eat when you don't have food in the house. But there can also be multiple social and cultural layers: it might be a first date, or it might be your ten-year anniversary. You might be meeting with a potential employer or someone you're trying to develop as a mentor. Each of these scenarios will affect other goals of the meal, such as which restaurant you go to and what you order. Asking for a fancy bottle of champagne would seem perfectly reasonable in the context of an anniversary, but it might seem out of place when meeting a potential boss. For example, when I first made the film *Headstrong*, I was introduced to a potential investor at a dinner. This man turned out to be the former CEO of Ford Motor Company. During that meal I focused less on the meal and more on finding the right opportunity to talk with him about my dyslexia, which allowed me to secure major support from him for my project.

With your help, your child can identify the best ways for doing a number of different things to reach her goals and dreams. This could include experimenting with different choices, talking with trusted people to figure out what the options are, developing a willingness to change paths, and noticing which dreams come to him from society and which from his own heart.

IDENTIFYING REAL DREAMS

Uncovering your child's dreams can be extremely difficult for any parent, because children can be fickle—at different ages, they may have a different fixation. In preschool your daughter might want to be a ballerina because she likes the tutu. In second grade she might announce that she wants to be a teacher. By fifth grade she may be convinced that becoming a professional athlete is the only way to go. And by tenth grade she may have decided that she wants to become a judge (possibly based on watching too many episodes of *Law & Order*).

Give your child permission to dream. Your child is already blessed with the advantages inherent in living in a free and democratic society, and her life is not prescribed from birth. As a parent, you have the task of bringing opportunities to your child so that he can explore individual interests and talents. You are also there to supply your own wisdom and experience as well as to reflect on who your child seems to be and what makes him happiest, as well as where his skills will fit into a competitive world.

The exercises that we completed in the last chapter should give you a good sense of your child's top three strengths. These offer a great place to begin to help her focus on her dreams. While there are certainly examples of people who have gone on to be very successful in fields where they did not initially have tremendous strengths, it is almost always the case that if you're good at something, you probably can find a variation on it that you enjoy and can build a life around. If you discovered that your child's top three strengths are verbal skills, narrative skills, and social skills, he might be cut out to become an actor, a marketing executive, or even a minister. These careers draw on these same three strengths. Given that profile, it seems less likely that he's going to be truly happy working as a librarian, a software engineer, or a graphic designer, all occupations that focus on nonverbal and more isolated activity.

Another way to help identify your child's dreams is to expose her to activities surrounding her core strengths. Use the lists in Chapter Three to find the right set of enriching activities that match a particular profile. By doing so, you can bypass the shame she can feel when she fails at something others are succeeding in. Dyslexic children are often drawn to activities that are designed to secure status, in order to prove to the world they are not dyslexic. Think back to my bookmark competition in third grade. I had no particular interest in bookmarks; they were actually a symbol of an eye-reading code that I couldn't crack, one that scared me. And that is precisely why I developed a passion for making one and winning an award. If I had truly loved books and reading, I would have made dozens of bookmarks, but instead I was highly strategic and made just the one; it allowed me to fulfill my real dream, which was to win some praise in a library, and then I moved on.

Here are some signs your child may be focusing on a dream as a form of camouflage:

- The dream focuses on or relies on an area that showed up as a weakness in Chapter Three.
- Any activity that is centered around spelling, reading, or looking like a "smart kid" is immediately suspect. Did she announce that she wants to win the calligraphy contest at school despite having terrible handwriting? Does he always carry around three books, but you never see him reading them?
- Your child gets injured during the activity in the process of doing what most people do without hurting themselves. This can occur when the stress level around a camouflage activity is high both because he wants it so badly and because he is relying on his weaknesses in order to succeed. Did he sign up for a play where he had to memorize lines, but then fall off the stage and bang his knee, so he had to drop out?

- Your child takes unreasonable risks around the activity in order to do it well. This might involve being reckless in sports, to the point that she hurts others or herself. Or it might result in her cheating to fulfill an objective.
- Your child focuses on the outcomes, not on the process of the activity. Does he measure his achievements only in terms of public recognition, such as awards or titles? Does she perceive herself as a complete failure unless she makes it to a specific level?
- Your child pretends to use an area where she is weak, such as eye reading, to complete an activity, yet is secretly using her strengths in order to keep up. Did she memorize stories based on you reading them to her and then pretend that she is reading them aloud? Older children may talk about books they have not read by giving vague details about major points in the plot, which they gleaned from a movie based on the book.

It is particularly important to look out for these warning signs because the more time students invest in an activity, the more they can convince themselves that it is their dream. It is a bad idea to get very good at something you do not like. I have seen lawyers who have been practicing for ten years but admit to never enjoying their job, feeling trapped in the profession and desperately wishing they had pursued a different degree. The same principle applies with your child. If she becomes adept at gymnastics, but only did it to stand out and not because of a deep love of time spent in the gym or at competitions, she is wasting a lot of time and energy to fit in.

Even if children are good at a camouflage activity, they may be ignoring what they could really thrive at. I played soccer all through middle school and high school, winning the award as the most valuable player in the playoffs and helping my team win a state championship my senior year. But as soon as I got to college, I dropped soccer and never played it again. It had been merely a means to an end—

credibility with my teenage peers—but in reality I never enjoyed it. I would have been happier if I had instead used my strong verbal skills and participated in high school theater or the debate club, something I only figured out when I got to college.

Your child may have a passion that is, at least in your mind, a little offbeat. But she can develop it into something that distinguishes her and makes her happy. Even the most obscure interests can become very powerful and joyful forces in a person's life and can ultimately lead to economic success. Willard Wigan is the self-described "greatest micro-sculptor" alive. As a child he was verbally abused by his teachers because of his dyslexia. Once a teacher told his elementary school class, "If you want to see failure, look at Willard."

One day Willard's dog tore up an anthill in his backyard. Feeling sympathy for the ants, he decided to build them little houses and even clothes. Whenever I think of this story, I imagine that Willard was sensitive to the ants because a massive destructive force swept in and attacked the small creatures, much the way the school system was attacking him. As he explains in the film *Journey into Dyslexia*, Willard then began making art so small that he had to learn to control his pulse in order to avoid damaging his work.

This odd obsession has also turned into a very successful career. Of his many masterpieces, my favorite is a sculpture of Charlie Chaplin that stands on the end of an eyelash! Today Willard has successfully put a sculpture of a camel in the eye of a needle—indeed, nine of them in one needle eye. When I met him at an awards dinner in Washington, D.C., he had appeared on Conan O'Brien's show the night before, showing off a sculpture of the White House that he'd carved from the end of a zip tie. He is now a member of the Most Excellent Order of the British Empire (MBE), an honor awarded by Prince Charles in Buckingham Palace, and when I last saw him he showed me a watch that he had made with a magnifying lens built into the face to allow you to see a personalized Wigan sculpture inside. These watches sell for over $1 million. Small stuff can be big bucks!

The key here is that Willard focused on his own dream and channeled all his creative strengths into something, not because he wanted to stand out or fit in, but because it was his true love. Art is one field in which this can happen. Entrepreneurship is another. My dyslexic friend Steve Walker played to his strengths with three-dimensional thinking when he was in high school, relishing his hours in the woodworking and metal shops when other parts of the day were far more frustrating. While in high school he was crushed when he learned that the shops were being shut down as part of systematic closing of these facilities, denying him and other students the opportunities he cherished. In a fit of entrepreneurial exuberance, he decided to buy all of the shop machines at auction shortly after graduation and put them in his basement, spending his last $2,000 to buy tools no one else wanted. He then spent the next few years trying out different business ideas using these tools, ranging from retooling landscaping equipment to handcrafting components for factories in his home state, Massachusetts.

One day a business associate told him about pellet stoves. That night he drove to a stove store and noticed that the pellets were manufactured in Montana. "Why would I buy wood pellets from Montana when I live in Massachusetts?" he asked. The storeowner issued a challenge: "So why don't you make them?" Steve went home and that night began building machines that could manufacture wood pellets locally. Even though he had no technical training in design or engineering, his spatial three-dimensional thinking allowed him to prototype the necessary equipment in his mind. Soon he had a functional machine, and twenty years later he is retiring to the board of the very successful company he founded so he can pursue still other entrepreneurial opportunities. With three factories running around the clock, New England Wood Pellet is the largest biofuels manufacturer in the region.

These two individuals doubled down on their strengths in order to fulfill their dreams. Willard Wigan understood that mastering the art of micro-sculpture involved using his visual and spatial skills.

Steve Walker harnessed his high school shop-class experiences and turned those skills into economic independence. By emphasizing nonacademic skills, these two men are now wealthy, well known, and—most important—happy and fulfilled. They have integrated their dyslexia, playing to their strengths so that they could fulfill a dream.

I lost count long ago of how many parents tell me that their child is obsessed with video games. While this is certainly often an escapist activity, it could also be a path into a lucrative career. These days the video gaming industry is on par with filmmaking in terms of the financial and technical investment necessary to make a winner. Major universities are developing video game programming classes within their computer science departments. And keep in mind that while Steve Jobs became a millionaire based on his success at Apple, he became a billionaire off computer animation by selling Pixar to Disney.

Many passions that your child will pursue may not turn into a world-changing career. David Flink, a good friend of mine, who is CEO and co-founder of the mentoring organization Eye to Eye, loved magic tricks as a child, and he had a lot of fun performing for neighbors and friends. He got positive feedback for his performances—astounded faces and applause all around. He is not a magician today, but having a skill that he could be proud of and which people around him obviously enjoyed meant that he was able to survive a lot of the other frustrations that came into his life as a dyslexic student.

ATTITUDES MAKE DREAMS BECOME REALITIES

Attitudes such as resiliency, proactivity, goal setting, and possibility thinking will help your child turn big dreams into success. Use the attitudes assessment in Chapter Three to track these attitudes over time. Helping your child develop success-correlated attitudes, even more than the skills, will allow him to turn goals into reality.

An entrepreneurship coach once told me that being a good entrepreneur means preparing for failure and recovery. All children would do well to be prepared for the possibility of failure and have plans for recovery, but this is especially true for dyslexic people: we are so starved for victories that getting close to a win and missing it can be devastating. For example, if your child's dream is to take the top prize at the science fair, he might see it as a catastrophic failure if his project receives only an honorable mention. Help him see that this is just another turn in the road on his path to success. You may need to help him step back, look at what happened, and figure out how he can do better the next time. It is also helpful to set reasonable, attainable goals up front and to have backup plans for most outcomes. Perhaps the goal is not to "win the science fair" but "get an honorable mention this year and try to win next year." It is this level of self-awareness that makes dreams tangible.

REALIZING DREAMS THROUGH GOALS

There are many different ways to achieve a dream. While you may see a clear path into a life that you believe your child will love, this path might not turn out to be straightforward based on his learning profile. I'm not suggesting that your child cannot reach his dreams, but rather that you may need to point him toward the metaphorical door with the ramp, which is not always the front door. You can help by setting realistic educational goals and coaching him on picking tasks that will make him better at achieving his dreams. For example, if your son loves comic books, you might suggest putting time into art and English class. You can also underscore that he is qualified to do anything that interests him and that he should dream big, regardless of the path the knowledge took into his head.

You will do your child a great service by looking carefully at what is material to his success in reaching his dreams, not what others may tell you is important. Everyone in your town might feel that a particular sport is the best. In some towns it's football, in others it's soccer, and in still others it might be baseball or basketball. You're going to want to figure out which of these sports your child enjoys, or if he enjoys sports at all, before you start signing him up for whatever is considered to be the standard path.

Reasonable goal setting is one of the keys to long-term success. I wanted to be a varsity athlete. My parents saw that I wasn't particularly fast as a runner. So they coached me toward positions and sports that would play to my strengths. I could be a good first baseman because for that position one has to catch a ball rather than chase it down in center field. I could be a good soccer goalie because I had quickness moving left and right, was tough, and didn't have to outrun the fastest striker on the opposing team. A striker I was not, but I was still a valuable member of the team.

SETTING CLASSROOM GOALS

Learning and enjoying school to a level commensurate with her effort should definitely be on your list of goals for your child. But keep in mind that educational goals are often driven by existing assumptions and biases, as well as the pressures that come from society. Establishing the right educational goals is critical for helping your child fulfill her dreams. For example, some teachers may insist that your child should be reading chapter books by fourth grade. Your own friends might boast that their children were reading them in third grade, and the really pushy ones will yammer about how their kids were reading at that level even earlier. But look deeper: what is the goal of reading chapter books all about? Is it so that your child has access to information and taps into his imagination, or so that he can be part of a peer group, talking about *Harry Potter* or *The Diary of a Wimpy Kid* with friends? All are valid reasons for wanting to be reading at that level, but couldn't audio or visual tools allow him to achieve all these goals? The key is not to accept that a book is the only way to learn. Instead, remember that the goal is almost always learning, and then pick the path that will best get your child there.

Part of what allowed me to navigate through all of my schooling as a nonstandard student was my parents' attitudes. They had the good fortune to join the Peace Corps in the mid-1960s, and their many years in Africa developing an expertise in local languages, music, and culture broadened their worldviews in many different ways. On their return to the United States, my father became a professor of art history, specializing in West Africa, and my mother published scholarly articles on Nigerian women's culture. Ironically, they had missed the 1960s countercultural revolution here in the United States. This made them that much more able to be true to their own dreams and goals, rather than following the herd, even when the herd wanted to break traditions. My father once told me that before he left for Nigeria, the social norm was to wear a tie when you went to see a movie; when they returned from Africa, they found themselves surprised by the shift to a more casual culture, so they adopted the changes they liked and rejected ones they did not. Suffice it to say that my parents were not set on a specific expectation of what was normal, in or outside the classroom. The joke in our house, adapted from the late humorist Erma Bombeck, used to be that "normal is just a setting on your clothes dryer."

My parents helped me to develop my own goals throughout elementary, middle, and high school. I was intent that I was going to follow my parents' path and go to college and graduate school. I did well in math as a fifth grader, so when I was in sixth grade I was put into the honors math class, taking algebra a year ahead of most other students. It did not go well. I eventually figured out that I'd done so well in fifth-grade math because the teacher talked about math in the context of things we did every day, as opposed to teaching solely from the textbook. In sixth grade we relied more heavily on a textbook, which required more reading. Plus there were lots of symbols that I hadn't seen before. I barely scraped out a C–.

My parents were called in for a parent-teacher conference to discuss the situation. They asked me to come along, and I sat through the session while my math teacher shared his concerns and walked them through the problems I was having. He then turned to me and asked if I had anything to add. I startled everyone by saying: "I should repeat this class." My mom was floored by this, but she could see that I could make decisions for myself—among other things, her acceptance that I didn't want a haircut at age four had taught me that my decisions were acceptable to my family. I knew I hadn't by any means mastered the material, and I knew that I needed to do so in order to have a solid foundation for the math I imagined I'd take in college. My request to take that algebra class again was based on my goal to get to college and succeed there and on the self-advocacy my parents instilled in me.

The teacher and my parents agreed, and the following year I retook algebra again and got an A. Two years after that I doubled up in mathematics and got back on the honors path, taking advanced algebra in my senior year. Repeating a class I had not failed was an unconventional way to do things, and other parents might have been worried about their child being "held back" a year (as might the students themselves), but my parents wanted what was best for me—to understand the material in that algebra class—and weren't worried about what others might think. If I wasn't worried about it, they certainly weren't going to be.

Your child's educational goals will be dependent on how old she is. In first through third grades, educational goals center around mastering basic skills such as reading, writing, spelling, and basic math. Most dyslexic children will have great difficulty with all of these. Yet you will want to encourage them to become as proficient as possible in the basic skills, and we'll discuss in the next chapter how to do so. Remember that reading, writing, and spelling are only a means to an end. We learn how to read in order to understand content and expand the mind. But your child can learn content and expand her mind in ways other than standard reading.

From fourth grade on, schools assume that your child has mastered the tactical skills—reading and writing—needed in order to start learning. However, a recent survey of the literature conducted at Brown University concluded that the conventional wisdom of a sharp division between "learning to read" (up through third grade) and "reading to learn" (starting in fourth grade) is flawed; even non-dyslexic students use reading to learn before fourth grade and are still learning elements of reading—vocabulary or the ability to track complex narratives—after fourth grade. Unfortunately, the conventional assumption still drives the curriculum at most elementary schools.

If your eighth grader wants or is assigned to develop an understanding of the scientific method, for example, he or she will need access to material on these subjects; the school will probably assume that the best access to these topics is through standard eye reading. You may need to advocate for a wide variety of educational accommodations so that your child is given the chance to comprehend the same material as his peers in a similar time frame and with similar outcomes. These accommodations will allow him to use his strengths to supplement any weaknesses he has in these areas. Advocating for these accommodations will help feed your child's mind—and, more important, her heart, by allowing her to keep up with her peers. (I will outline accommodation options in the next chapter.)

When children become young adults, they begin to choose a specific path toward their interests. By the time they are in high school they may specialize their education toward one particular area, such as science, math, a foreign language, or history. If they decide that they're going to go to college, they will pick a major and, beyond that, a career that will combine both the skills they have developed and the knowledge necessary to succeed in their specific field. In early education, however, all students are generalists and all should have an opportunity to master the basic ways of learning. If your child is dyslexic, this is going to mean using alternative methods to get access to the general curriculum.

In a well-accommodated educational environment, your child's strengths should allow her to succeed. Any child should be able to get respectable grades if she puts in a good effort, regardless of whether she is using eye reading, ear reading, or finger reading. Put another way, do not accept lower standards on the basis that your child is dyslexic, and do not allow your school to water down the curriculum, lowering expectations because the institution is unwilling to provide appropriate accommodations. Schools would never bar kids in wheelchairs from attending an honors English class because the school didn't feel like building a ramp into the room. The same should be true in the case of non-obvious disabilities such as dyslexia. Yet if all the students are being issued textbooks and being quizzed with a pen and paper, the school may resist alternative models because they might be difficult to administer.

A dyslexic's dreams should be as bold and powerful as anyone's. It is at the level of day-to-day tasks that we run into a challenge. This draws on the forest-and-trees metaphor. Unfortunately, the elementary school years are almost entirely about tree activities. As an adult dyslexic with full accommodations, I never use a pen to write out my thoughts; I am never evaluated on how well I spell or asked to read a test off a photocopied sheet of paper. Yet these are the tasks of daily living as an elementary school student. Given that these tasks are the first ones on which children are evaluated, teachers may jump to the conclusion that your child will not be able to do higher-order thinking or that her goals and dreams aren't reasonable given her skills. The next chapter will focus on how to begin to tell your child's story so that you and your child can begin to turn the system around, making it possible for her to do the tasks that will help her find, and achieve, her dreams.

CHAPTER FIVE

Tell Your Story

One of the fundamental issues for dyslexic adults and children—as well as anyone else who has a non-obvious disability—is recognizing when to disclose this information, and figuring out the best ways to do so. There are going to be many different times when you'll need to tell people about your child's dyslexia. You also need to figure out how your child can do this for himself. Whether you are the one to clue people in or your child is, there are important practical and emotional considerations to the process. Practically speaking, quick and effective disclosure is key to developing your child's Individual Education Plan (IEP) and later for how it is implemented. An IEP is the legally mandated framework for starting your child in special education and getting her the services she needs. I'll discuss it in detail in Chapter Seven, but for now, view it as the plan of record for your child's education, one you and she get to help write.

But don't underestimate the emotional considerations. While it's tempting to see the process of disclosure as a means to an end (getting your child resources), it's important to understand that you are doing this for the psychological well-being and long-term happiness of both your child and yourself. The most important people for you to consider when approaching a disclosure is yourself and your child and the benefits of telling the story. Keeping a secret often means that you are also holding on to fear and shame. Not only is it emotionally unhealthy, but it creates an enormous amount of extra effort: it's like trying to hold a beach ball under water. Instead, you can look at disclosure as an opportunity for you and your child to embrace yourselves and stop hiding from other people. Once you get comfortable showing the world that you have a beach ball (dyslexia), you can stop doing all this extra work of hiding it. With practice, telling your story will become easy, and eventually you'll get to the point where it will be almost second nature to help other people understand what's really going on with your child.

The two most important barriers you are going to encounter in conversations about dyslexia are ignorance and uncertainty. Very few people know much about dyslexia, even within the school environment. In general, I've found that when people don't know much about something they quickly become risk-averse. The good news is that it is rare that you run into someone who is genuinely bigoted about dyslexia. Instead, you'll find that because people really don't understand this disability, they make a jump in their minds to a number of inaccurate assumptions. The real problems occur when they are either unsure of what to do or unaware that they have to do anything in order to support your child. Engaging people in a conversation to unpack and rewrite their assumptions into valid ones is the key to an effective disclosure conversation.

Think about it from the perspective of your child's general education teacher. Most schools divide their staffs into "general education" and "special education." The general education teachers are the ones in the mainstream classrooms. When the general education teacher hears the term *dyslexia*, he might worry that the dyslexic child's issues will disrupt or negatively affect the entire class. As a result, he may conclude: "I don't know what to do here and it probably would be better for this child if I just moved her over to special ed." Worse, he'll make a decision based on the limited knowledge he has, perhaps that dyslexia means that a person "sees her letters backward." He might think he just needs to teach the child not to do that and then she'll catch up. Well-meaning, but very wrongheaded.

The ability to share your story is therefore critically important. You need to present your information so that you can get what you want and so that other people can understand where you're coming from. The best way for you to engage with your child's school in terms of accommodations, programming, and equal educational opportunities is to be able to talk about what your child needs in a professional yet caring manner. The ultimate goal is to give other people context that is relevant to providing an environment in which your child can work independently.

Yet at the same time I know that disclosure isn't always easy. Even though I was well accommodated in public school, when I went to college I thought I would start with a clean slate and keep my dyslexia a secret. And because I was dead set against asking for accommodations, I made all kinds of warped choices in my education.

Thanks to my course selections in four years at Wesleyan University in Middletown, Connecticut, I have a deep knowledge of film. I took classes in Japanese film, French film, Western film, and New Age film. I realized that I could get college credit and be able to fully participate in college thinking and classroom discussions by watching movies. However, I completely denied myself a math and science education. When I was in high school, I was very good at math and science. I was an honor student who got A's. But when I got to college calculus, the teacher handed everyone a textbook and assumed we would work the problem sets out of the book on our own. Knowing no better, and scared that I would fail, I limped through one semester, cheated my way to a low B, and quit halfway through the year, disgusted with myself for breaking the honor code and frustrated that I could not master the math with ease. I didn't even have the language to say what was going wrong. I couldn't figure out why I was having such trouble, so I just abandoned math, which turned out to be a problem when I got to business school years later. But the worst part is that I now know I could have gotten a great math and science education if I had had the skills to ask for the accommodations I needed and a knowledge of the tools that would have given me independence.

As you begin to put these pieces together for your child, consider yourself an educator for the rest of the world. Your job is to spread the philosophy that your child (and everyone else) deserves to learn in the environment best suited for him. Yet even the most expensive private schools in the country that focus on dyslexia may not subscribe to my Empowerment Plan way of thinking. You're going to have to become an explainer and an advocate, and eventually your child is going to have to become her own explainer and advocate, because that is where true independence lies.

When you and your child get more comfortable with his story and begin to share it with the world, you're also doing an important public service. Every time you bring someone to a better understanding of dyslexia, you will have smoothed the path for the next person who needs to have this same conversation. Social movements are built on one-on-one relationships. People get comfortable with someone who is of a different background or who has a disability when they get to know that person. Once they see the human side of dyslexia, they will often become an advocate to help others. Take pride in the work you're doing and recognize that even though going first is sometimes hard, other people will appreciate your efforts and may well continue to pay it forward in other environments.

THE SPECTRUM OF SCHOOL CULTURE REGARDING DYSLEXIA

Schools are filled with teachers who care deeply about their students' learning. Yet even well-intentioned teachers sometimes miss the point. As you prepare to have conversations about your child's dyslexia you should expect that teachers will fall into one of five groups: knowledgeable, good-hearted with bad methods, well-intentioned but underfunded, uninformed and discriminatory, or unreachable.

Knowledgeable. There are a limited number of public schools throughout the country that handle this issue well. There are also a handful of private schools that focus on dyslexia and other specific learning disabilities. It's possible that you can move your school into this category by having the right conversations: many of these schools started as less than ideal but with the right motivation were able to change gears and help children learn. I've listed some of the best independent schools in Appendix B.

Good-hearted with bad methods. There are a lot of teachers and administrators who care and are trying hard to help. But in the majority of cases they are highly focused on the remediation model, thinking they should focus on fixing your child rather than accommodating her learning style. You will be able to recognize them by their use of phrases such as "diagnosed with dyslexia" or by their offer to provide your child with an "intervention that will fix this problem." They really are trying to help, but their orientation is off. Even if they are able to get your child up to standard eye-reading levels, they often overlook the underlying emotional experience and the toll that their drilling has taken on your child. In these cases you will have to use some of the techniques in this chapter to convince teachers that they need to focus on your child's emotional health and broader literacy through other techniques (such as ear reading), rather than getting her to fit into a standard learning model.

Well-intentioned but underfunded. The budget battle in public schools is brutal. In the case of a non-obvious disability such as dyslexia, good teachers are put under strong pressure, either implicitly or explicitly, to ignore the disability. I know of a large number of public schools where teachers are told they are "not allowed" to use the word *dyslexia* in talking to parents for fear that it will trigger legal obligations to provide accommodations. In this case you'll have to use some of the techniques in Chapter Seven to engage them in dialogue and, if necessary, to press the point that the law demands that public schools must provide a free and appropriate education for your child.

Uninformed and discriminatory. Some teachers still labor under significant misperceptions about dyslexia. They might privately believe that it's the result of bad parenting or, worse, that it is a phenomenon invented for kids who don't quite measure up. Be sure that you are taking time to engage these teachers in conversation and try to bring them over to your worldview with science and logic. If you find after repeated attempts that they're not willing to listen to reason, then you need to use the legal techniques in Chapter Seven.

Unreachable. There are a small number of teachers and administrators who are downright belligerent about this issue. Rarely you may come across someone who feels it's her personal mission to stamp out "laziness" or other characteristics that she perceives to be associated with dyslexia. If you find yourself up against someone who after repeated attempts will not get on board with your worldview and legal rights, then it's perfectly reasonable to use some of the techniques in Chapter Seven.

TALKING TO FAMILY

One of the most important audiences for the story of dyslexia is your own family. As you craft a compelling story (which we'll discuss later in this chapter), you'll want to try it out with your own parents and siblings. On one hand, you may find out that everyone is extremely supportive and interested to learn more about a member of their family. On the other hand, I've seen instances where grandparents or aunts and uncles, even those who are dyslexic themselves, are resistant to this story. This can be in part because of generational or cultural norms.

Potentially the most critical members of the family to talk to are your dyslexic child's siblings. I've seen the needs of the dyslexic child dominate family time. It's important to recognize that siblings who have a mainstream learning profile also need your love and attention. At the same time, be sure that the child who is dyslexic, even if he is older than the other children, is not made to feel less capable or hardworking. The best way around this is to have a family discussion about what dyslexia is, and share some of the myths and facts that you've uncovered in this book. One private school focusing on dyslexia hosts a sibling day each year to bring the brothers and sisters of the dyslexic students into the school so they can understand the issue better. You can re-create this in your own home by working with all of your children to develop stories that you'll tell outside the home.

My overall advice is to go slowly when dealing with dyslexia and family dynamics. It's a good idea to have a professional psychologist involved if possible. Don't be surprised if other family members resist the revised story. People have a lot invested in their concepts of the past and in the concept of normal, and any challenge to these may cause them to become uncomfortable. This can be as unsettling as trying to discuss the history of alcoholism in a family. While the two have totally different profiles and epicenters, both involve a tremendous amount of shame and hiding which can result in some very strong emotions coming to the surface.

In the long run, it is valuable to have these conversations and to unpack past history, but it is also something that you don't have to do in one day. In fact, it may take years before you're able to really integrate it into everyone's lives. And you may never be able to get everyone on the same new page. Focus on the present and trying to get accommodations for your child and these other conversations can happen whenever you are ready.

HOW TO CRAFT A COMPELLING STORY

As you think about how best to explain your child's learning profile to others—and as you help him become comfortable explaining it himself—it's important to think of the crafting of your explanation as you might the crafting of a story. This obviously isn't fiction you're inventing, but rather you're looking for a way to explain your child's situation to people who have the power to help or stand in the way of her learning. Being persuasive is important.

Specifically, your story has to be honest, full of specific details, and delivered in a humorous and engaging way. Picking memorable and real details from your life and that of your child will make your case stick in the minds of those you are speaking with. Humor is important because the concepts of disability and the institutional frameworks we are discussing can be dehumanizing. Being able to crack a joke here or there or keep the conversation light brings life back into the narrative.

Along with humor, timing is key to good storytelling. I encourage you and your child to take a public speaking class, an improvisational acting class, or even a comedy class. Many of the best actors started out as comedians: Tom Hanks, Jamie Foxx, Robin Williams—Oscar winners all—crossed from comedy into serious acting by knowing how to read an audience.

Above all, your body language and your ease with the topic will positively impact your ability to have a productive conversation. People can pick up on your emotions, and if you approach this conversation with a matter-of-fact attitude, people will respond positively. On the other hand, if you approach your story about dyslexia as a deep, dark secret, something you feel embarrassment about, they'll take their cues from that and see your requests similarly, as something to hide. For the best effect, you'll need to rehearse telling the story and to unpack your emotional baggage around it to the point where you can tell it as a meaningful personal anecdote rather than a formal or uncomfortable disclosure.

Start by drawing on your child's personal experience or an experience you've had with your child. The first anecdote you tell should be three to five sentences, max. This short introduction will allow you to feel out the person you're speaking with and determine by his response whether he can be your ally. My version is three sentences:

My name is Ben Foss and I'm dyslexic. It wasn't a big deal when I was a kid because my mother would read to me. At college, I would fax my term papers to her in New Hampshire so that she could read them out loud to me over the phone, helping me find my own mistakes.

I've found that this cluster of information is just enough to get people oriented. It sets a context quickly and helps the listener understand how difficult it is to be dyslexic. The few details I include are important because people have a lot of things to do and my needs may not be on the top of their list. In your case, you will be dealing with teachers and administrators who are definitely pressed for time. You want them to be able to hold on to the facts you've given them so that you get what you need.

Subtle things can really make a story stick or totally disappear. If I told you "I sent my papers home to my mom," it would be less effective than saying "I faxed them home to my mom in New Hampshire." The element of faxing creates a picture in your mind of a concrete experience. There is the hissing and beeping noise of a fax machine. And then there is New Hampshire. Everyone thinks of New Hampshire as cold and far away (including people from Vermont). If I said "to New York" it wouldn't seem as far away or as difficult. Those two little phrases improve my story significantly.

Consider a few of the other subtle elements. I've indicated to people that I went to college. For someone who thinks dyslexics must be stupid, this gives them evidence otherwise. Of course, going to or not going to college does not mean someone is smart or stupid, but most people equate college with intelligence, so I use that detail when telling my story. I also fill in the blank as to why I am faxing these papers home to my mother. I note that I can't find my own spelling mistakes and that she's helping me.

Find something in your child's life that summarizes where he is vulnerable and where he has strengths. You want to look for something that has memorable details, like the fax machine or New Hampshire. Think about your own child and what games he enjoys, what he is good at, or what he is known for in the community. If you tie a story to an instance when misinterpreting some small piece of information made a big difference in his life, people will likely remember your story. In terms of its effectiveness in getting your child noticed, remembered, and accommodated, you've likely got a winner with that kind of story.

My friend Steve Walker told me a great story that he uses to set his context. Steve lives in Peterborough, New Hampshire, a town of six thousand people. Recently he complained to his wife about how hard it was to get groceries. She asked why he was whining when the grocery store was just down the road. "Down the road?" he said. It turned out that he'd been driving an hour round trip to a store in another town—for seven years!—because he couldn't read the part of the local store's sign that said "groceries."

This is a great story because it's true, it's full of details that will stick in people's minds, it's amusing, and you can get how Steve's dyslexia led to a very real problem. It's important to remember that Steve is a successful businessperson. The story of him not being able to find a grocery store when he runs a large company and flies his own plane is amusingly disarming.

One dyslexic nine-year-old who uses the Intel Reader had a perfect story about why he needed assistive technology. He explained to me that he had used the device to read the instructions for his favorite board game, Risk, which he had been playing with the same group of friends for years. The first time he heard the instructions read aloud by the device, he figured out his friends had been cheating all along. "They're mad at me," he told me, "but I'm glad I did it!"

Again this story is brief, real, and has some memorable details: the familiar board game Risk, a nine-year-old using a high-tech device, and his friends getting mad. It also shows the vulnerability that comes with dyslexia—his friends had been duping him—as well as the empowerment that can come from having assistive technology. When I heard this story, I couldn't help rooting for this kid. You want your child's story to elicit that kind of reaction too.

Don't be afraid to use hard science to get your point across. Explaining that dyslexia happens in the "language processing center of the brain" and then pointing with your finger to a spot right above your ear is one of the most effective openers I use. Remarking that "this region is called the temporal parietal lobe" makes people think, "Oh, he must know what he's talking about." You might want to show people the MRI images from the Introduction that show a non-dyslexic's brain while reading and my brain while reading (I've included that scan in Appendix A as well so that you can tear it out and show it to people as part of your communication). Visuals help underscore the power of science in explaining dyslexia.

You can also bring along a piece of assistive technology. I have found that demonstrating text-to-speech on my iPhone or laptop allows people to understand that my brain works differently. It also shows that I'm willing to work with tools that allow me to be independent. Finally, it makes you a realist and an expert when explaining this issue: instead of saying "I have a problem and I need help," you are saying, "I'm aware of my child's strengths and weaknesses, and here are some solutions that I would like you to allow him to use."

Using statistics and numbers is also compelling and helpful to your cause. I give people this brief shorthand: "Dyslexics are 10 percent of people, 35 percent of entrepreneurs, and 41 percent of prisoners." Each time I get the same response: people nod when they hear 10 percent, their eyes widen when they hear 35 percent, and then they cock their heads to the side in genuine surprise and interest when they hear 41 percent. These three numbers tell a story of our community, and they will provoke a conversation, which is really your ultimate goal. A good gag line following this is to say, "Of course, entrepreneurs and prisoners are not mutually exclusive!" Try this out on someone you are just meeting and I'll bet you get a big smile.

Before the disclosure of your child's dyslexia, assume that the people you are speaking with know nothing about the term. That's especially important if they tell you they *do* know something about it. Ninety percent of the time, that means they've got bad facts. This situation is worse than if they had no facts at all. On the other hand, don't be surprised when people you are speaking with end up disclosing their dyslexia to you. Remember, 10 percent of the population is dyslexic, and 30 to 40 percent have a family member who has some sort of specific learning disability. Even if the person you are talking to is dyslexic or has a family member in the club, he may still need to be convinced that your view of dyslexia as an identification and not a disease is the right one, so build the relationship based on what you hear. If the person does mention that he has a related experience, this will be a great opportunity for you to let him figure out how he can best assist your child. Sit back and listen to his perspective so that you can find out how much work you need to do to bring him over to the dyslexia-as-identity rather than dyslexia-as-disease worldview.

Another great technique is to show some vulnerability when you are disclosing, such as "I'm nervous telling you about my child's dyslexia because many people believe that a dyslexic child must be lazy or stupid." When you put people on the spot like that, they have to respond more positively. They might say, "Oh no, I don't think that. I appreciate your telling me." Even if they do have negative preconceptions, they now specifically say they don't think it and are less likely to behave badly toward you or your child. Openness about your feelings is a wonderful way to approach any disability issue.

Most of all, practice your story before you go public. Don't assume that you can tell a great story off the cuff. Consider Bruce Springsteen. In his sixties, he still does four-hour concerts that are nonstop. Most people would never know that he rehearses his concerts down to every single move he makes onstage. The audience thinks that when he's jumping up on a chair and pointing to his horn section in the fifth song it's spontaneous, but all the while it was timed down to the second, including when the spotlight's going to hit him, when he jumps on a chair, and even the flash of a smile at the audience. The first time he went onstage his act was likely more spontaneous, but it was not as effective because the spotlight didn't know where he was going, or he stumbled because one horn player was sitting where he wasn't supposed to be.

The same thing will be true of your story. Initially you're going to be a little clumsy, so try it out on multiple audiences. Start with your family or friends—you are focus-grouping this story. Tell them the story, and ask them to repeat the story back, including as many details as they remember. The details that come back first consistently are the specific details: they stick in people's minds. When they repeat the story back to you almost verbatim after the first time hearing it, you know that you've landed on just the right way to express yourself. Eventually you will have a well-rehearsed story that you can roll out every time you speak with a stranger.

You can also use two or three different metaphors I have found work well to introduce the subject of dyslexia. I've used them myself in this book. The first involves explaining dyslexia in terms of having a "bad cell phone connection to the page." By using this language you can explain that using accommodations "is like having a landline." This is an effective way to replace the myth that people who are dyslexic see words or letters backward. It is an inconsistent signal that is the problem, not a consistent reversal of it.

Another metaphor that I find works well is that of describing the accommodations you will be asking for as "a ramp into a book." If you can get people talking about students in wheelchairs in the same context as students with dyslexia, you immediately have a compelling narrative that addresses why your child's needs should be met. No one would want to exclude someone in a wheelchair, so why would they exclude your child? And then you have them hooked.

Similarly, you can introduce the old name for dyslexia: word blindness. With my own mother this was the metaphor that finally sank in. In my late twenties, when explaining to her the difficulty I had with text I said, "Imagine that I am partially blind when it comes to reading words." After she heard that, she remembered it each time she considered handing me a menu or buying me a book, thinking of a better way to get me the information.

SETTING THE STAGE FOR "THE ASK"

The story you are developing sets the stage for having a deeper conversation about dyslexia. The next step is to build a relationship that will ultimately serve your child well. In the context of school, these conversations will set the stage for an individual plan, or IEP.

When you're attending a meeting with people whom you're ultimately going to look to for accommodations, you don't want to come into the room with guns drawn. Indeed, the first meeting with your child's teacher should not be about accommodations or IEPs at all. Instead, make it a general conversation about your child, as in, "How's my son doing? Where do you think he needs to improve? What can I do at home to help with his homework?"

People love to be asked for their advice, so if you haven't yet gone for the formal identification but have completed the questionnaires in Chapter Three and Appendix D, you can engage your child's teacher around dyslexia. Try something like, "You clearly care about your students. I'm pretty sure my child is dyslexic. I've been reading up on it. These are some markers: difficulty connecting the sounds of spoken language to written words, and errors in reading or spelling. He is also very good at [*pick from this list the three that apply most to your child:* verbal, social, narrative, spatial, kinesthetic, visual, mathematical, or musical] skills. What do you think I should do?"

Teachers will react very differently to you depending on their own attitude and the school's position on this situation. Some teachers are quite open to the concept of dyslexia. Others may be open-minded but have been explicitly told by their administration to avoid the terms *dyslexia* or *learning disability* in communications with parents, or at least to avoid putting them in written communications, so that the school can avoid taking on the financial and legal obligations of accommodating a child who's been formally identified. Even though this is a violation of the law, it nonetheless happens. I have also seen situations where schools will avoid identifying students as having dyslexia because they don't want to change the number of kids in special education; there are some provisions within the No Child Left Behind act that give schools an incentive to keep the number of children identified with disabilities low (basically, if administrators keep this number below a certain threshold, they can exclude these children from the numbers used to assess their yearly progress, which is the basis for future funding). In sum, there can often be an incentive for schools to not identify your child as dyslexic.

After you've said your piece initially, you want to listen, pay attention, and learn. If the teacher seems sympathetic, press the issue just a tad more: "Do you have any advice on how to deal with this issue in the larger school context?" See whether the teacher is interested in discussing teaching in relation to dyslexia, or whether she pulls back and suggests that you speak with the learning specialist rather than with her. In a good negotiation, you make your counterparty move first and see what she puts on the table without you asking for it—it helps build a positive relationship if you let people come toward you as much as they will on their own. When you do find someone who seems like a strong ally, ask that person to help you navigate the institution you're working with.

FINDING ALLIES AND BUILDING RELATIONSHIPS

You will need to begin building a relationship with your child's teacher and school administrators before you choose to disclose. There is a wide range of responses teachers and administrators can give you. They can do the minimum required by law, not giving you anything you fail to ask for and following the rules scrupulously even if it's not in your child's best interest, or they can be really strong advocates for your child if they understand that you are interested in becoming a long-term partner in your child's education or if there is a connection between you that goes beyond the classroom—you need to increase the odds in your favor by making and reaffirming every connection you can. In general, the anticipation of dealing with another person in the future is what drives people to build relationships. A good relationship can be the greatest incentive to productivity, so try to highlight the ways in which you'll be able to help them down the road.

One great technique for navigating your child's school is to meet with teachers your child really likes. If your child likes somebody, odds are that she likes your child too. This might be a teacher from a previous school year, or someone outside of the core faculty, such as a teacher in the art or music department. In my case, my kindergarten teacher noticed that when the class was discussing opposites, I said that "was" was the opposite of "saw," and "dog" was the opposite of "god," because the order of the letters was inverted. Because the teacher liked me, she took the time to mention it to my mom, giving my parents an early indication that something might be up.

To build these relationships, always approach people with dignity and respect. This will spur them to respond to you in kind. The secretary who sits in the front office of a school is an incredibly important person. If and when your child gets in trouble, this will be the person he'll first meet with. Whenever I walk into an administrative office I strike up a genuine conversation with the people answering the phones or getting the coffee. Generally people view the office staff as just a step on the path toward a more powerful actor in that organization, such as the principal. However, because I put in the time to get to know them, I find that those folks are actually looking forward to talking with me. My phone calls get put through and they get me on the calendar when I need to make an appointment.

Advocates can also be found in the middle tier of an organization. The top people often don't have time to deal with your issues, but their immediate underlings can become wonderful allies. In a traditional school district, this midlevel but important person might be the district learning specialist (as opposed to the school principal or the district superintendent). Alternatively, it might be the head of the English department or the career counselor: people who have some influence but who will still take the time to meet with you. For example, when I was at law school I made a point of getting to know the assistant dean for student affairs, who was three levels below the head of the school and two levels above the assistant registrar. She had been born in West Africa, and I realized that I could connect with her because my parents had lived in Nigeria for many years. Two years later this alliance came in handy when I needed to get the attention of her boss in a high-pressure situation involving a missing accommodation: because of our previous conversations she knew she could trust me and that I was not crying wolf.

Also remember that not everyone will respond to your kindness. It's important to determine early on whether a person you need to cultivate is with you or against you. If it becomes clear after one or two conversations that someone is not particularly friendly to the identity concept of dyslexia and does not seem open to persuasion, it's best to just step around him or her. Chapter Seven will lay out ways to use legal language to compel people who are not friendly to do what they're required to do. But in your initial interactions it's better to simply put a mental wall around them and see if there are other routes to your destination.

Key signs that someone may not be particularly supportive may be the use of phrases such as "Your child just doesn't seem to want to try hard" or "Your child is clearly intelligent but needs to stop goofing off." Another signal that you're dealing with someone who may not be a good ally is resistance to changing his teaching methods or including accommodations. This can be seen in subtle statements such as "That's going to take a lot more time. I'm not sure if we can fit that in" or in more direct ones such as "We really do try to maintain standards at this school, and if your son is not up to them, maybe you need to lower your expectations." I've included a series of comebacks for these types of comments in Chapter Seven.

The final place to find allies is among other parents and kids in the school. It's possible that the school will make an introduction to other parents, especially if you are in a private school focused on dyslexia. However, they may not do this because of confidentiality concerns (or because they do not want parents getting together to organize against the school), so you may need to work through the grapevine to see if you can identify the right target parents.

A middle ground here involves asking the school to share your email address with parents with kids in special education generally, perhaps with a cover note from you explaining that you are mainly interested in finding a community, and see if people contact you back.

Any parent with a child in special education can be a good start—for example, the parent of a deaf child can tell you a lot about how the district and the school handle things—but parents of kids with non-obvious disabilities will have a more on-point description of what will happen. While you do not have to name your child at this stage, especially if he or she is uncomfortable with this—you could be interested for any number of reasons—it helps if you can say you have a child who might be seeking services, just to establish yourself on equal ground with the other parents. Before you take this step, you will need to develop the storytelling skills discussed in this chapter and work with your child so that she does not feel exposed. For example, if your child is still nervous about this issue, you do not want to make an announcement at a PTA meeting that you are looking for other parents who are in the club.

It's also useful to form a community between your child and other students with IEPs, in particular those who are receiving services you would like your child to have. If your child feels comfortable, ask them who their friends are in the special education classes and look for ways to build a relationship with that family. If your child is younger, this could be as easy as setting up a play date and gently raising the topic with the parents, introducing them to the dyslexia-as-identity model. You can also look at some of the organizations discussed in Chapter Nine as a path to finding this sort of community.

TEACHING YOUR CHILD TO BE HIS OR HER OWN ADVOCATE

Before I was able to express my frustration about my dyslexia, sometimes it came out in unproductive ways at school. One day when my father came to pick me up he was asked to visit with a learning specialist. I was in fourth grade and had been going to a separate room for one-on-one help for an hour a day for a number of years. The specialist explained that she had been working with me on writing out words by hand. She had written a word on a green chalk easel and asked me to copy it. In a fit of rage I rushed the chalkboard and flipped it up in the air, yelling and having a tantrum. She had not called my father in to ask that I be punished; rather, she wanted him to know that I was having real trouble at school and was frustrated.

Other days I would come home from school furious. This might have been because a teacher gave me a low mark on a spelling test, or another student taunted me for being sent out of class to special ed. So my mother and I made a deal. When I came home from school I could destroy anything in my room, as long as I dealt with the consequences. I was not allowed to destroy things outside my room (in the car, at the dinner table, etc.). On one particularly frustrating day I came home and decided to open up the window and throw my new stereo out onto the pavement. Result: I blew off a lot of steam, and I no longer had a stereo.

My mother's insight here was that she allowed me space to vent my anger, while also teaching me to deal with the consequences. She did not buy me new stuff—that was on me. As an adult I learned to speak up in situations in which I was frustrated, and I learned to avoid getting angry. But as a kid I didn't have that poise. Don't get me wrong: My mother has since told me that there were many times when she wondered whether she was raising a hooligan. But she trusted her instincts and saw that I was able to get along well with others better when I had the space to let go of the anger.

Regardless of whether you think this type of parenting is the best solution, you want your child to be able to talk through his frustration and, more important, to develop the skills involved in telling his own story. It is essential that he learn how to be a strong self-advocate because you will not always be with him when he needs to have these conversations, and it will allow him to feel confident about who he is and thereby break the cycle of shame. Advocacy starts at home around daily choices. What does he want for breakfast? What does he want to wear? Allow your child to have his opinions and make decisions about his own life. He doesn't need to, and shouldn't, make every decision, but let him make some where he can. This reinforces his ability to speak up, and that's what advocacy is all about.

Remember that you're often doing a favor for people when you explain the full context of dyslexia. Make sure to convey this to your child. People are nervous that they will say the wrong thing or offend you. Your child's job then is to be clear and direct and to tell her story with confidence. On the Headstrong Nation's website (www.head strongnation.org) you'll find a video on how to demonstrate assistive technology to a person who is unfamiliar with it. Use this script as a model when having these conversations yourself. Even better, let your child take the lead. If, for instance, your child is able to use accelerated text to speech, she can incorporate that ability into her own demonstration, making it that much more compelling. Your child will be the expert in the room and wow her teacher.

I want to share with you an example of how my friend Mark dealt with his disability, even though he wasn't dyslexic, because it offers some good pointers for having a conversation with someone about a disability. During the first week of classes at business school, Mark sent an email to the entire school in the first week of classes that said (in paraphrase):

Re: Mark: The guy with no hands
   My name is Mark. I was born with no hands. I didn't have an accident. You're going to see me in the hallway and you aren't going to know what to do in terms of shaking my hand.

So here's what you do: shake my wrist. It will feel like grabbing someone else's wrist. It won't hurt me and it will make me feel welcome if you do shake it. If you see me in class and I have my bag with me, I don't need your help carrying it out—I brought it in in the first place!

A few lines of introduction and explanation and a well-placed joke completely changed the way people dealt with Mark. Before he sent this email, I saw people avoid him in the hall; they didn't have any animosity toward him, but they were simply uncertain of what to do when they encountered a person with no hands. After years of experience, he knew what questions were in their minds and he gave them direct answers. After he sent the email, I saw the shift the next day, people crossing the hall to seek him out.

Your child should be proud of who she is. She is working really hard to do something honorable: get an education. A free and appropriate education is her legal right. But if she can't speak up, she is less likely to secure that right.

Advocacy can take many forms. One friend I know who is dyslexic came up with a novel way to avoid being asked to read aloud in class when she was young. She was enrolled in a very strict private school in San Francisco. When her mother went in for her second-grade conference the teacher asked why her daughter was always singing in class. The teacher went on to explain that every time she asked the children to stand up and read out loud this young child would simply break into song. The girl did not have the language to say, "Pardon me—I have difficulty with text and I would appreciate if you would provide me with an alternative way to participate in this activity." So she defended herself in a novel and amusing, albeit disruptive, way. You will want to look and listen for these incomplete early elements of advocacy, ones that you can develop as a way to help your child be heard.

In the film *Headstrong,* a fifteen-year-old boy named Jason approaches his high school math teacher and explains to him that he has dyslexia and ADHD. The teacher listens carefully and asks if he might need extra help in class. Jason replies that he'll come to the teacher and ask for help if he needs it. Then the teacher, picking up on Jason's articulated needs, generates a new idea: would Jason like to have someone read the test questions aloud to him when he's taking an exam? Jason gladly accepted the offer.

When it comes to advocacy, earlier is better. A child who approaches a teacher ahead of any problems in class and explains his unique profile is viewed as a proactive student interested in learning. The kid who comes in after getting a bad grade and explains that it was "my dyslexia that caused this" is seen as someone who's trying to make excuses. In Jason's case, speaking up allowed him to create a dynamic relationship that enabled him to ask for help when he needed it and gave him an ally. He went on to graduate from high school and earn a college degree that would help him focus on music producing, his lifelong dream.

In just the same way you need to rehearse explaining your child's story, you'll want to help your child rehearse his interactions with his teacher. For this you can try a role-play at home. In Chapter Seven I've included information about how to help your child create a PowerPoint presentation that she can use for more formal environments such as an IEP meeting. Children can become really powerful public speakers, and even the quietest and most unassuming child can have a profound effect when he speaks the truth about his own needs. And once children begin to feel positive about themselves and their dreams, they'll be able to start to figure out what they'll need in order to achieve them. That's where accommodations, highlighted in the next chapter, really come into play.

CHAPTER SIX

A Tool Kit of Accommodations

Information is like water to me, and the learning process offers just as many ways to consume information as there are ways to consume water. Water can be liquid, ice, or steam; it can be delivered intravenously, sipped by mouth, or even absorbed through the skin.

The knowledge in a conventional book is like ice to me. It has been put into a solid state to be preserved, allowing it to be consumed by a standard reader at any time. Most people can pick up a book and, like transforming ice into liquid water, quickly transform it into the information that they need to learn. I cannot do this with my eyes, but I can do it with my ears. So I have to transform books into audio, which is the equivalent of liquid for me. This can involve someone reading a book aloud to me in person, getting the same book in an audio format, or even having a computer speak it to me. I read dozens of books each year, meaning I listen to them—it is all learning to me.

When it comes to learning, every child needs her own tool kit, her bag of tricks. The tool kit that standard learners carry around includes their skills for reading, spelling, and handwriting. But as you know, the dyslexic child is going to need a different set of tools in order to help her get through school. In a perfect world, classrooms would be filled with all of the learning tools available, including those that facilitate audio learning, visual learning, and eye reading. But in the real world there's an existing legacy in which eye reading is considered to be the best way to learn, and consequently all children have to learn how to thrive in this system—easier said than done for anyone whose skill set doesn't include eye reading!

That's why I created the shopping list of educational tools detailed in this chapter. If they are well implemented, these accommodations will reduce your child's anxiety levels. But there's a paradox that you'll need to navigate. At the outset, using the accommodations will highlight that your child is different, and can create anxiety for him. This is why attitudes are so important, because once your child masters these accommodations, they will help him reduce his anxiety level at school so that he can thrive.

You have already identified the best ways for your child to consume information based on the Strengths Star in Chapter Three. For some children, it will be visual or kinesthetic; for others, it will involve verbal or even musical pathways. Not all accommodations have to be super-fancy high-tech devices. Sometimes it can be as simple as getting a couple of pieces of butcher block paper, putting them up on the walls, and working through ideas with colored markers. The key is to look for the ways that your child naturally learns and use them to accommodate his schoolwork. If your child is very kinesthetic, when it comes to science class you might get 3-D models of molecules that he can play with and see how they click together. If your child is particularly musical, it might involve singing elements of her history lesson so that she can incorporate them, or connecting her to the music of that era so that she has a feel for the context. The critical element here is not to accept that a book is the best or only way to teach. Think about your child and what he enjoys, and try to structure learning according to his strengths.

Initially you're going to have to give your child many options, to see which work best. However, once you find the right tools that allows your child easier access to learning, he will be able to fully participate in the classroom, which is the ultimate goal. Accommodations, then, are simply tools for leveling the playing field.

Before you head into your child's school and demand accommodations, you need to know what is available; teachers and administrators often have no idea these tools exist, or worse, know of them but play dumb to avoid paying for them or changing the flow of the classroom. Familiarize yourself with the choices I've outlined, and then make a list of the ones that you think will have to be included in your child's IEP. You can also begin to familiarize your child with these tools by starting to use them at home. That way, you'll know which ones are the most successful before you begin to make requests from your school.

Unfortunately, some children and many teachers are uncomfortable with students using accommodations. This was certainly true for me. When I was in school I felt a sense of stigma because the accommodation meant that I was getting something "extra" that the other kids in my class couldn't have in order to do the same work. But now I know that a better way to think of this is that some people were not given a key to the building, and the accommodations were simply a way of getting them into the school. That metaphor might help your child understand the value of accommodations and be comfortable getting them.

I cannot count the number of adult dyslexics I've spoken to who have genuinely traumatic memories from their years in elementary school. Many were belittled or made to feel inept based on a grueling regime of teachers trying to—in some cases literally—beat reading into their head without accommodations. I have seen teachers "co-read" with students, with the teacher and student taking turns reading a paragraph aloud. In my experience, teachers who do this point out how much the child enjoys reading when she is being read to; they get this one right. They also believe that modeling gives the child an incentive to keep working through the material and will push the child to eye-read on her own. What these teachers are missing, however, is that the child is usually feeling embarrassed and stupid as she watches someone else glide through what she finds so hard.

My friend Matthew Bickerton once told me very earnestly that his teacher had used a specific tool to try to teach him to read. He then held up a shoe: "He used this to hit me in the head." Today Matthew is a very successful entrepreneur who owns a home in the United Kingdom that has its own moat, but he still looks back on his early school experiences as tremendously damaging. Any school or teacher who tells you that the only way for students to demonstrate their capability is to read in a standard way not only is wrong but runs the risk of doing serious psychological damage to your child. It's doubtful they will employ the same technique as Matthew's instructor, but even a stern look and a red pen can do a lot of damage if they are all the child sees day after day.

EYE-READING METHODS

Many people assume that if you push a student hard enough he will learn to read in a standard way. I can't repeat often enough that this is absolutely untrue for someone who is dyslexic. However, every child should be given an opportunity to learn to eye-read, and learning accommodations should begin with methods of teaching eye reading.

For dyslexic children, the most useful method for teaching reading is the Orton-Gillingham (OG) method. Samuel Orton, the grandfather of dyslexia research, and Anna Gillingham, a psychologist and educator, created this model in the 1930s. It involves a multisensory approach that helps students develop the ability to break down the written code of language. It is often delivered as one-on-one tutoring or in small-group instruction, and it has been adapted, updated, and repackaged into a number of different methodologies. For example, the Wilson, Lindamood-Bell, Barton, and Slingerland reading programs each rely heavily on OG, and all are good models that a school can adopt for eye-reading training for dyslexic students. Note that proponents of a specific model will claim theirs is the only one to use. There can be some turf wars between the methods, but if you find a good teacher working with one of these, you are on the right path.

A high-quality, in-person teacher is the best "delivery system" for these teaching methods, though online learning is also an option. In my opinion the best home resource for Orton-Gillingham-based teaching is by Verticy Learning (www.verticylearning.org). As of this writing, Verticy offers online classes priced between $250 and $1,700 a year.

The core of any OG program guides children through the sounds associated with letters and then provides step-by-step training to turn those sounds into words. For example, in this approach the word *hat* has three phonemes: "ha," "aa," and "tu." Starting at this most granular level can help dyslexics learn to pull a word off the page.

OG will not turn children with dyslexia into standard readers; it is more likely to help your child develop a somewhat stilted process for doing what other people do fluidly. To use a metaphor, it teaches them the most efficient way to crawl up stairs. This is better than not getting in the building at all, to be sure, but I still believe that a ramp is greatly preferable.

Unfortunately, OG teaching is usually presented as a "remediation" program. This label quickly forces dyslexic students down the dyslexia-as-disease path. This is a risky expectation for three reasons. First, it reinforces the sense that your child is broken. Second, even if your child makes real improvement from OG training, she is never going to be as fluid an eye reader as her mainstream peers. Why is this dangerous? If you have gone from being in a wheelchair to being able to hoist yourself up stairs by leaning on a banister, you might start to think of yourself as cured and therefore start refusing ramps. All the while, standard learners will be jogging effortlessly up the stairs, gliding with the ease you could have had with your wheelchair on a ramp. This is especially true if she is going to move on to a higher education level. She might match her fifth grade peers, but will she be in the top 50 percent of eye readers in college? No. And that is fine. Ironically, we should want our children to do so well that they will not be the best reader there. This is proof that their poor reading has not held them back! Finally, there is the risk that your child will not reach mainstream standards and will therefore conclude for herself—or have others conclude for her—that she is lazy or stupid.

I had OG-style interventions from second grade onward in order to improve my reading, but I still am in the bottom 15 percent in my broad reading score and the bottom 1 percent in my ability to name a letter when I see it. I value the reading I can do, but I do not, and your child should not, take on the shame that comes with thinking that reading with your eyes is the only way to learn.

There are numerous other remediation programs that you may be tempted to try with your child. Some are clearly unhelpful. Beware of outrageous claims such as "Try our simple system and you'll cure dyslexia in a week." Or, worse, they will tell you that with the right intervention, dyslexia can be a Gift with a capital G!

You may also come across providers who will charge thousands and thousands of dollars for consultations, with no evidence that they can change outcomes. When I was a child, my grandfather asked me to try a methodology that he'd heard about: play a piano keyboard while humming and reading at the same time.

There are some strategies that may provide a certain amount of incremental benefit. One of these uses colored filters or colored paper, which is thought to make the process of eye reading easier. Proponents of this approach ask you to try out blue, yellow, or red glasses, or colored transparencies held over the page. Your child may find that it makes a slight improvement; for many years I used a blue filter over my text and convinced myself that it made reading better. Using my wheelchair/stairs analogy, however, I think of colored filters as equivalent to putting some sand on the stairs for a person who cannot climb with ease—it gives you more traction, but the stairs haven't become a ramp. A recent variation on this is tweaking text to make it better for the dyslexic reader, such as making part of a letter fatter or putting color around it. The worst part is that these kinds of incremental strategies can end up diverting your child from finding a better path. Getting a 5 percent increase in access to text by putting a filter over it can prevent you from looking for the 95 percent improvement your child might get through proper accommodations.

Sometimes a methodology improves your child's eye reading capability slightly because it is implemented through one-on-one tutoring. It's not that the methodology is working; rather, the child drinks up the attention and praise or believes he is improving because of the effort he is putting in. I have seen modern-day snake oil salesmen simply substitute their made up catch phrases for the eye of newt in concoctions of old, in some cases calling dyslexia a gift, in other cases calling it a condition, always insisting that they have the cure. In the worst cases, the charlatans take thousands of dollars in seminar, tutoring or therapy fees from families.

The upshot of all this? Make sure what you pick is well researched and validated, like the accommodations listed below.

MOVING BEYOND EYE READING

The best path to learning for dyslexic children is to use an Orton-Gillingham-based reading method for the first two to three years after having been identified, while simultaneously employing the best accommodation technologies described in this chapter. This approach guarantees them an alternative way to learn when they hit their maximum eye-reading capability or reach a plateau that is below what they are capable of. For example, even if your child achieves average eye-reading ability by fifth grade, she might be able to digest intellectual content that would be appropriate for a tenth grader. If this is the case, you are doing her a disservice by shackling her to standard reading instead of freeing her to race ahead as her mind allows. Put another way, standard reading is not the goal; learning should be. And the following accommodations can help you achieve that goal.

In Chapter Three, you identified your child's top three strengths.

We now want to map the right accommodations that will play to those strengths and use them to support the weaknesses. There is a core accommodation environment you will need to build regardless of your child's specific strengths. I'll also name ones to avoid because of their ineffectiveness or, worse, the likelihood that they will reinforce stigma.

TECHNOLOGY CREATES ACCOMMODATIONS THAT WORK

Your child's accommodation tool kit needs to support a learning environment that can change with the times and be adaptable. In technology circles, this means that a product has "universal design." For our purposes, this means we need to look to digitization, using both hardware and software to accommodate dyslexic learners.

Generally speaking, schools are massively behind on adopting new tools. Teachers often resist the arrival of technology in their classroom. There's often an unfounded fear that the students could use the technology to cheat or that they could get some unfair advantage by using these tools. Over time, however, institutions slowly come to accept new technologies. For example, when calculators first became cheap enough that almost every student could afford them, many teachers voiced the same old but unwarranted concerns: that students who used calculators would never learn how to add, multiply, divide, or subtract. Consider Ohio, where it is now common practice to allow students in sixth grade and up to use calculators as an accommodation to take their standardized exams. The state figured out that it was better to spend the time testing students on more complicated mathematical concepts than to waste it on doing routine calculations.

It's important to look at your own anxieties about technology and figure out whether they have to do with your own nervousness about new things or whether they come from your child. Nine times out of ten, children are excited to try out new technologies, especially if a device gives children an opportunity to put down an unfair burden that they have been carrying. Think of it this way: even Betty White is on Twitter, and if she can tweet, you should be able to embrace an iPad and your child's teacher should be able to handle a word processor in the classroom.

HARDWARE TOOLS

The best private schools whose mission is to educate students with specific learning disabilities, including dyslexia, issue hardware to their middle and high school students, including iPads or Windows-based tablets or netbooks. This may seem impossibly expensive at first glance, but consider that for about $400 your child's education can be dramatically enhanced. At the cost of one iPad or netbook per student every three years, you are talking about less than 40 cents a day—and the price will keep falling. Students can carry these devices with them to record lectures, take images of notes that are scrawled on a board, and have instant access to a spell-checker, a calculator, and a computer engine that will read aloud text on a screen or even allow them to talk to the device and have it write down what they say. For the younger child, managing and supporting these tools may be beyond her ability, but having the technology platforms in the house or working with someone in school to have these technologies available is a good starting place for many of the most effective accommodations.

The Kindle and iPad, as well as a number of other e-readers, are hit or miss in terms of audio accessibility. When the Kindle was first released, it had a built-in speech engine that would allow it to read content aloud. Publishers fought back: they were concerned that consumers would use the computer-voiced audio function (think robot, not a human recording) on a Kindle rather than buy an audiobook. Amazon, which produces the Kindle, now leaves it up to the publishers whether they will lock the audio content on this platform. This information is often listed on the specific book's information page. For example, on Amazon.com, on the Product Details listing for each Kindle eBook, look for the words "Text-to-speech: Enabled."

In the case of the iPad, there is a workaround that will allow you to use the "VoiceOver" feature for the blind, as opposed to the "Speak Selection" option, to read content in an iBook. However, this is complicated to explain. Separately, many of the publications in the "Newsstand" cannot be read aloud at all. I recommend you go to the Headstrong Nation website if you're interested to learn more about these functions and the accessibility of e-readers in general.

One gadget that will make you and your child both feel like Maxwell Smart is a recording pen. Livescribe manufactures the Smartpen, which is a computer embedded inside of a pen that will record everything you hear, say, write, and draw. It can then wirelessly sync notes and audio to an Evernote account (see page 169) where you can replay, organize, search, and share your notes. These pens can hold up to two hundred hours of audio and are compatible with both PCs and Macs, as well as a variety of smart phones. It also has a number of embedded functions that can be helpful to dyslexics. Check out www.livescribe.com.

Another piece of equipment that you may want to invest in is a flatbed scanner. There are some that retail for less than one hundred dollars and will be indispensable for digitizing all types of text into speech to be read aloud by a computer, as outlined later in this chapter. Currently I'm a fan of the Fujitsu Snap Scan S1300i. This market moves fast, so check product reviews before you make a purchase.

I also like document cameras for scanning. If they have a 5-megapixel camera and a lighting source built in, these can be the fastest way to capture a page. NuScan, Epson, and Elmo manufacture models that take clean, crisp images, or check out the following: www.thehovercam.com.

Mobile phones that have powerful cameras will be a key tool in your kit. These cameras can take a scannable image of text so that it can be used later with text-to-speech software. It's incredibly useful for a student to have a text-to-speech engine built into a phone. It allows your child to access texts, emails, or websites on the go, or to be sure that her Facebook postings are spelled correctly. This may seem like a trivial matter, but being able to keep up with her peers and communicate easily is as much a part of daily life for a teenager as was attending a school dance back in the day. Indeed, much of the stigma a student can feel over an inability to spell well can be about what people will think when she comments on a social networking site, rather than what grade she gets in school. You will find text-to-speech functionality built into iPads, iPhones, and Android phones; Kindles too. Visit www.headstrongnation.org to see a tutorial about how to turn this functionality on.

You may have already heard about Siri, the voice function on Apple products running iOS 5 or higher; I have found that the latest version of the Android speech functionality is even better. And of course this will change as the market evolves. This technology provides tremendous potential to reduce barriers for people who are dyslexic. The best part is that they are completely without stigma. I recently saw an Apple ad in which a movie star used Siri to help cook a meal. Accommodation technology has clearly moved out of the basement and up to the penthouse, becoming something desirable for everyone. While standard readers may use the personal assistant to schedule an appointment while they're jogging, a dyslexic student can ask Siri to write a text message to a friend and then to read the text message back for accuracy. If you have an iPhone, try asking Siri to "send a text message to [someone in your contacts]." When you are done speaking the message, ask Siri to "read that back to me." No more sending messages that read "I'll tax you about sinner" when you really meant "I'll text you about dinner"!

Since audio reading is a key accommodation, headphones are also important. I prefer to get inexpensive earbuds, as I tend to crush or lose them often in my travels. Standard earbuds also have the benefit of looking the same as any other set a young person might be using to listen to music, thereby reducing any stigma your child might feel about ear reading rather than eye reading. However, you may want to purchase a higher grade, over-the-ear model to use at home: these are much better for blocking out surrounding noise. This will allow your student to focus on what he's hearing and also ensure that the audio does not disturb others.

SOFTWARE: TEXT-TO-SPEECH

The most flexible audio accommodation is the ability to transform any printed text into digital text and have your child access a "talking computer" via text-to-speech software. This technology has been around for decades: Ray Kurzweil built the first optical character scanning system with a built-in voice engine for musician Stevie Wonder in the 1970s. Back then it cost $50,000. These days both Apple and Microsoft operating systems have built-in speech engines that are pre-loaded onto most any new computer you can purchase. Either of these two speech engines will meet about 80 percent of your child's text-to-speech needs, and given that they are free with the purchase of the overall system, they're hard to beat in terms of value for money.

When you think of text-to-speech voices you probably think of terrible computer-generated voices or the canned voices you hear when talking to an airline's recorded voice system. The quality of text-to-speech voices has gone up dramatically, however. Voices can now sound quite human, and can even have remarkably localized accents such as British-, Australian-, or even Punjabi-accented English, as well as foreign language options in the hundreds.

One critical benefit of text-to-speech engines is that they enable independence: you can quickly listen to something when you need it. By contrast, relying on a human reader to deliver material, even if it's a downloadable MP3, has some inherent limitations. The first issue is availability. A work has to be popular enough to justify creating the audiobook. The handout that a teacher gives out in class or the instructions for your child's favorite board game are unlikely to be available from a service where people read it aloud onto tape. Scanning at home and using the speech software discussed here allows this.

The main reason that you want to start training your child to use text-to-speech, however, lies in the long-term ability for him to level the playing field with eye readers in terms of time. Standard human speech is substantially slower than standard human eye reading. A radio commentator speaks at between 100 and 120 words per minute. Most people can read text at more than double that speed, and strong readers are typically clearing 300 words a minute. If your child is using standard human speech as her main alternative to reading, she will forever be at a major time disadvantage.

I discovered this firsthand when I went to law school. In my first year I started using audio in the form of books on tape. I eye-read at one-fifth of the standard speed. My law school was assigning five hours of reading a night. At my eye-reading speed, this meant that I had twenty-five hours of work a night! Using standard human voices reading to me, I still had fifteen hours of work a night—clearly not practical. I realized that the only solution was to speed up the tape player to a rate faster than what you typically hear from a human being. I learned that blind people have been using speech at extremely accelerated rates for decades, so I began to train myself to do the same, using their tools for my "word blindness." Today I can listen to text at over three hundred words a minute. This is not merely an interesting party trick but is fundamental to my ability to keep pace with my peers. You can hear examples of these voices on my website.

It is extremely important that you begin training your child to use text-to-speech technology if she has reasonable strength in listening ability. However, be prepared for the difficulties she may encounter at the beginning. It takes at least a month before a child becomes comfortable with this tool, and it can take more than a year before she has genuinely mastered it. When you consider that a standard reading curriculum allows three to five years for students to become proficient in eye reading, this is not at all an unreasonable expectation.

The best starting place for text-to-speech is in the operating system of your computer. If you're using an Apple computer, you'll find it in the systems preferences screen. Look on the left for the word "System," and find the picture of an old-fashioned microphone, which is the "Speech" icon. You can watch me do this at my website. Of course, these menus are likely to change over the long term, but here are images of the menu as of publication that should help you get started:

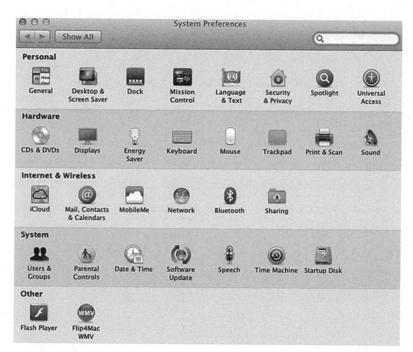

Once you have selected the "Speech" icon, click on the "Text to Speech" button at the top and you will pull up the menu shown on the next page.

If you click "Play," you'll hear the device read the standard Apple phrase "Isn't it nice to have a computer that will talk to you?" You can select a male or female voice, and you can even download additional voices from Apple by choosing the customize option within the "System Voice" menu:

Victoria is my favorite. In general, most people find that female voices register more easily than male voices: their higher pitch is easier to hear. Any of the voices will sound better when you listen to them with headphones.

The last step is to create a customized keystroke that will trigger this voice anytime you highlight text on the screen. I use Option + Escape in combination, as this is a keyboard function not currently assigned.

Set a key combination to speak selected text.

Type one or more modifier keys (Command, Shift, Option, or Control) and another key below. Use this key combination to hear your computer speak selected text. If the computer is speaking, press the keys to stop.

Option+Esc

Cancel   OK

Announce

Announce when an application requires your attention

Speak selected text when the key is pressed
Current key: Option+Esc   Change Key...

To have clock announce the time: Open Date & Time Preferences...

To change VoiceOver settings: Open Universal Access Preferences...

With this keystroke enabled, all you have to do is highlight text on the screen and hit the combination on the keyboard. You'll instantly hear the material read aloud regardless of whether it is a Web page, an email, or a document, as long as it is digital text (as opposed to an image of text). The technical term for this is *ASCII text*, but you can think of it as any text you can cut or paste as opposed to a picture of text on the screen that is solely an image.

On the Windows operating system, go to Control Panel. You can find the text-to-speech function listed (counterintuitively) under "Speech Recognition" (look again for the old-fashioned microphone icon). The speech recognition function within the Windows operating system is not very good (ignore it in favor of the Dragon Dictate option presented below), but the text-to-speech function works just fine.

Once you have opened the "Speech Recognition" item, you can make adjustments to speech properties, including the voice and the speed, in the "Speech Properties" menu:

When using a PC, I use Microsoft Word as my default speech engine, cutting and pasting text into Word in order to read it. This means that if you are reading text on a website or in an email, there is an extra cut-and-paste you have to do in order to bring it over into Word. You'll need to elevate the speech icon within the Microsoft Word menu structure to make the speech function easy to find. You can find the "Customize Quick Access Toolbar" in the upper left corner of the screen once you launch Word. It will look like this:

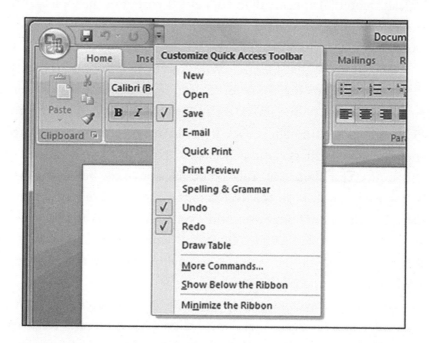

Select "More Commands" and you'll see this menu come up:

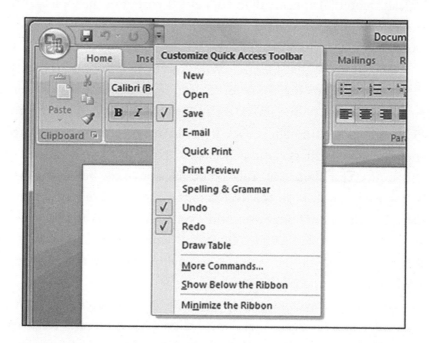

From within the "Choose Command Format" menu you will then need to select "All Commands" and scroll down to "Speak." Add this to your customized toolbar, and then whenever you highlight text in Microsoft Word you can have it read to you by pressing the "Speak" icon that appears in the upper left corner of the toolbar. The speed is controlled from the "Speech Properties" menu found in the Control Panel, as described earlier.

Keep in mind that the Microsoft voices are older and therefore more robotic than the Apple ones. You can buy new voices from NextUp or other online providers and then download them to your PC for about $35, though you are likely better off getting a dedicated speech engine such as Natural Reader or NextUp (described later in this section) for about $50. You should use one of the better voices to introduce your child to this technology—she will likely reject anything but the more human-sounding ones. Given that the basic version is free and provides incredibly useful access into printed material, it is still an okay option. You can get help understanding how this works through videos on my website.

There are, of course, other higher-end speech engines that you may want to consider using. Some schools have adopted Kurzweil 3000. The software was one of the first widely commercially available applications. These days, its pricing is out of line with the market, coming in north of $1,200 for an individual license. However, it does offer a tremendous amount of functionality, including the ability to scan and read any document and highlight directly to the scanned documents. It may be that your school has already bought Kurzweil 3000, in which case it is a good choice for you given that it's free for your child. Still, the learning curve for this software is steep, and the teacher who understands the full functionality well is rare.

A better option would be software such as Natural Reader or NextUp, both of which provide streamlined text-to-speech solutions for about $50. A middle ground would be ClaroRead, which provides much of the interactive speech engine qualities of Kurzweil at a lower price. You can pair any of these with off-the-shelf optical character recognition (OCR) software that you can use to scan documents into electronic form. OCR software has been around for decades and has become so sophisticated that it allows you to turn virtually any font into a digital file that can be read aloud or cut and pasted. The primary ways to use it are either with a 5-megapixel (or better) document camera or a flatbed scanner (see "Hardware Tools" earlier in this chapter). ScanSnap from Fujitsu is a more expensive version if you have a large amount of scanning to do.

Once you have a document scanned you'll need to turn it into speech. The two leading engines to OCR material are OmniPage by Nuance (www.nuance.com/for-individuals/by-product/omnipage) and Abbyy FineReader (www.abbyy.com). OmniPage OCR software, which is at the high end of this market sells for roughly $90. Alternatively, an OCR engine is available as part of Google's Drive suite of software. You can do this by uploading a high-resolution version of the document to Google Drive. See their instructions online and make sure to consider your privacy needs when uploading documents. The resulting capability will allow you to take any worksheet or instruction manual your child might want to read, turn it into digital text through imaging, and then have your computer read it aloud.

I invented the Intel Reader in order to streamline this process. It was released in 2009 and allowed you to take a photograph of any printed material on the spot, quickly turning it into speech. When it was released it retailed for $1,600, 50 percent below the price of the closest competitor. These days it retails for $550; by the time you're reading this it's likely that the price will have fallen further. There may also be a new generation of this technology on the market. The Intel Reader can be purchased on the Internet (www.careinnova tions.com/products/intel-reader-text-to-speech-technology). There are also training videos that can help you use this device. Thirty minutes of expert introduction will make it highly effective for any student. I recommend the Intel demo training: www.youtube.com/watch?v=sNJQuZv-RO8.

TEACHING TEXT-TO-SPEECH

Once you have a text-to-speech engine you'll need to go through a number of steps to help your child learn how to use it. For starters, it's probably easiest to stick with the default speed. Start your child using text-to-speech in the context of content that he will enjoy. If he is a sports fanatic, get him access to material regarding his favorite team. If he is into video gaming, get him access to the latest news on his favorite gaming platform. You can typically find this content on websites and use the speech engine on your computer, tablet, or smart phone to access it.

Explain the use of this software in terms of how much time your child will save: "Imagine if your homework took you an hour less each night and you could use that time to play with your friends." Or "How would you like to be able to skip sessions with your after-school tutor and just do this on your own?" You can listen to speech software with your child and make it a joint project. This will help in addressing the other reason students will not want to use text-to-speech: stigma.

It may take as much as a month before your child is willing to entertain the idea that this technology will be useful—this is what I have learned from talking to assistive technology coordinators at schools and watching the adoption curve for the Intel Reader with test users. It is only an estimate, but what's more important to keep in mind is that you should not expect this to happen instantly. Keep up the campaign, trying different products and voices and selling the idea as hard as you can. Learning this skill is a huge help for your child's overall literacy—that is, access to text.

It is useful for many people to visually track the written word as they listen to it. Apple iOS6 will highlight words as they are read, and ClaroRead or Kurzweil products come with this tracking capability built in. On the other hand, some people find the highlighting distracting. Similarly, many of these programs will allow you to adjust foreground and background color for reading text on-screen.

This can help some folks; you should experiment with these settings to see what your child likes best.

When you get to the point where your child asks to use the text-to-speech software in reading something on his own, it's time to start accelerating the rate at which text is read back. First try increasing the rate by 10 percent to see if your child can follow along. Every time your child increases her speed by 10 percent, it will take her 10 percent less time to get through material. You may find that your child can use different speeds in different contexts. For example, if I'm reading an article in *Sports Illustrated* from its website, I'll be able to listen to it at my highest rate, which is about 400 words per minute (this is well beyond where you will start). On the other hand, if I'm reading a new piece of scientific literature that I don't understand very well, I might slow it down to 300 words per minute. And if I'm reading over an important contract, such as documents for a mortgage on my home, I might read it at a much slower rate.

A good rule of thumb is to increase the rate 10 percent every week, which will get a user to roughly a 50 percent increase within a month. If you can keep this up for another month you can get your child to a full 100 percent increase, which would be outstanding. This is unlikely to happen for anyone who does not have strong auditory skills to begin with, but if you can get there, it means your child will have better comprehension and will be able to more easily keep up with (and maybe even surpass) eye readers.

Digital versions of text with text-to-speech software are more useful than audio recordings for other reasons. Students often need to quote from a book for their papers. If you have an audio version, listening to someone speak and having your child transcribe the information can be a very tedious task. It's better to have material that he can cut and paste out of the digitized version of the book. This allows your child to both see and hear, while having an accurate transcription of the content for quoting.

A great way to make your dyslexic child feel more at ease adopting this and other tools is to run the following experiment: ask your entire household to live without text for a week, and if you are successful, work up to a month. What if there were no more books or instruction manuals? What if you had to learn everything through another set of strengths beyond eye reading? This is the experience that a dyslexic person lives with daily. For your child to succeed as a dyslexic learner you will need to walk in her shoes and try to abandon what seems safe and easy in order to incorporate these new methods.

I came up with this experiment after I learned how the National Federation of the Blind (NFB) trains its members to use a cane. Many people who are legally blind have partial vision. They can see light or dark or perhaps read the headline of a newspaper, but not the article. The NFB found that people with some sight will cling to it, which means that they will be less independent in the long term. For cane training sessions, the NFB requires that people wear light-deprivation goggles. These are similar to ski goggles that have been painted black, cutting out all light and forcing the person to rely on her other senses. In the exit exam, the participant is dropped off on a random street corner in inner-city Baltimore, where the NFB national headquarters are located. The trainees are allowed to ask only one person where they are. Then they have to work their way back to the headquarters on their own, figuring out the bus system or walking all the way. Difficult and scary, no doubt—but confidence-building and important as well. The same is true for your child. As she grows up, getting a teacher or a friend to work with her will be important, as will mastering a faster rate of ear reading so that she can learn independently.

The no-text-household experiment has two important benefits. First, you will discover how much people rely on text, gaining empathy for your child's situation and perhaps even insights about how to include him better. Second, it will communicate to your child that the whole house is with him on this, meaning there is a community. Again, community is the chief antidote to shame and critical to long-term success.

SPEECH-TO-TEXT SOFTWARE

Speech-to-text software is also extremely useful for creating and, just as important, editing written prose. I used a headset microphone and dictation software to write this book. But even then I still had some inaccuracies. The phrase "text-to-speech software" was transcribed as "Texas Creek" when I first started. Listening to what I wrote down, I corrected the error and taught my speech-to-text software to understand me the next time. You can see a demonstration of this process on the Headstrong Nation website.

Far and away the best provider of speech-to-text software is Dragon, a brand owned by Nuance. They produce Dragon Naturally-Speaking for Windows and Dragon Dictation for the Mac, which retail for between $50 and $100. As with text-to-speech software, mastering speech-to-text is a skill that your child will have to work to learn, and you'll have to determine whether the time spent learning it would be beneficial. If you can work with your child on developing his ability to speak as he would write, you will find that it can dramatically accelerate the writing process. It also opens up the possibility of using vocabulary that he might have been reticent to explore. (Note that I have no idea how to spell *reticent*, but my speech software does!) In general, you should expect it to take at least a month before your child is fluidly using this tool. In the first week have him practice at least thirty minutes a day, writing about anything he likes. Then have him try it in place of standard writing for school activities. Be sure that your child is comfortable and competent using the tool before you have him use this technology outside of your coaching reach.

One important tip for using speech-to-text software is to get a high-quality microphone. Do not count on the basic microphone that typically comes with the software. You will want to get a USB microphone that plugs directly into the USB port on your computer. These will start at about $35 and can go up to $300 if you want to get wireless units or other features.

When you begin using Dragon software, the setup process asks you to read aloud roughly five minutes' worth of text (they do have child-friendly material). This is obviously a challenge for someone who has difficulty reading in a standard way. It may make sense to have a strong eye reader actually record the audio first and then allow the student to listen and repeat it into the computer in her own voice so that the computer can build a profile. I have seen speech software work for students as young as nine years old, and I would encourage anyone from third grade on to attempt using it. There is also a Dragon Dictation app for the iPhone that allows you to transcribe information into your phone via voice.

Android and iPhones also have an excellent speech function. When you look at the keyboard, there is a microphone button in the lower left. Tap it and it will record what you say and transcribe it. Quality can be mixed but it is getting better and better and it soon will be superior. This is great for texting or posting on social messaging sites. They also have a workable iPhone app called Claro-Speak.

Ginger (Gingersoftware.com) provides a contextual spelling and grammar engine that learns in response to dyslexics. Don Johnston, Incorporated (www.donjohnston.com), was founded by a gentleman who is dyslexic and focuses on creating products that help with learning. Their Read Write Gold, Read Outloud, and other products are excellent.

At school your child will likely need to have a private space in order to write, given that she will be speaking out loud. This creates a challenge in the classroom, though it is rare that there are extended periods of writing in elementary school. Requesting a separate room during exam time is a fairly standard element of many IEPs. While there is some stigmatization to being in a separate room from the other kids, being able to use the software is absolutely worth it. Lastly, be sure your child has access to a high-quality USB microphone to ensure that he captures the best input of sound. This will create the best text output.

Core Accommodations for All Dyslexics

- Appropriate language instruction for two to three years: Orton-Gillingham (OG) method
- Digital platform: iPad or laptop (includes spell-checker, keyboard for writing, and device for recording audio)
- Access to free audio versions of text material: Bookshare and Learning Ally outlined below
- Speech-to-text software: Dragon NaturallySpeaking products and a high-quality USB microphone
- Text-to-Speech Software: Native Apple or Microsoft speech engines turned on

ADDITIONAL AUDIO TOOLS

The central premise of accommodations is for you to pay attention to how your child learns and to try to bend the environment toward his strengths. As a general rule, most dyslexics are stronger in ear reading than they are in eye reading. Therefore, the core elements are built around the assumption that listening is a relative strength for your student even though it may not be the strongest aspect of his profile.

If your child excels at learning through hearing and speaking, he will thrive using many of the excellent learning tools that deliver information via audio. Some people raise the concern that dyslexic students will never learn to read if they have access to audio. The research suggests quite the opposite: the two together actually expand vocabulary and keep students interested in developing both skills, as well as offering a differentiated path to learning, adapting the content to the kid, not the kid to the content. Exposing an average reader to audio content can have benefits even after she has mastered the basics of reading, allowing her access to vocabulary that she might not be able to read yet. For a student who is dyslexic, using audio to access content is even more critical. Dyslexic students can often be two or three years behind in their acquisition of eye reading. Shall we ask a sixth grader to stick only to material we would assign to a third grader? Would you expect a blind student to be cut out of all the content that is generally available to eye readers?

The critical insight here is that reading is not an either/or situation. Both text and audio, as well as visual and kinesthetic learning methods, should be available for all students. I recently visited a school in Portland, Oregon, and heard a fifth-grade teacher make a novel suggestion when I brought up the idea of providing audiobooks for a student who was dyslexic. She suggested it might be a good learning opportunity for all the students to try using an audiobook. The teacher recognized that every student in the classroom could benefit from developing the skill of focused listening. She also understood that it would destigmatize ear reading versus eye reading. Setting the norm that everyone could use audio some of the time and books at other times created an opportunity for all the students to see these two mediums as equally valid ways of learning.

There is a significant self-esteem component to incorporating ear reading early on for the dyslexic child. While crawling up the stairs into a building (eye reading) can be very frustrating, gliding up a ramp (ear reading) allows the student to know that school can be fun. It also helps her know what is in the building. There is a tremendous amount of social pressure for students to learn to read with their eyes, and therefore they may want to learn how to do so even if the results will be less than perfect. Many situations in life are not immediately designed for audio access—consider medicine bottles or cooking directions on boxes of food—and therefore having even the most basic eye-reading skill will be useful. However, your goal is to create an atmosphere where your child will accept with ease all options as equally useful depending on the particular situation.

BOOKSHARE AND LEARNING ALLY

Access to audio material begins with two sources for content, both free for dyslexic students: Bookshare and Learning Ally. Both of these services provide audio versions of printed material for individuals with print-related disabilities. That includes people who are blind, but the vast majority of their clients are dyslexic, given that dyslexia is ten times more common than blindness.

Learning Ally, originally called Recording for the Blind and then later Recording for the Blind and Dyslexic, has been around since 1948. They provide digital download services to more than 300,000 users nationwide. The services target texts that are most commonly used in elementary, college, and graduate school education. They rely on an army of volunteers who create high-quality recordings of everything from the Harry Potter books to fifth-grade social studies textbooks.

Bookshare receives funding from the federal government to create an archive of textbooks. They provide digital downloads as well, though they use a different method to create their content. Their content is almost entirely e-book DAISY files. This is a special format designed for people with disabilities that allows software to read the book aloud.

Both Bookshare and Learning Ally rely on the 1996 Chafee Amendment to the Copyright Law, which guarantees people with disabilities access to printed material. In order to qualify for these services, your child will have to have a formal identification of a print-related disability. Both of the services are sympathetic to the high cost associated with these identifications and will often accept a letter from your doctor or from a school learning specialist who will certify that your child is qualified. Bookshare or Learning Ally books are available as MP3s, so they can be downloaded onto an iPod or any other digital music player. You can find out more information on their websites: www.bookshare.org and www.learningally.org. As I mentioned earlier, an Amazon Kindle or an iPad can be great for digital books, though because of publishers' restrictions not all material can be read aloud.

Audible.com is another great source for audio content. This is a commercial service that is probably most useful for high school students and older because it delivers audiobooks for adult fiction and nonfiction as MP3 files for a smart phone, tablet, or laptop. However, it's always good to search their database to find out whether a particular title is available. This software uses human voices that can be accelerated, but not as much as with text-to-speech.

Last but not least, there is Project Gutenberg (www.gutenberg .org), which offers free digital downloads of e-text that can be placed in a speech engine and read by a synthetic computer voice. They have a deep catalog of material that is in the public domain, e.g., works by Shakespeare or Melville.

For years I listened to other people discussing books they'd read for pleasure, and I would know neither the books nor the authors' names. I had not read *Harry Potter*, *The Great Gatsby*, or any other recreational book. There was a giant desert in my intellectual life around pleasure reading. After fully integrating audiobooks into my life, I went to Audible.com. Then I called a friend to help me narrow down my options. I was thirty-five years old and didn't know what I liked to read. Walter asked me what kinds of movies I like and suggested that I try those categories in books as well.

Books were just so foreign as a medium that they seemed a different world. It never occurred to me that my television or movie life could correlate with something I really wasn't comfortable with. When it comes to pleasure reading I had to start from scratch to develop a world and a skill that nearly all of my peers have had since they were ten. I note this not to complain, but simply to illustrate just how far apart your child's world can be from the mainstream without anyone, including him or her, noticing unless someone brings it up.

As a result, your child may fight you on giving her tools and skills for independence because the path to get there involves standing out from the crowd and recognizing that she is in a minority. Many children will resist using assistive technology if it labels them as "different." However, if you can show your daughter the benefits to her daily life, she is likely to adopt it and begin using it regardless of the potential stigma. She can even become downright proud of using it once she sees herself solving her own problems. When I was testing the Intel Reader, I met with a boy named Tim, and when we explained how the device worked to him, we asked him if he would use it if it was available in his school. Before he answered, he shot back, "How many other kids are using it?" I said, "Let's say that fifteen of the kids in your class were using it." Then Tim asked a critical follow-on: "Which kids?" He wanted to know if, in this theoretical class, the cool kids were using it. We told him that the cool kids were using it. Then he said, "All right. I guess I would probably use it."

When he tried it and realized that he could access printed material and so didn't have to stay after school for tutoring or rely on his mom or dad to read stuff to him, Tim got really excited about the product. At the end of the demo he asked if we had figured out what to call this machine, and when we said that we hadn't gotten to that part of the project, his response was, "Well, you can name it after me!" I was shocked to see this quick transformation. Tim, who had grilled me on the social context of using this technology, was willing to literally put his name on a machine he would be using in front of his friends, once he knew that the device was useful to him.

EVOLUTIONARY STEPS TOWARD ACCOMMODATION

These hardware and software tools and audio libraries form the core set of accommodations for your dyslexic child. There are, however, a number of low-tech options that you can use as a bridge before you have an entirely digital system set up, or as a backup for those occasions when the digital options are not available.

The most obvious accommodation is reading aloud to your child. Parents typically do this with their children early on, and you'll want to extend the practice until your child is comfortable with speech technology. Strive to make the transition to speech technology as soon as you can, as it ensures independence for your child—he'll be able to read whenever and whatever he wants (which in turn frees up your time as well).

Another great accommodation is to allow your child to study in groups and to work with other students on projects. When I was in elementary and middle school I regularly hung out with other students while doing homework or talking about the material from class that day. It was a good way for me to integrate what I'd learned. You will want to structure environments where your child is encouraged to partner with people by using her strengths to help the other student, and vice versa.

A popular accommodation is requesting that take-home papers be assigned instead of in-class exams. Having your child create a paper can make him feel just as capable as the students taking an in-class test. It also gives him extra time to get help with proofreading or to discuss the material. You should push for full accommodations during exams, but this is a good first step.

Supporting your child with proofreading is also important. As you move toward using speech-to-text software, spell-checkers and other elements will improve written output, but it's useful to have a human intervention as a backup. It is also likely that dyslexics will never produce flawless material on their own (I certainly don't). As he gets older, your child will have to produce more and more written material. It may be useful to identify a professional proofreader whom he can work with, especially for term papers or college essays. Creating a professional relationship around this by employing a local college English major or a copywriter is useful. For a student who may be embarrassed about getting help, having to rely on Mom or Dad constantly is not ideal. Further, working with a professional ensures that your child will not have to impose on his friends or rely on a proofreader who doesn't have the required skills. Make sure that the proofreader will enter the changes directly rather than ask your child to enter them. Standard proofreaders assume that your child will be able to accurately perceive the markup on a paper version. It is better to have the editor work directly on an electronic version and then accept changes after your child has reviewed them, preferably with text-to-speech software reading it aloud. You'll reduce anxiety, and it's worth every penny to have a document fully cleaned up.

Verbal, Social, Musical, and Narrative Accommodations

- Alternative assessment: Instead of turning in a paper perhaps your student can perform a monologue or create a film.
- Film and audio learning: Students with these skills often thrive by learning through film and high-quality television. Look for documentaries and performances related to classroom activities.
- Musical: The Suzuki method for music is well suited to dyslexics, allowing us to avoid reading sheet music. This Japanese method emphasizes learning music by ear, not sight.

VISUAL TOOLS: ENHANCED PERSONAL ORGANIZERS

Keeping organized can be a major task for students who are dyslexic, because many, like myself, have a built-in aversion to paper. For kids who are also ADHD or have an executive-function-related disability profile, which is quite common with our population, accommodations for organizing can be a lifesaver for both parents and their child. Filing systems often rely on an ability to read labels in order to keep stuff in alphabetical or category order. To keep track of papers that are important to me, I rely on free software called Evernote and an iPhone. Evernote allows you to capture and organize information and access it from anywhere. This wonderful tool can also be used to keep track of webpages, emails, receipts, photographs, and more.

This tool is especially helpful for students who think of information visually. On the desktop interface for this software you can sort your information as you might album covers in the iTunes interface, flipping through whiteboard images, emails, or audio content easily. But for a dyslexic person there are some especially useful features. You can use Evernote to capture images of printed material that you might need to reference later. This includes handwritten notes on a blackboard or whiteboard in a classroom. The premium software is so sophisticated that it can allow you to search those images later simply by recalling a piece of content. For example, if you had a photograph of a whiteboard that referenced Abraham Lincoln in writing, you could merely hold up your phone and say the words "Abraham Lincoln" into the search field using speech capability, and Evernote will dig out all documents with the name on it, including those that are handwritten. Instead of frantically looking for notes or trying to recall what the whiteboard said three months ago, it's all in your phone or on your desktop! Google Drive (formerly called Google Docs) can also be a great organizer, allowing your child to have one place to keep documents, calendars, or images. The program allows you to access them from any computer with an Internet connection and to export as needed. You can find Google Drive at the top of the menu when you log into Google, and you can download it for desktop access while offline.

Maintaining a calendar can be an important tool for someone who's dyslexic. There is often some extra effort that needs to go into coordinating accommodations, and a calendar will come in very handy. It might be that you need to talk with your school librarian about getting an accessible version of a book or schedule time with the teacher to have a conversation about exam conditions. Empowering your kid to be part of this planning process will help him feel in charge of his world.

The low-tech version would be to get a large calendar that you can write on in order to keep track of your child's homework, projects, and assignments. You could also have your child use an Android or iPhone calendar as an organizer. This will be too much for a young student, but starting in about sixth grade, being able to pick up your phone and say to it, "Remind me to do homework in three" can provide a helpful reminder when the phone buzzes three hours later with the prompt.

Digitizing in general—that is, starting to use a laptop or an iPad, and moving off pen and paper—also opens up a host of other tools that can be helpful to a visual learner. One of the most obvious is spell-checking. When I was in elementary school, teachers became very upset about the invention of spell-checkers. They were concerned that students would "never learn to spell." These days, if a student turns in a paper without having run the software on it, the teachers become frustrated: "How could you be so lazy as to not use spell-check?"

There are a number of other niche technologies that are extremely useful for students in high school and beyond. These include products such as WordQ prediction programs, which help with writing, or even using the Google search engine as a way to spell-check words you can't figure out how to look up in the dictionary. These technologies are constantly changing, so Headstrong Nation maintains a section on its website where you can learn more about them.

ACCOMMODATIONS FOR KINESTHETIC LEARNERS

Many students who are highly visual or kinesthetic like to work on a whiteboard. Learning mathematics where you can scrawl out information and draw pictures about it is often more useful than sitting with a small worksheet. This can be higher-tech if you like, such as using a Smart Board that integrates into a computer. Or you can go low-tech, simply putting blank sheets of paper on a wall and allowing your child to draw ideas as part of the process of learning and communication. Similarly, for students who are kinesthetic, being able to play with objects can greatly improve their learning. Who decided that science is best learned from a book? If your student is studying birds in her fourth-grade class, be sure to get her out to listen to and observe birds.

Incorporating motion into learning is extremely helpful. This may involve creating a dance that is associated with a specific concept—for example, understanding the history of plate tectonics by moving around the room in the way the continents shifted. Three-dimensional models can also be integrated as a way to communicate learning. For example, if your child is learning about mathematics, counting out marbles or stacking up blocks when learning abstract concepts can help reinforce the physical implications of an otherwise hard-to-read formula.

Simple behavioral accommodations for home and classroom can also be extremely helpful to kinesthetic students who are dyslexic. For example, those with ADHD in addition to being dyslexic often benefit from permission to stand up and politely walk to the back of the class while the teacher is still teaching, or to play with a squeeze ball in their hand. These simple steps can allow them to work off a little bit of energy while still bringing their attention back to the main activity.

Kinesthetic, Spatial, and Visual Accommodations

- Lab and field work: Look for opportunities to have hands-on and interactive experience typically limited to book reading—science in a science lab, history on a field trip, English class at the theater.
- Movement time: Make arrangements with your child's classroom teacher to allow your child time to get up and move about during standard lessons. It's also helpful to get

a squeeze ball that your student can use to work off excess
energy while sitting in class.

- Alternative assessment: Instead of turning in a paper, perhaps your student can deliver a 3-D model, a painting, or
another type of art project to demonstrate her knowledge
of the underlying material. It is important to learn the skill
of writing as well, but only after your child has demonstrated mastery via the alternative method.

- Mathematical: Math-to-speech mark-up (Math XML) is a
good tool for high school and college students. Live Math
(www.mathspeak.org) provides speech software plug-ins
that allow computers to read mathematical equations. This
is only relevant for algebra, geometry, calculus, and higher-
order math.

- Whiteboard discussions: Working a problem through conversation rather than out of a textbook can be a great way
to play to a math student's skills. Use lots of color and
shapes to make the learning fit this profile.

POORLY DESIGNED ACCOMMODATIONS

While there are many accommodations that will make a big difference in your child's life at school, there are some that do not work well.
Unfortunately, these are often the first your child will be offered. The
most common is extra time for test taking. Extra time can be a useful
accommodation, and you should ask for it to the degree that it will be
helpful in managing time-consuming elements of *another* accommodation. It should not be used merely as a way to allow a student to
labor through a standard reading, writing, or spelling approach. Giving a person in a wheelchair extra time to get up the stairs makes no
sense. If, however, going up the ramp takes longer than going up the
stairs, or you need to spend time building a ramp before you can get
into the building, then the extra time is appropriate.

I had extra time for my exams in graduate school, primarily in conjunction with other accommodations that took extra time. For example, I had a person sit with me and spot homonyms in the exam. Lawyers care a lot about whether you use the term *council* or *counsel*. We did not have a piece of software that would spot these words efficiently, so I had to rely on another person to comb through the exam with me and find the instances where my spelling of a word was inaccurate. That took extra time. Therefore, the time accommodation made sense.

There are three unsaid reasons for giving extra time that are not in your child's best interest. The first is an assumption that the metaphorical gears in the mind of a dyslexic are moving slower than in a non-dyslexic. Do not for one minute believe that this way of thinking adequately describes your child. We dyslexics are able to draw the right conclusion quickly when we have the right path to the information. Think back to my Tylenol PM story, when I took over-the-counter downers before a big speech because I hadn't noticed the "PM" on the label. Having a pill bottle that would read itself out loud to me (audio), a color-coding system for the bottle (visual), or a rough versus smooth label (tactile) would've allowed me to get the right information fast, but extra time was not the issue.

The second reason that extra time is often given is because it is the lowest-cost accommodation for a school to provide. It presents the least bureaucratic hassle and is designed to make administering a test easier on the school's part. It would be much easier for an institution to say to all people in wheelchairs: "Tell you what—since you're a special person, we will give you extra time to get up the stairs, at no charge!" when what they actually want to say is "We will not spend money on concrete and architects to figure out how to make this easier." Extra time is really in the interest of the institution: it places the burden on the individual to correct him- or herself rather than on the institution to improve the manner of testing. On top of this, the school administrators can say they have met their obligation and limit legal liability.

The final reason to be cautious of extra time is that it can be one of the most socially stigmatizing accommodations. There are two primary impacts. The first is that a student who is using extra time does not have an obvious symbol to represent his need for his accommodation, and other students will surmise that they too would benefit from extra time. Yet this is not the case. A 2006 study from the University of Massachusetts shows that while students with disabilities make great gains when given extra time, students without disabilities do not see a large improvement when given extra time. One might conclude from this that extra time is in fact a useful accommodation, but that would be wrong—a person in a wheelchair can get herself into a building if she is given enough time to drag herself up the stairs with her arms, but what would be the point? A better question is, what would best ensure that a student can perform well on a test? In 2011, the National Conference of Bar Examiners lost a federal case in which they refused to allow a blind person to use speech software while taking the bar exam. All of the major testing agencies, including the people who administer the SAT, LSAT, and MCAT, wrote briefs claiming that it would be too difficult for them to provide certain accommodations. The court concluded that the administrators had an obligation to ensure that students were being accurately assessed, not simply to do what is easiest for the test givers.

Under the No Child Left Behind Act and in many state educational systems, there is an expectation that your child will regularly take standardized exams. If he is planning to go to college, he is likely to take the PSAT and SAT. Your student has a right to accommodations in these environments. You'll need to have established documentation both of your child's specific learning disability and of his use of accommodations. For example, the College Board requires at least four months of using the requested accommodation in a classroom setting before they will allow use of the accommodation on the SAT, and they generally look for more than that. It's critical to make sure that your child's IEP ensures access to accommodations for these tests.

Hopefully your child will have begun using text-to-speech software by the time she needs to take one of these exams. However, the administrators of statewide exams or the standardized tests for college may not be prepared to allow her to use this technology. Because the 2011 precedent mentioned above is relatively recent, you may be the first parent to ask for these supports. A human reader for your child (with extra time, given that human reading is slower than standard eye reading) is a good backup plan. Many states develop specific standards to articulate what accommodations are acceptable for their testing. You can find out information about your specific state at the Headstrong Nation website. Remember not to let administrators leave you with only extra time, which is the cheap and lazy approach to inclusion.

Extra time outside this context has other negative impacts. It requires that your child work on a different schedule than the other students in the classroom, thereby segregating her. When I was in business school I would regularly get extra time for exams, which often meant that I would not show up for the celebrations at the end of the semester because I was still grinding through my economics final when my classmates were enjoying themselves in the courtyard. As a result, I learned to lie to my friends (not a good idea) in order to avoid being seen as different. Your child may also try to keep hidden that she gets extra time, which only increases her shame. Remember, your child has a right to the best accommodations. That is the standard that you should be seeking; it's what is best for your child, and it is also what is best for the school that is trying to accurately assess your child.

Another common and ineffective form of accommodation is for evaluators to promise that they will "not take off for spelling" or "not take off for any mistakes related to dyslexia." When I was growing up, I had not figured out how to ask for appropriate accommodations and would sometimes go to teachers and explain that I was likely to make spelling mistakes on the exam. They would assure me that they would not take off points. However, the exam would inevitably come back marked up with red ink for all my grammatical or spelling errors. When I went back and spoke with the teacher, he could never explain to me what *content* I had failed to understand. The default bias is that if you can't spell *Napoleon*, you don't understand who he was.

Don't set your child up to have to rely on the goodwill of others. Always have access to the tools that your child needs in order to produce a high-quality exam. It's better to have some uncomfortable and direct conversations before the exam than to wait until afterward to try to clean up a mess.

DON'T ACCEPT MODIFICATION AS ACCOMMODATION

A second common model that schools will offer is modification rather than accommodation. Modification involves altering the standards of performance or the content that the student is expected to learn, rather than developing the methods that will allow your child to gain access to the same content everyone else has to master. In the stairs metaphor, this would be the equivalent of allowing kids who are dyslexic to enter only the first floor, when all other students are given access to the second floor. If students in fourth grade are being asked to master state history and your child is told that she can have a modified exam in which she will be asked more basic questions than the other students, this is a major red flag. It puts her on a path to falling behind her peers in learning. In some states, schools will even offer a modified high school diploma based on a modified curriculum. Oregon offers such a diploma; a statewide newspaper, the *Oregonian*, took to calling it "Diploma Lite." Modifications represent the school system's unwillingness to create a pathway into knowledge that will give your child independence.

Substitution of content versus modification of content is a better alternative for students to meet school standards. For example, if your child's high school guidance counselor believes that completing four years of a foreign language is important for college applications, you might look into your child learning American Sign Language (classes are often available in the community) as a way to meet this requirement. Learning to sign is a non-text-based way to learn a language and works great for many dyslexics. Working with your school to set up a program of independent study can satisfy a college looking for skills in multiple languages and can also demonstrate your child's willingness to do things differently, which can be attractive in a college admissions scenario.

THE RIGHT ATTITUDE ENSURES THAT TOOLS ARE USED

Your own response to doing things differently, as well as how open the school will be, can change the way your child perceives his tool kit. What's more, your child's attitudes will be the primary booster or barrier to adopting accommodations. Depending on age, your child may be hyper-aware of how other students perceive what he's doing with his accommodations. I've seen instances where children who have IEPs that allow them to have a teacher read test questions aloud skip this access on the day they have a substitute teacher. They do this because it allows them to grab a small window of opportunity to blend into the rest of the class, even though it resulted in losing substantial points on an exam later on. The fear of being seen as different is that strong.

In the initial phases of adoption you want to provide your child with enough camouflage so that she can handle learning how to use the accommodation well and understand its benefits before the issue of stigma blocks adoption. This could include allowing her to use speech technology at home while not forcing her to use it in public places. Another way is to combine accommodations with things your child already does: a great way for a child to blend in is to simply download school audio content, perhaps from Learning Ally or Bookshare, to an MP3 player, because who else will ever know what is on her iPod? For the initial introductory phase of any accommodation, whatever you can do in order to get your child to start using it is beneficial.

Many of the tools you will try out will not initially work, or you may find that they could work better if you make a slight variation. This will require experimentation. When you try text-to-speech and the voice isn't right for your child, try a different one until you find one that works. Try out different headphones. Try using it slightly faster or slightly slower. I guarantee that once your child has that "aha moment," when learning becomes easy, it will be worth all the hours that you put in helping your child get comfortable with it.

By definition, using an accommodation is doing something differently than other people do it. Given the level of shame dyslexics feel, and the resulting instinct to hide, this can mean that students will not seek the support they need, or possibly reject it when it is offered. The child may even put in place a far less reliable support to avoid being noticed. For example, my shame around the fact that I couldn't read in fifth grade was so great that I created an elaborate and cumbersome work-around that was at best hit or miss. I would talk to my friend Ross while we rode to school on the bus each morning about what had been in the book we were supposed to be reading. My reliance on my friend was not a great accommodation because it left me completely dependent on someone else: if Ross didn't show up on the bus, I had no idea what was in the book. In fact, this is what my attitude matrix looked like for my bus ride accommodation period:

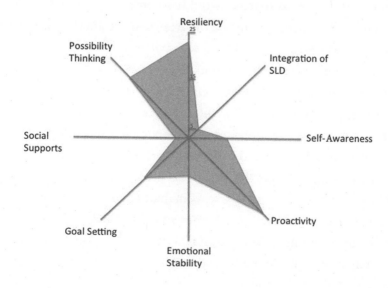

Fast-forward to law school. By my second year of law school I had built a strong set of accommodations I knew how to use well. But things still went wrong. At the end of my first semester, I showed up at the registrar's office only to be told that they did not have evidence that I needed an electronic version of the exam. "Can't you just take it on the paper version?" the person at the desk asked.

Exhibiting a much higher degree of self-awareness than I did when I was in fifth grade, I said "No, I have a right to the electronic version." Over the next two hours I was bounced around from the assistant registrar to the registrar to the assistant dean for student affairs and eventually to the dean of student affairs. Each of these conversations was triggered by an unexpected barrier that popped up: when I finally got the electronic version on disk, my computer disk drive broke! I suggested to the registrar that she email me the exam. She was concerned that this might violate the honor code by allowing me to forward the exam to other students. I pointed out that the exam had begun an hour before, so everyone had it already. Looking ahead, I noticed that I was going to miss the scheduled time I had with my "homonym spotter," a person who would come in to meet with me and help me find similar sounding but differently spelled words; I had to step out of the exam room and get permission to make a phone call to her so that she wouldn't come to campus two hours early and sit idly while I finished my exam. My resilience and proactivity skills were solid.

Once the exam was over—I had been delayed a total of four hours by the various mishaps that had befallen me—I found myself rushing across campus to make it to my finance class at the business school. That particular day the professor called on me to get up in front of the class with a small group and present the problem set. Rather than tell my presentation partners the long (true) story, I lied to them, saying I had been out at the big party everyone had gone to the night before, and I just hadn't gotten to my homework. I failed to use social supports or to fully integrate my dyslexia in the situation. That day the devil-may-care attitude that I used for camouflage let me slide by for the presentation, though I'm sure some of my peers thought I was a freeloader. That night I was in tears talking to friends about how stressful the day had been and was startled to hear them say in amazement, "I had no idea you had to put in that much effort." You can see in this diagram of my attitudes matrix that I was now filling in more area inside the attitude map. But there are still some holes:

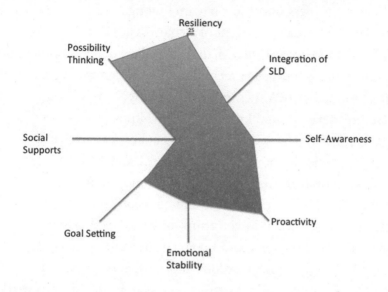

Now jump to my fourth and final year of business school. At this point most people around me knew that I was dyslexic. I was skilled at using my accommodation technologies. Indeed, I thought I had built a complete system that allowed me to be independent. That semester I was taking a class from Andy Grove, the former chairman and CEO of Intel. I was told by the staff at the university's Disability Resource Center that they would be unable to get me the reading packet in a scanned format until about three weeks after the start of classes. They explained that they had seven blind kids this semester and that they were overwhelmed with scanning work. Knowing that I needed a long-term relationship with them, I let this poor excuse slide and went to class assuming that I could use another strategy to keep up. In this situation I completely gave up independence, but I was thinking it would be better in the long term.

The case being taught was about Intel's leaving the memory business and switching to microprocessors in the early 1980s. This was a decision that Andy Grove had made and one that had required him to fire thousands of people in one day. When Andy asked in his thick Hungarian accent, "Why did Intel get out of the memory business in 1984?" I popped my hand up and answered, "Intel was in the horse and buggy business and the car came along." Andy is known for being the intellectual equivalent of a chain saw. He looked at me and said, "Horse and buggy? DRAM, distributed random access memory, chips are a horse-and-buggy technology? Your laptop sitting in front of you, how many DRAM chips are in it today?"

Getting nervous now, I replied, "I don't know."

"Eight. Today. Horse and buggy? What do you call that!?"

Hoping to use humor to slip the noose, I said, "A mistake."

He was not amused. He came back to me seven different times over the course of the class to ask me questions such as, "Well, Mr. Horse and Buggy, what do you think of your Japanese competitors' financials?" Or "Mr. Horse and Buggy, what would you tell [Intel co-founder and Andy's boss] Gordon Moore when he points out that 80 percent of the research budget for next year is already invested in memory chips?" By the end of the class I was devastated. As Andy had intended, all of the other students in class had seen the example he made of me, and they had learned an important lesson: don't come into this classroom unprepared.

I went immediately back to the Disability Resource Center and asked to see my accommodations officer. She again politely explained that they were overworked. I pulled a seat over in front of her desk, sat down, looked her dead in the eye, and said, "I'm not physically leaving your office until you hand me the readings for Andy Grove's class." With this statement I was emphatically declaring my independence, ensuring that my system would work for me. Thirty minutes later, she had the document scanned. Two days later I went back to class ready to do battle. Again I stuck my hand up after he asked the first question. But this time I knew what I was talking about.

For the next six classes, I was always the first person to stick my hand up and always knew the information well. Eventually I gathered my confidence and went down and spoke with him about dyslexia. It turned out he was keenly interested in speech software because he had experimented with it himself for other reasons. On the last day of class I went down to thank him for a great semester. He asked me what I was doing after graduation in the spring. I told him I didn't know. He handed me his business card and said, "Come work for me."

A situation that had started out poorly had turned into one of the most important professional relationships of my life, and led to me developing the Intel Reader and writing this book. It was the attitudes underlying my approach that made that situation successful. Here's how I would map that phase of my life:

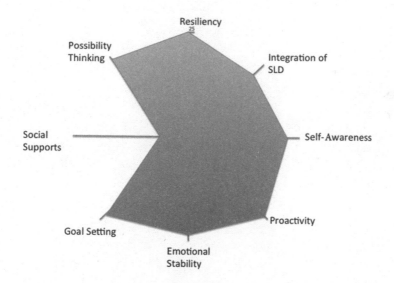

My use of social supports was still not as high as it could have been. I was not talking openly with my classmates about what had happened. Looking back on it, I bet they were perplexed: *One day this*

guy gets his head handed to him, the next day he's on his game? One's attitude toward accommodations and use of supports is always evolving. You want to keep track of your child's reactions, but these stories show that the time and energy you put into creating a good set of accommodations and the underlying attitudes to utilize them can lead to great things.

CHAPTER SEVEN

Assert Your Rights

Now that you've mastered the pitch and have your shopping list for your tool kit, it's time to engage your child's school to pursue appropriate accommodations to help your child learn. This will involve navigating often complicated bureaucracies in order to secure the resources needed to reshape your child's school environment. Keep in mind that you may be a pioneer at your child's school—you may have to train the teachers and the administration regarding what is legally and professionally necessary. That said, this chapter is not intended as a guide for legal action. I do include information on how to select legal counsel if you get to that point, but you should not use this information as your guide for court. Instead I want to give you a basic vocabulary for asserting your child's rights, as well as prepare you for the common pitfalls many parents face.

The law functions best when it acts as a bodyguard; people tend to pay attention when you walk into a room accompanied by a big guy in dark sunglasses! You don't want your bodyguard to do much beyond look menacing: if he acts, it may encourage others to get their own bodyguards, aka lawyers and bureaucrats. Merely noting in a passing comment that you have a bodyguard is more effective than boasting what he could do if you wanted him to. When I confronted the Disability Resource Center in graduate school in order to get scans of the reading I so desperately needed to do, I didn't threaten a lawsuit. I simply told the woman at the desk that I was not leaving the office until I had my needs met. My actions made clear that I understood my rights and was asserting them. My bodyguard was definitely doing his job.

Understanding the school's legal obligations and how to obtain what you need for your child is your chief goal. In many cases the best path will be to avoid a legal battle, because they are costly and emotionally draining, and they take a long time. The best scenario is that you'll be able to keep 90 percent of the knowledge in this chapter in your back pocket and only have to display it from time to time in order to signal to others that you know what you're doing. In Chapter Five I noted the range of teachers' practices you are likely to encounter, spanning categories from knowledgeable (rare) to good-hearted with bad methods (common) to unreachable (rare). I suggest you go in there assuming the best but prepared for the worst. In this context that will mean being engaging and polite with the school, but keeping detailed notes and documenting their actions at every turn in case you get to a point where you need the records.

HISTORICAL CONTEXT

To this day, the most prominent example of a person with a disability achieving access to education is Helen Keller, who lost her vision, hearing, and speech when she was nineteen months old. It's easy to view Keller as a two-dimensional hero, or what people in the disability movement call a "super-crip." But as I was researching her life story I realized that her hurdles were our hurdles. Over a hundred years ago, she had to make the same pitch and create her own accommodations tool kit, and you should feel connected to her proud tradition.

Keller battled for acceptance at Radcliffe College. Once she had gained admission, the administrators there didn't feel it was their responsibility to provide her with Braille versions of her course material, nor did they want to provide her with a translator for sign language. They clearly doubted that she would be able to keep up with their standards at all, even with help.

Helen Keller grew up in an era before women had the right to vote (a right she would help secure), and although she was severely disabled, she not only graduated from Radcliffe but also authored twelve books, learned to read and write in English, French, and Latin (among other languages), and became close friends with many of the most famous individuals of her day, including Alexander Graham Bell, Charlie Chaplin, and Mark Twain.

Legally, the right to a free and appropriate education that your child now enjoys can be traced directly to the principles of the 1954 Supreme Court case *Brown vs. Board of Education*. A case that focused on racial integration in schools, *Brown* established that "separate is not equal." In the late 1960s, a group of parents in Pennsylvania who wanted access to the public school system for their children with developmental delays used *Brown* to make their case. Along with another case called *Mills vs. Board of Education of District of Columbia*, which was decided in 1972, the Court declared that students with disabilities need to be included in the public school system. The legislative history of the resulting Education for All Handicapped Children Act, made law in 1975, points directly to *Brown*:

> "The Supreme Court of the United States (in *Brown v. Board of Education*) established the principle that all children be guaranteed equal educational opportunity." The Court stated, "Such an opportunity . . . is a right which must be made available to all on equal terms."

The main purpose of the 1975 act, retitled the Individuals with Disabilities Education Act in 1990, was to fund programs and the teacher training needed to include children with disabilities in classrooms. Unfortunately, most schools made poor choices about spending these government funds (for example, investing in remediation at the cost of accommodation), and the legacy of those choices, as well as other bureaucratic legacies means the strained funding persists today.

There also are a number of court cases that are more specifically focused on the issue of dyslexia and accommodation. In 1997, a seminal case taken up against Boston University underscored that dyslexic students are entitled to the same rights as all students with disabilities. The president of the university had previously stated that he thought people who are dyslexic or had specific learning disabilities were "lazy fakers." The university lost this case to the tune of millions of dollars in legal fees, and the precedent that was set has made it standard for all universities in the United States to include students with specific learning disabilities and dyslexia in the group that gets accommodations.

Dyslexia and other specific learning disabilities are now considered "high-incidence" disabilities, meaning that those with this identification are a large portion of the total number of students with disabilities in public schools. "Low-incidence" disabilities include most of the ones the mainstream thinks of as a disability: blindness, deafness, autism, needing to use a wheelchair, and so on. Autistic children make up only about 6 percent of the special ed population, and those with visual impairments less than 0.5 percent. U.S. Department of Education data from 2010 suggest that specific learning disabilities affected roughly 40 percent of the special ed. population, with speech and language impairment (SLI) affecting an additional 25 percent of those receiving special education. The categories are fuzzy, but it is safe to assume that dyslexia is half or more of the subcategory of SLDs and some part of SLI.

Today, the total identified population of students with disabilities is over 6.5 million, much higher than ever contemplated by the Individuals with Disabilities Education Act. If funding was stretched then, it is stretched all that much thinner now. This is the main reason schools will resist an identification of dyslexia or other specific learning disabilities. It is nearly impossible for a school to reject the claim that a student is blind or has a hearing impairment, but dyslexia can be ignored more easily. This is, in part, why I support the notion that we should have mandatory screening for all children regarding dyslexia at first grade or earlier, in much the way we do for auditory processing at birth or for vision in annual nurse exams at school.

One recent educational methodology is called response to intervention (RTI, sometimes referred to as response to instruction). Ideally, it is designed to help all learners get access to good instruction without needing a label, but more and more RTI has become a school's way to reduce the strain on budgets involved. The guiding principle of RTI is that a student should be kept in a mainstream classroom as long as possible; teachers should provide your child instruction within a general education context. Some critics have come to call RTI "watching them fail," meaning that by waiting until a student is in a real crisis, teachers will "watch" him but not extend full IDEA supports. If a student shows indications that she is dyslexic, a school will sometimes argue that it is better to delay labeling the child and to keep her in a general education environment. This is attractive to parents who are scared of the label. However, be very cautious of this program; it can be a bureaucratic sleight of hand designed to keep your child from receiving additional resources or accommodations that she may really need. The key issue is that if your child is in an RTI program rather than an IDEA-funded one, she is not protected by the legal due process procedures that come with the IDEA funds. Unless your child has an IEP, you have little recourse if your child does not make progress. Be especially vigilant about this issue if your child is eight or younger. In this window, the school has a more plausible case to claim that it is meeting your child's needs, suggesting you wait rather than test for specific learning disabilities. If you are seeing the markers for dyslexia outlined in this book, push hard for a referral for services per the process outlined in this chapter. If there is no dyslexia, then the testing will show this, but waiting a year to find out dyslexia was an issue is a year lost to the school's delay.

The problem has gotten bad enough that the U.S. Department of Education issued a memo in January of 2011 in which it reported that "local education agencies (LEAs) may be using RTI to delay or deny a timely initial evaluation to determine if a child is a child with a disability and, therefore, eligible for special education and related services pursuant to an individualized education program."

If your child's school takes longer than the mandated limit of sixty days to conduct a "referral evaluation for a disability" for your child, you're running up against the very thing reported in the 2011 memo. In your defense, you should feel free to quote the memo's further commentary: "It would be inconsistent with the evaluation provisions at 34 CFR §§ 300.301 through 300.111 for an LEA to reject a referral and delay provision of an initial evaluation on the basis that a child has not participated in an RTI framework."

In a world of limited resources, there can also be tension within the disability community. School administrators are not above pitting people with low-incidence disabilities against people with high-incidence disabilities. It's very important that all students with disabilities see themselves as a community, and that you should do everything you can to stand with parents of children with other types of disabilities. If you can work together with other parents in your school district to generate resources for *all* students with disabilities, everyone will benefit.

My own experience forming community with people with disabilities other than dyslexia has been critical to my current level of integration for this issue. When I was in business school, my friend with no hands invited me to sit on a panel of students with disabilities. At first I didn't want to see myself as part of a larger disability community and was nervous about presuming to have the status. After sitting on the panel, I understood that the frustration that a person with a hearing impairment feels trying to keep up with a spoken conversation is very similar to the experience I have when the classroom discussion is based solely on a text that everyone is assumed to be able to eye-read. I understood that their experiences of being an outsider and having to ask for accommodations are similar to mine.

These days, I work with Lime Connect, an outstanding program for college students with disabilities (www.limeconnect.com). The organization gets funding from Google, Target, PepsiCo, and Goldman Sachs, among others, to fund summer internships at these corporate offices. Working with students who have a range of disabilities, including those with obvious ones such as the need to use a wheelchair and non-obvious ones such as dyslexia, is eye-opening still. Year after year, the students enjoy allying with others, whether they share their specific disability or not, forming the type of powerful community that exists when people with disabilities work together.

EXISTING LEGAL FRAMEWORKS

Today there are three major legal frameworks that directly affect children with dyslexia. You don't need to master the content of each, but you do need to be able to cite some key pieces of legislation in conversation and understand some core precepts from them in order to deal with your child's school most effectively. In order of importance to the education of your child, they are the Individuals with Disabilities Education Act, Section 504 of the Rehabilitation Act, and the Americans with Disabilities Act.

IDEA provides federal funding to public schools to support a "free and appropriate education" (FAPE) to students. It defines thirteen categories of disability and applies to children ages three through twenty-one who are determined by a multidisciplinary team to have a disability. Dyslexia falls squarely within one of the thirteen categories: "specific learning disability." IDEA and U.S. Department of Education regulations regarding Section 504 explain that this statute applies to "any person who:

(i) has a physical or mental impairment which substantially limits one or more major life activities,

(ii) has a record of such an impairment, or

(iii) is regarded as having such an impairment."

For a person with dyslexia, the relevant "major life activity" is defined in law as "learning" and, under recent amendments to the ADA, specifically, "reading." Note that the regulation points to the importance of a record of the impairment, so getting the certification and a formal record (identification) of your child's disability is extremely important.

Under IDEA, it is the obligation of elementary, middle, and high schools to find all students with disabilities within their district. Legal experts call this provision "child find." In theory this means that your school should be looking hard for students with disabilities. In practice it means that while they'll do their best, you're going to need to highlight this issue for them to take notice, given the non-obvious nature of dyslexia. Once the school is made aware of your child's identified disability, they are legally obliged to provide you with services and accommodations at no cost to you.

Section 504 and the ADA are both civil rights laws, as opposed to federal funding acts (which is what IDEA is). Section 504 protects people with disabilities from discrimination in private or public programs that receive federal funds. Private schools that receive money from the U.S. government are also subject to Section 504's guidelines, even if these funds are unrelated to special education (for example, if the school has subsidized meal programs or scholarship funds from Washington). The ADA applies more generally to employment, public services, and accommodations such as buildings and facilities. In the context of schooling, you would rarely use ADA claims, instead relying on Section 504. However, the ADA applies to nonsectarian private schools (but not to religious organizations) even if they do not receive federal funds, a narrow space where it would be the relevant law rather than Section 504. If you get to a point where you need to understand this level of detail, it is likely time to get a lawyer.

Both IDEA and Section 504 require that a student be educated in the "least restrictive environment" (LRE). This is generally interpreted to mean, to the maximum extent appropriate, that students are to be educated with their peers who do not have disabilities. The effect of this provision is that schools are not allowed to segregate your child from the mainstream classroom unnecessarily. While it might be appropriate to ask that your child leave a classroom for one-on-one sessions with a learning specialist once a day, it would not be appropriate for your child to have a totally different set of classes than her peers unless there was something specifically identified in her IEP that made this the most appropriate way to educate her, and therefore something you have agreed to. If your school proposes this accommodation, consider it a red flag, and dig more to determine the benefit of pulling her out of the mainstream. I am mainly concerned about students being left out of the social and academic life of their school, rather than in them leaving the mainstream school altogether. Generally, I have a bias in favor of inclusion, the term experts use to describe keeping students with disabilities integrated into the general education classroom setting. There are circumstances where a public school simply does not have the programming or resources to provide an appropriate education. In these situations, shifting to an independent school focused on dyslexia is a good option, providing you can afford it or you are able to strike a deal with your district to have them pay the bill in lieu of services they should be providing.

Most of the enforcement for IDEA and Section 504 is overseen by the Office for Civil Rights in the U.S. Department of Education. The reality is that people in these offices have too much on their plate and you're unlikely to get a lot of help from them unless you get yourself into a legal wrangling of national significance, not something that will be much fun. It is more likely that if you have a dispute you will end up using the arbitration mechanisms built into these two laws, and if you find yourself in that position, you're going to want to consult a legal expert.

STATE AND LOCAL POLICIES YOU NEED TO KNOW ABOUT

The federal government generally delegates decisions about education to the states, and so it's important that you understand local dynamics. State laws are constantly shifting, so do some homework on your specific state. For example, as of this writing, Michigan has extended funding for students in special education through the age of twenty-six. In many states, based on a precedent called *Florence County v. Carter,* school districts have determined they will pay private school tuition for students with disabilities who qualify. While this sounds like a great opportunity, it turns out that you may have to file a lawsuit against your school district in order to secure the funds before they release them, a process which can take years. Check out the website for your state's department of education, where they often have more details. You can find additional state-by-state resources at http://nichy.org/state.

Sadly, there is no knight in shining armor who is going to arrive and provide your child with the accommodations that he desperately needs. Instead, you need to build a constructive relationship with your school district, beginning with your child's current teacher and school principal, only using aggressive legal tactics if it is absolutely necessary. That said, as in most things, the squeaky wheel does get the grease.

INDIVIDUALIZED EDUCATION PROGRAMS

IDEA requires the development of an Individualized Education Program (IEP) for each of the thirteen classifications of disabilities. An IEP will be the cornerstone of your child's accommodations in a public school setting. The guidelines require that the plan include a specific set of evaluations, objectives, and accommodations. It even specifies the people who need to attend meetings to prepare the plan. If a school identifies your child as having a disability, the law requires written notice to the parents, as well as a reevaluation of your child every year. The IEP team, which includes you and your child (as well as others I mention below), must agree on a plan before it is implemented.

As soon as you believe that your child may be dyslexic (see the dyslexia assessment in Chapter Three), it's important to start a conversation with the staff at the school. Even though you might worry you'll be viewed as uptight or litigious, it's *essential* to document everything you're discussing in writing. While your initial conversation with your child's teacher or an administrator can be casual, following the principles outlined in Chapter Five, it is important to follow up with a letter documenting what was agreed on and to submit a formal request for evaluation and accommodations. Some tips:

- Be very cautious of administrators who say that they will "take care of things" and then take no action. The written record will allow you to go back and establish exactly what you requested and when.
- You should take detailed notes on every meeting that you attend, and if possible bring a witness with you, such as a family friend or an outside specialist in learning issues. This may seem extreme, but it will also communicate to the school that you are not someone to be trifled with and make it more likely that they will respect your "bodyguard" (aka the law).
- It's also a good idea to talk to other parents in your community and find out what their experiences dealing with the school district have been like. This will help inform your posture.

The path to getting an IEP for your child will look like this:

GET A REFERRAL FOR SERVICES ON FILE

Initially you want to speak with your child's classroom teacher and with the special education coordinator for your district. After your first meeting, follow-up with the sample "request for referral" letter below. Send this letter even if the meeting went very smoothly and you're greatly pleased with the outcome. If that's the case, add a cover note to this letter communicating how happy you are, including some warm and supportive comments. If the meeting went well, the basic tone of the cover letter should be, "I know the following letter is formal, but I want to do what is right for my child and make sure we are on the same page. I am so happy you and I are communicating well. I look forward to working with you in a collaborative manner." The form letter triggers some important legal rights that you want to preserve, and it is important that, while being cordial or even gracious, you get it on file.

Here is a sample of the "request for referral" letter you can use after you have met with your child's current teacher and administrators (you can download it from the Headstrong Nation website as well). It is adopted from a number of forms on the web and draws greatly from the ones offered by the Disability Rights Education and Defense Fund (DREDF), an excellent resource for parents looking for information on how to talk to their school:

Director of Special Education
[Local School District]
[Address]
[City, State 00000]

Re: [your child's name]

Dear Mr. [Ms.] [Name]:

Thank you for the time on [date of initial meeting] to discuss my child, [child's name]. I would like to formally refer [child's name] for assessment to determine if [s]he is eligible for special education services and support as allowed under the Child Find obligations of the Individuals with Disabilities Education Act (IDEA). [S]he is not progressing in school. [S]he is [age] years old and attends [child's school].

I also request that my son [daughter] be evaluated under Section 504 of the Rehabilitation Act of 1973 for the presence of any educational service need that may require any accommodation or program modification not available under special education or if my child is not found eligible for special education. I would like to have an Individualized Education Program meeting as soon as an evaluation concludes that [s]he is qualified for services.

I also request that the Section 504 coordinator for [name your school district, as opposed to your school] be present at the initial IEP meeting to discuss the results and recommendations of the Section 504 evaluation. However, I do not agree to substitute a 504 assessment for a special education assessment.

I also request that the [name of your school district] conduct the following evaluations of my son [daughter]: a psychological evaluation to determine his [her] learning potential, and his [her] expressive oral language, expressive written language, receptive oral language, receptive written language, intellectual functioning, cognitive processing, and educational achievement, respectively.

I would like to ensure that this test includes:

- *Developmental, medical, behavioral, academic, and family history*
- *A measure of general intellectual functioning*
- *Documentation on cognitive processing (language, memory, working memory, auditory processing, visual processing; visual motor integration, reasoning abilities, and executive function)*
- *Tests of specific oral language skills related to reading and writing success, including tests of phonological processing*
- *Tests to determine level of functioning in basic skill areas of reading, spelling, written language, and math*

My concern is based on testing and conversations I have had with [child's name]'s classroom teacher, [teacher name]. Further, I am concerned about his [her] abilities in the following areas: [In this section, include only the ones from the following list that are appropriate to your child. You may want to include state test results, samples of written work, report cards, and other data that support your reasons for concern. You may also have your own expert deliver reports that you can include in this communication. You may want to get the classroom teacher to give you concrete examples and work products in writing that support the need for further investigation of your child's problems.]

☐ *Expressive language disorder*
☐ *Attention difficulties*
☐ *Inattentiveness*
☐ *Planning and the organization of information*
☐ *Monitoring task-oriented activities and self-monitoring*
☐ *Interpersonal behaviors*
☐ *Ability to initiate, or begin a task without being prompted*
☐ *Social skills*
☐ *Working memory*

I look forward to receiving an assessment plan in a timely manner [in California, the law is in fifteen days, but this may vary from state to state]. I hope that these evaluations can be completed promptly. Thereafter, we can have an IEP meeting to discuss the results of these evaluations within sixty days and plan for [your child name]'s continued education. Please ensure that I get copies of the assessment reports at least five days before the IEP meeting.

Sincerely,
[Your name]
CC: [School superintendent's name]

If the district's special education coordinator does not communicate with you within roughly fifteen days or does not provide your child with an assessment within sixty days of your first contacting them, it's time to escalate the pressure. Time is important here. If the school is not going to work with you, it is better to find this out quickly; each week that goes by is another in which your child is being cut off from the mainstream education she deserves.

Your next step if you do not receive a satisfactory or timely response is to reach out to the principal of your school as well as to the superintendent for the district, requesting a meeting and sending them a copy of the letter that you sent to the special education coordinator, making clear when it was originally sent and expressing your frustration with the delay. Paperwork is a huge part of this process, so keep dated and detailed notes on all phone conversations and in-person meetings. After every meeting send a follow-up letter confirming the agreements that were made. If you still do not get a response or you are not satisfied with the response, send a letter to the head of the school board that presents your concerns, and include copies of the previous correspondence. If even this does not work, it is time to engage a lawyer, switch districts, or both. I'll explain those processes later in this chapter and in Chapter Eight.

If the district's special education coordinator does not get back to you after the initial fifteen-day period and you have the means, identify a local psychologist in private practice who can provide the necessary testing that will serve as a follow-on to the initial screening in this book (later in this chapter I give some tips on how to pick an expert). Share with this person the initial letter you sent, and use that to build a list of the appropriate tests for your child's needs. Keep in mind that I am skeptical of the usefulness of even the full battery of testing, as I explained earlier, but you will need this documentation to move things along for your child.

SEEK DOCUMENTATION

Hopefully your initial request for referral was acted upon and now your child will be evaluated. The school should provide an evaluation free of cost. You are entitled to receive a copy of the school's evaluation at least five days before the scheduled IEP meeting.

However, you may not agree with the school-appointed expert's evaluation. This disagreement could be over the identification of dyslexia (or lack of one), or over more subtle issues, such as if the plan emphasizes remediation with no support for accommodations, a common default. The school's expert might not recommend Orton-Gillingham training or could suggest outdated methodologies, such as phonics training.

You are allowed to have your child also evaluated by an independent expert, and to bring your own expert to the IEP meeting. Even if you trust the school, getting testing done by your own expert is a good idea if you have the funds. As my mother told me, "Getting our own testing was very important. The expense made me hesitate. But knowing what I know now, I would have eaten cereal for a month to save up that money."

The main thing my parents gleaned from the testing was a deeper understanding of my learning style. The testing helped my mom realize that, in her words, "I did not have to think there is something wrong with him—he is just an auditory learner."

If you do not like the school's testing options, your expert can provide a second opinion. Find someone who is reputable and can point to a number of instances where his or her reports have been used as a basis for an IEP with a public school in your area. The best-qualified individuals are likely to be a child psychologist or a learning specialist with at least a master's degree. You can contact the private schools in your area that specialize in dyslexia as a resource. Every major metropolitan area in the United States has at least one and sometimes two or three of these private schools. They will typically be able to point you to a local expert whom they trust.

The testing process can be quite stressful for children, and in seeking your own evaluation you are now asking your child to go through it twice! He's going to be asked to do a number of things that he is not good at, including working through reading and writing tasks, so make sure that you pick someone who shares your philosophy that your child deserves to be happy with who he is; your chosen expert should be respectful of your child's needs and be someone with whom you can build a long-term relationship. Warning signs that an expert you may be considering is not a good match include the expert's emphasis on "fixing" your child. The expert should be able to write in plain language and should make clear and definitive identifications that will fit cleanly into the category of specific learning disability (e.g., dyslexia, central auditory processing disorder, etc.). It is a good idea to see sample reports the expert has written to get a sense of whether you can understand her writing and if she speaks to the issues outlined in the form letter above.

IEP STUMBLING BLOCKS

If the school is not willing to identify your child as someone who has a disability, and therefore is unwilling to schedule an IEP meeting, you have a legal right to receive "prior written notice" that encompasses all of the following:

- A description of the actions proposed or refused by the school
- An explanation of why the school is taking this action
- A description of other options the school is considering
- An outline of the evaluation procedures, records, tests, and reports the school used to make this decision

- A description of the factors that were relevant to the school's decision
- A specific written legal statement that the school acknowledges you have protections under procedural safeguards

Furthermore, you have the right to this information in your native language; schools must pay for translation if English is not your first language.

I would hope that you will not have to go this route—most schools are responsive to parents who they see have their information straight—but if you do not receive this information, you should send a letter to the school superintendent requesting all of the above and citing the law involved in the "procedural safeguards outlined in 20 U.S.C. § 1415." At that point it would be a good idea for you to select an attorney and to prepare for mediation with the school.

THE IEP MEETING

Ideally an IEP meeting is a collaborative session where mutually interested parties come together to create a plan for your child. You can be prepared by bringing in a list of accommodations that you think would be helpful, based on the ones listed in Chapter Six. Even better would be to bring examples of these technologies. If you can show them an iPad reading text aloud or speech-to-text software being used by your child, this would be very persuasive.

Some administrators will often push back on the expense of the technology you suggest or demonstrate, so you should highlight that much of it is free: for example, if your school has Windows-based PCs, then they already have a speech engine they can turn on easily, and they can get free audiobooks from Bookshare or Learning Ally. That said, keep in mind that the cost is not your problem and you have a legal right to these tools. I touch on ways to discuss this below.

Here's a list of everyone who is entitled to attend the IEP meeting and common issues that come up in relation to these individuals:

Your child. Make sure to spend time talking with your child before the meeting about what will be covered and what your mutual goals are. It is extremely important to make sure that your child understands that she is not broken and that this meeting is an opportunity for her to get the tools that will help her learn. It is likely that your child will resist attending the meeting. However, I've seen outstanding results when children have an opportunity to be present and explain who they are and what they need. If your child can speak for even a few minutes about why she likes to learn and what her strengths and weaknesses are, it can completely change the tone of the meeting. It is not uncommon for these meetings to get tense and even hostile, and if you feel that it's going to be an unwelcoming environment for your child, or your child is unable to make a presentation, it may not be a good idea for her to speak. But I have also found that the presence of a child at the meeting tends to reduce the hostility. You may want to have a way for her to come but leave early gracefully (for example, "We would like you to come for ten minutes, and then your dad is going to take you for a walk"); you can always invite your child to stay if it is going well. As a backup, you might videotape your child talking about her needs, but the power of her being there in person should not be underestimated. A tailored PowerPoint presentation that you can create to help your child present her story is available at www.headstrongnation.org.

Parent(s). If yours is a family where both parents are engaged in the child's life, either as one household or as two, it's a great idea for both of you to attend. It might be a good idea for you to designate one of you as the note taker and the other as the speaker. This will allow you to focus on your respective tasks, both of which are very important. Your goal is to establish that you are a reasonable person who can be worked with and that you have an understanding of the legal frameworks available to you. You might indicate how happy you are that everyone attended and that you are excited to work together to secure a "free and appropriate" education for your child in the "least restrictive environment." Make clear that you are really hoping you can take a strength-based approach and find some "supplemental services"; these are the reasonable accommodations such as a talking computer or books on tape. These key phrases will signal that you know what you're doing and invoke the bodyguard of the law in a gentle manner.

General education teacher. If your child is in fifth grade or below, he is likely to have one main teacher—someone we call the general education teacher (as opposed to the special education teacher). Having this teacher be part of the meeting is essential to success. For an older student who switches classrooms, the faculty will usually assign the child's homeroom teacher. This person is likely to have a major say in your child's progress into the following grade, and hopefully your child will be spending a majority of his time in this teacher's classroom. Unfortunately, general education teachers often skip the IEP planning meeting because many believe that special education is not their primary task and that they can hand it off to the designated special education teacher. If you arrive at the meeting and find that the general education teacher is not there, ask to reschedule the meeting. Politely make it clear that you will not hold the meeting until the general education teacher can be available. Obviously it's best to confirm ahead of time that she will be there.

In addition, if there are specific teachers that you want to attend, it is important to invite them in advance. It could be that an art or science teacher has a good relationship with your student and you would like one of them to be there, or it could be that there is a problem teacher who you want to make sure is on board with the accommodation plan. Think through the dynamics and decide who is important to have in the room, and do not proceed if you do not have that person there.

Special education teacher. Most schools have dedicated special education teachers. Often these teachers have an overwhelming load, and therefore it's good to try to meet with this individual before the IEP meeting so that you can understand her general approach. Is she someone who believes in "remediation" for your child's dyslexia? Note that you do want to get access to OG tutoring and it is possible the school is using the term "remediation" to refer to these services. While you should not share their view that this will "fix" your child, make sure to unpack what the school is telling you lest you reject something useful over imprecise language. This is quite common, and you're going to want to make it clear that your goal is not to make your child "normal" but instead to make him a successful learner.

School district administrator. This could be a district-level special education coordinator, the school principal, or another member of the district staff. This person's primary role is to make sure that all of the procedural safeguards are being met. He or she may also have oversight over the school budget. It is likely that this person is more of a veto rather than an affirmative voice in the meeting. If the meeting does not go the way that you anticipated, this is likely the person you're going to need to follow up with.

Other experts (optional). You are also allowed to bring experts to the meeting. Your experts could be involved either in the identification of the disability (e.g., a psychologist) or in setting up a good school experience (e.g., an accommodations or technology expert). There is a group of professional advocates who work on behalf of parents seeking special education status for students and who can be quite helpful if you have the funds; having someone coach you through the process one-on-one is always useful. Make sure that this person meets the criteria outlined earlier; especially important is that he or she subscribes to the dyslexia-as-identity worldview. Again, contacting a local private school that specializes in dyslexia is a good starting place to find an advocate whom you can trust.

Witness/friend. It is a good idea to bring along a third party who can be a witness to this important meeting. This could be the expert you have hired or a professional advocate. If you cannot afford those, it's worthwhile to bring along a friend or relative you trust. You can explain to others at the meeting that this person is there to help you take notes so that you devote your attention to the discussion at the meeting. This should be someone you should feel comfortable drawing into very personal conversations about your children—and someone who would be willing to testify if you did get into a formal mediation dispute hearing or even a full-scale legal battle. Having this person attend is a signal to the school that they are not going to be able to say one thing in the meeting and then do another thing later. Again, the law-as-bodyguard metaphor applies.

Unless you have major warning signs that this meeting is going to be hostile (e.g., other parents have told you that the school rejects all claims for special education for dyslexia and you've received communications from the school district that are highly aggressive) it is not a great idea to bring a lawyer to the first meeting. If you have already experienced this level of hostility from the school, it can be advisable to consult with an attorney but not have him or her attend the first meeting. Having an initial meeting without a lawyer present might give the school administrators and teachers a chance to come around to your point of view and begin to collaborate with you. At the very least, the administrators and teachers will be less guarded without a lawyer present and may therefore reveal their biases—information that will be helpful to you if and when you do engage an attorney.

If you think you might have trouble taking notes, or you want a more complete record, you can ask to record the meeting. I have used an iPhone or a small tape recorder to avoid having to take detailed notes. This is entirely within your rights. I would suggest you opt for notes if you can, as the recording can cause the school officials to be more guarded, but it is important to have a clear record of the meeting. Be sure to discuss and confirm on tape that people understand the meeting is being recorded before doing so.

DRAFTING THE IEP

The outcome of the meeting should be the drafting of an IEP. Some school districts will come into the meeting with an IEP already written. As with your child's evaluation, you have the right to have received the plan five days in advance of the meeting, so if you have not had five days to review that document, it is perfectly acceptable to say that you would like to take it home and look it over it before proceeding. In that circumstance, the gathered school team may pressure you to sign the plan, but you do not have to do so and should not unless you're comfortable with it. There are even instances where school administrators will insist that you have to sign a document in order to prove that you attended. You can sign an attendance sheet instead, indicating that this signature "does not constitute approval of the IEP." Most IEP meetings don't come to this; I mention these extreme cases just so you'll be prepared.

An IEP should be a "living document" in that it can evolve and adapt as your child's needs change throughout his school years. The law requires that it be updated every year, but you should plan to review it with your child's special education and general education classroom teachers each semester in order to see that it's up to date.

The school will typically have a boilerplate IEP form. You can get a copy of this blank form ahead of the meeting. If they have begun filling out the form in advance, make sure that you have an opportunity to review it before discussing it with the school, to ensure that the description of your child includes both his strengths and his weaknesses and is an accurate statement of what your child's needs and goals are. Again, five days for review is the legal standard.

The IEP should include a list of appropriate accommodations for your child. Even in the best of situations, I find that schools rarely provide enough information about the accommodations that they intend to offer your child. Administrators will often give lip service or suggest that they will "look into that" in response to your specific suggestions for accommodations. Do not accept these answers. If it's not written on the IEP, it's not enforceable. Remember, it is your child's school's obligation to provide you with a free and appropriate education. Spending a significant amount of money on your student is their problem, not yours. When you consider the legal costs that they would take on fighting you over these accommodations, providing them without such a fight will seem pretty cheap. This motivation is not something you would want to mention in the first meeting, but keep it in mind.

The IEP should also include specific metrics to determine your child's progress. Do not accept mere opinion as the basis for evaluation. This could allow the special education teacher or the general education teacher to later come to the conclusion, based on no concrete data, that your child no longer needs the support or that an accommodation is not appropriate. You want to have measurable goals, including performance on standardized tests and evidence of the school using the accommodations in class and during standardized evaluations.

The IEP should also include a plan for standardized (sometimes called "high-stakes") testing. Dozens of states now use these tests as a way to grant diplomas or promote students to new grades. Be sure that high-stakes testing does not have what legal experts call "flagging." If students receive accommodations on a test, it is sometimes the case that they will get an asterisk next to their score indicating that they took the test under "nonstandard conditions." This mark flags the score as unequal to others. The College Board, the governing body that administers the SAT, agreed in a legal settlement in 2002 (it took effect in 2004) that they would no longer do this. The ACT soon followed of its own accord. There are still organizations that will flag a score, however, and if your school has this policy, you want to fight aggressively, up to and including legal action, to prevent it. Keep in mind that the accommodations were given to level the playing field, so the asterisk is merely a way for them to stigmatize your child. You should also be sure that there are no caps or quotas for the number of students who can receive accommodations on a high-stakes test, or at least that this is not used as a rationale to deny your child an accommodation. Some states limit the number of students who can receive accommodations. This macro concern is not your problem, and your child should be afforded accommodation based on her individual profile, not the school's concern about testing rules.

You'll also want to make sure that the high-stakes test is assessing your child's skills and not his disability. This is where accommodations come in. If a portion of a high-stakes exam requires writing an essay, presumably the point is to determine whether your child can make a valid thesis and support it; no one in this context should be interested in your child's handwriting. So getting an accommodation to complete that section of the exam using speech software (or at minimum a keyboard) would be a good way to avoid testing your child's disability rather than his knowledge.

COMMON ADMINISTRATION RESPONSES DURING IEP MEETINGS

Your school will negotiate with you over the terms of the IEP. In many cases they are negotiating based on a genuine interest in the long-term outcomes for your student. However, there can be ulterior motives, such as budget or biases about what is and is not a disability, that can influence the conversation. Here are a number of common arguments that schools will use to block or delay providing accommodations, as well as some good responses that you can use.

"Your child is so smart! She is performing wonderfully for a student who is dyslexic. She doesn't need this much help."

Getting good grades does not preclude a student getting services.

Your comeback: "Thank you for that compliment. I'm interested in seeing my daughter perform to the best of her ability. The Department of Education issued a 'dear colleague' letter in 2012, saying that good grades do not preclude a student from having a disability protected by the law and getting accommodations. How can we establish accommodations that will allow her to work to the level of her intellectual capabilities?"

"You're out of touch with your child's skills. You're just going to have to lower your expectations given his disability."

This is the inverse of the "your child is too smart" argument. You will want to push back equally hard on this one, underscoring that you have reasonable expectations for your child and you merely want to provide an environment where he can do his best.

Your comeback: "I don't believe we have an appropriate accommodation in place, so we don't really know what his level of performance could be. I'm committed to helping him do as well as he can."

"If we give your child accommodations, he will never learn to read like a normal student."

Reading like a mainstream person is not the goal. Learning via ear reading or finger reading is acceptable. What you want to secure is access to information and independence for your child.

Your comeback: "I think the goal here is learning and literacy in a broad context. If my child had a visual impairment, you wouldn't suggest to him that using Braille would mean he never would learn to read, would you? How can we work together to get appropriate accommodations in place?"

"Your child has a behavior problem, and these accommodations will just make him distract other students more."

It is not uncommon for students who are dyslexic to act out in class. Talking about your child's discipline problems in the context of accommodations is irrelevant.

Your comeback: "I know you have a lot on your plate, and I know that my son can get frustrated. But I believe if we put appropriate accommodations in place, he will be successful in school."

"Our budget is limited and there are already too many kids with disabilities requesting services. We're not going to be able to support the cost this semester."

The law is crystal clear that it is the school's obligation to provide a free and appropriate education. In most cases the accommodations that you're asking for are relatively inexpensive. Many students with disabilities get full-time aides in the classroom as well as occupational and physical therapy that costs thousands of dollars. You are not asking for that level of expense for dyslexia. Even if you were, what the school administrator may have to deal with in answering to his or her superiors is not your concern.

Your comeback: "I understand how much pressure you're under. It's also my understanding that we are entitled to this level of service under IDEA. This IEP meeting is not the time for us to discuss the cost of these accommodations. It's the time for us to establish which accommodations are best suited for my child."

Once the meeting is concluded, you should have the basis for an IEP plan. Request that they deliver a copy of it to you as soon as it is complete. If you have retained an expert, give that person an opportunity to review it before you sign the document. You can work with the school to make changes later on, of course, but it's better to have the right plan to start with.

The most important accommodations or supplemental services you should be looking for with a young child are (1) Orton-Gillingham intervention for two years in order to support the child's learning of standard eye reading and (2) access to audiobooks. These two components will help stop your child from falling behind and allow you more time to get other accommodations in place.

You may be faced with a difficult decision if the school offers you part of what you want but not everything. Fight them for at least four weeks to get what you think is necessary before compromising in any way. If you wait longer than this, you are risking your child falling further behind on the key material he should be learning. You may want to accept a core set of accommodations and then push for other ones through appeals, mediation, or legal action.

CHOOSING A LAWYER

There will be various junctures in this process that may necessitate your securing legal counsel. My own preference is to try all of the polite (and even the pushy) options before retaining a lawyer, but you must judge for yourself how comfortable you feel in the process of advocating on your child's behalf. If you're making no progress after three months of badgering the school, it's definitely time to consider bringing an attorney on board, factoring in your own finances and ability to cover the costs. If you have the economic means, get counsel earlier, but as I've mentioned before, I would suggest that you keep the lawyer in the background until you have tried every means of communication with your school.

Choosing a lawyer is much like choosing a doctor or a mechanic. You need to be able to trust this person to make judgment calls on issues that you don't fully understand, and you're going to want to have someone who has your child's interests at heart. Understand that if you do get into a formal legal dispute, in many cases the settlement will include an award to the prevailing party to cover attorney's fees, but these cases can take months or years to resolve, and you may have to pay out-of-pocket for the costs in the interim (or permanently if you do not win your case).

Much like selecting an educational expert, a good approach to finding an attorney is to contact a local private school that focuses on dyslexia and interview at least two or three attorneys the school recommends. As with the educational expert, you will want to make sure your attorney generally shares your philosophy when it comes to securing accommodations. Lawyers are supposed to represent your interests and should follow your lead on this, but it is good to be sure there are no squabbles over this issue within your own team.

Be certain that you and your attorney are also on the same page about timing. Ultimately your lawyer works for you, and he or she needs to serve you and your child's best interests. Just as surgeons like to cut, many lawyers like to litigate, and in some cases they might suggest they can do extra work that is unnecessary, secretly hoping to increase their billable hours (this unsavory practice is called "churning fees"). Make sure that you have a clear expectation about the amount of money you are willing to commit and what your short-term goals are. Your attorney may be able to secure you a fabulous win, but it could cost you $300,000 and three years. Alternatively, he or she may be able to get you 75 percent of what you want in three months for $10,000 in fees, or even 65 percent of what you want for $1,000 worth of letters and phone calls. You'll need to figure out which of these paths is best for you and your child, keeping in mind that the best win is a fast win, given the stress to you and the delay in services to your child that come with a protracted battle.

EDUCATIONAL SLEIGHTS OF HAND AND OTHER FAQS

Is it illegal for a school to retaliate against me or my child for raising concerns about my child's education or for requesting accommodations?

Yes, it is illegal. However, many districts will penalize your child in subtle and not-so-subtle ways in order to discourage you and other parents from asking for support. In extreme cases, a school's tactics can be quite nasty. I have seen districts demand that students attend remedial reading classes with children younger than them, in order to embarrass them. I have heard of schools that allowed a child to attend a special Orton-Gillingham reading program off-campus and then docked him for truancy for not making it back on time for gym class. In this way the school can establish a record that your student didn't show up for school when in fact the school intentionally scheduled activities that make it impossible for the child to receive the accommodation of an outside learning specialist. I have even heard of instances of schools labeling children with other identifications such as oppositional defiant disorder (ODD) to give them a legal basis to segregate the child, or, worse, instances in which schools try to pin made-up or exaggerated charges (graffiti, bullying, etc.) on the student to give the school a discipline-based reason to punish the child.

If you feel that you are being unfairly treated, retaining a lawyer who can communicate with the school is an excellent idea. Writing a letter to the Office of Civil Rights at the U.S. Department of Education outlining the specifics of what is happening is also an option, though likely to be less effective given the demands on that office's resources. Still, writing the letter to the Office of Civil Rights and sending a copy to the district superintendent, the school board chair, and your child's school principal can spur action. You want to make sure that you highlight the specific actions that you asked for (referral for an IEP, for example), the retaliation that happened (for example, "My son was held after school on suspicion of graffiti with no evidence"), and why you believe that the two were related. If you do not get a quick response, you will want to retain counsel and then review Chapter Eight so that you can begin to think about other educational opportunities for your child.

What do I do if my child is being bullied?

Many students in special education find themselves being bullied. This can range from quiet but painful teasing for being "a retard" to stuff as rough as people shoving them into lockers and even beating them up after school. Unfortunately, one of the consequences of the stigmatizing nature of disabilities is that it allows people to feel justified in taunting and excluding others. I mention practical approaches to bullying by other students in Chapter Eight, but in the legal context make sure to contact your child's school in writing as soon as you hear about this activity. Ask them to provide you with the school's written policy on bullying and how they plan to address the issue. If they do not respond to your letter in writing, send another letter outlining the conversations you have had with any school officials (teacher, staff, etc.) to the district superintendent. In the same letter, request that the school create a safe environment for your child, and request a written response to your letter. If the school does not resolve this issue, you may want to contact a legal advisor or even your local police department; this last step should be taken only if you think there is a real risk to your child and after you have pressed the issue with the authorities in the district in writing.

What if my child is a teenager or older?
For a child in his teenage years you will want to put that much more effort into providing accommodations and be sure to get documentation as soon as possible in order to enable him to have a track record of these accommodations before he begins applying to colleges or trying to make the transition to work. At an extreme, if your child has dropped out of school, you will need to begin by getting him one-on-one tutoring in Orton-Gillingham and accommodations that give him the confidence to return to school. Getting back into school is important, as the funds from the federal government for support are available only when he is enrolled and, in most states, twenty-one years old or younger.

If your child is having great difficulty in his first semester in college because of issues related to spelling or reading, it may be that in the jump from a high school environment many of the students who were performing below him are no longer there, thus revealing his dyslexia. If he is no longer in public school, you may need to seek alternative ways to get an identification such as talking with the disability services center at a college. Colleges have an obligation under the ADA and Section 504 to provide accommodations for enrolled students, as discussed earlier in this chapter. If your child is employed, he is covered by the Americans with Disabilities Act and has a right to reasonable accommodation in the workplace. You will want to coach him on how to have this conversation with an employer, substituting the director of human resources or his manager for school district officials or a teacher in the conversations outlined in Chapter Five.

When is it time to leave special ed and go mainstream?

Once they have a full set of accommodations in place and have mastered using them, many dyslexic students do not need to spend hours outside of a general education classroom during the day. It is likely that between second and fifth grade (or within the first three years after she is identified, regardless of age), your child will spend time with a reading specialist, who will help her acquire eye-reading skills to the best of her ability. Thereafter, if she is receiving appropriate accommodations, such as books on tape and a talking computer, you may be able to have your child reintegrate into the mainstream school population. This is preferred, as it reduces stigma and will keep her on grade level with peers. You should make this decision with your child. It's very important to allow her to have a say in how this will go and to encourage her to advocate for herself at school.

My mother exhibited this practice with both of her children even when we were young. My brother, who is three years younger than me, was having difficulty in kindergarten, and the school proposed that instead of going into first grade, he enter into what they called "pre-first." Given that I was dyslexic and that my brother was left-handed (cross laterality that can be linked with dyslexia), my mother thought it might be a good idea. After a month in the pre-first class, however, my brother was exceeding all of his classmates. When the school approached my mother and asked if she wanted to move him to first grade, she told them that it sounded like a good idea but she wanted to talk to her son first. The teacher who was meeting with my mom just about fell over: "Why would you want to talk to a six-year-old about this?" My mother replied that while my brother was not going to make the decision, he was going to be consulted. He and she discussed it and he thought it was a good idea, so they made the change.

If you do come to the conclusion that mainstreaming is appropriate, be sure to maintain the IEP in relation to the accommodations for exam taking. A critical factor in whether the administrators of the SAT and other standardized tests will grant accommodations, as well as the prospective use of accommodations in a college environment, is the record you have of your child's use of these accommodations. If your child had an IEP and accommodations through eighth grade and then completely left special education and stopped using accommodations, it could impact the child's chances to get accommodations on exams later on. Good record keeping is important! Remember, too, that even if your child is "declassified" for special education purposes, she is still protected by disability civil rights laws (Section 504 and the ADA) and entitled to accommodations under those laws as well.

If you think it's a good idea to move your child back into the mainstream environment, you will want to maintain the accommodations that were agreed for the IEP (e.g., use of a laptop in class or audiobooks for ear reading). You will need to make sure as well that your child has the advocacy skills to use those tools. Discuss with your child that while he might stop attending special education classes, he should keep using the accommodations listed in the IEP. In this case, he would be in mainstream English class but get books on tape and a separate room for exams if he needs speech-to-text software. Your child is very likely to want to try to dump all affiliation with special education as soon as possible. This is a major mistake, and you should work with the school to ensure that he has access to the tools he needs—and that he uses them. This transition will be dependent largely on his attitudes (see the mapping in Chapter Three, especially integration of SLDs and use of social supports).

Is my private school obligated to provide special education services?
As with many things, the legal answer is "that depends." Technically, if a private school receives federal funds in any form, it is subject to Section 504 of the Rehabilitation Act. This could be funding received in subtle ways, such as through anti-drug programs or federal loans. If the school is a non-religious institution, they are also subject to the Americans with Disabilities Act.

Private schools that do not receive any federal funds do not have an obligation to spend money on an IEP. They do still have to provide accommodations, such as books on tape or extra time, but they do not have to have a special education program and staffing for it per se. And even if they are taking federal funds, they still have a lower obligation than a public school. Overall, they are not required to provide "a free and appropriate education"—private schools are never free for all. In general, if Section 504 is triggered, the school is only required to make "minor adjustments" to the curriculum or their policies in order to support a student with a disability. Note that they do still have to provide accommodations. It is reasonable to expect them to provide your child with access to audiobooks from Bookshare or Learning Ally, for example, but they will not go significantly out of their way. In a private school setting, the legal context is less clearly in your favor than in a public school context. If you have the means to have your child attend private school, you may want to consider shifting her to another one if the school is not being supportive.

Generally, I find private schools can be much more judgmental about dyslexia. Those that do not focus on dyslexia as their primary activity may turn their nose up and be quietly dismissive of anyone requesting that support. In purely economic terms, it's not a good business model for them to accept students who require more time and attention. Sadly, a number of my friends who run private schools focusing on dyslexia note that when the economy turns bad every private school claims that it has a great program for dyslexics as a way to fill empty chairs. Your dyslexic child may find himself shunned when the economy picks back up and the school has its pick of non-dyslexic, tuition-paying students.

There is a group of outstanding private schools that specialize in specific learning disabilities. Check out Appendix B for a list of schools that I think are excellent.

REMEMBER THE BODYGUARD

My sincere hope is that none of the legal action I've covered in this chapter is in your future. Familiarize yourself with the basic frameworks and the key pieces of legislation, and then make sure to document all actions and communicate clearly with your school. Push hard for accommodations, and above all make sure that your child takes part in advocating for his needs, so that very soon he'll develop the skills and have the self-confidence to do so for himself.

CHAPTER EIGHT

Is It Time to Exit?

We've reviewed finding your child's strengths, getting your child the tools she needs, and asserting her right to a free and appropriate education. A harsh truth that I've learned, however, is that even when you do all of these well, things at your school might still not be right. One of the challenges of being dyslexic is that you must learn to accommodate the world around you. This can lead to losing track of your own needs and putting up with unsustainably high levels of frustration or pain that result from not having access to the same information everyone else does.

The worst lies related to dyslexia are the ones that we dyslexics tell ourselves. Our internal monologue often sounds like this: "If I just try harder, I can catch up with everybody else." Or "This is easy for everybody else, so there must be a way that I can figure out how to do it like them." At a number of points in my life I've had to realize that no amount of trying to blend in would make a specific situation workable. In short, I've had to realize that for me, it was instead time to move on. In this chapter, I'll discuss how to monitor your child's happiness and stress levels, how to teach your child to report on her own needs, and how to recognize when it may be time to look for an alternative way to do things. I'll also walk you through how to scout out new options and make an effective transition to a new educational context.

One of the most important things I try to do every day is to listen to myself and pay attention to my needs. This is rooted not in selfishness but in survival. Trying to fit in, like a square peg in a round hole, is a mistake that I have made more than once in my life. The most severe example occurred when I was in law school. In my first semester there, I ruptured a disk in my spine. There were a number of factors that led to this. First, I had arrived in an environment that had a higher standard for text-based perfection than I had ever seen. Second, I didn't know how to use my tools well or to ask for enough help to be able to handle the workload. Finally, and most important, I didn't know how to pay attention to the early warning signs my body was sending that the environment might not be well suited for me. This allowed me to develop a warped sense of what levels of strain and pain were acceptable in day-to-day life. I was willing to push through the warning signs and work around any pain until it was way too late.

I had a minor injury halfway through the first semester that I now realize was caused by trying to function while enduring high levels of stress, such as going without sleep or forgoing exercise because I had to spend so much time in the library in order to catch up with my classmates. By the end of the semester I landed in the hospital and had to have surgery on my spine. All this could have been avoided if I had learned how to tune in to my needs and stop trying to accommodate the system around me.

This issue is extremely common and problematic for dyslexics. I've seen young children get to the point where they are cutting themselves or acting out in ways that are quite dangerous to them or their friends. As I mentioned earlier, a majority of the adult dyslexics I know report having reached some very dark and low points during their school years. At an extreme this can get to the point where children will have a plan for suicide, so this is not an issue to take lightly. A majority of the adults I know who are major figures in the dyslexia movement had specific plans to take their own lives, planned down to the level of what chemical or ammunition to use. In my experience this doesn't happen until the tween/teenage years, but it's extremely important to get ahead of it for young children and create channels so that they can communicate and not feel hopeless. You want to be able to have an open dialogue with your child that allows him to report how he's doing in school. By using the techniques outlined below to monitor your child's behavior and maintain a dialogue with him, you will be able to keep track of his stress and anxiety, and increase the likelihood that you both will have good outcomes.

THE RISKS OF AN ONGOING NEGATIVE ENVIRONMENT

Beginning in the 1930s, Kenneth Clark and Mamie Clark, a husband-and-wife team of psychologists, created an experiment called the Clark Doll Test. In this experiment children were shown two dolls. The dolls were identical in terms of shape and clothing, but one had brown skin and brown hair and the other had fair skin and blond hair. When asked which dolls were the "good" dolls, which were the dolls that the children "liked" more, and which were the dolls that they would prefer to be like, both black children and white children picked the white doll. These data were used in arguments before the U.S. Supreme Court as part of the *Brown v. Board of Education* case. In their 9–0 decision, the justices cited the data as evidence that segregated systems were inherently damaging to children's self-concept.

The same negative pattern can be instilled in children with specific learning disabilities if they are learning within a school system that segregates them and treats them as second-class citizens. We can all agree that it would be completely unacceptable for a teacher to make an attribution about a child's work ethic or intelligence based on race. Yet I've frequently run into these assumptions when it comes to dyslexia. When someone in a school system says that your child is "lazy" or "less intelligent," he or she is making a deeply damaging attack—on you as well as on your child. Even if these words are not used, being asked to ride the "short bus," leave class when reading time happens, or go to the "special class" for half the day tells everyone that your child is less good than the other kids. The focus of your efforts and of this book is to get your child the services he needs without the stigma.

For this reason, your child's academic achievement is not the primary criterion you should be using to determine whether your child's current school is a good fit for him. Instead, his psychological experience should be the single most important element in assessing the fit. With the right tools and accommodations, your child may be able to catch up on reading, but it will take years of therapy to unwind "I hate myself" or "I'm a bad person." The heads of some of the best private schools for specific learning disabilities have told me that they not infrequently have to spend the first year with a new student just undoing the psychological damage that was inflicted before the student changed environments. This chapter shares the signs of this problem and ways to respond.

BULLYING

Students with dyslexia are particularly susceptible to bullying. While a school may have its feelers out to identify bullying based on gender, race, or sexual orientation (and because of high-profile and tragic cases, schools are increasingly taking notice of bullying and then taking action), teachers can often miss the more subtle jabs against students with disabilities. Schools have to walk a fine line, getting students additional help without fully segregating students with dyslexia in special education classes. Helping a student, if the help is not delivered with sensitivity and an emphasis on the diversity of learning styles, can become a form of institutional bullying.

The website StopBullying.gov defines bullying as unwanted, aggressive behavior among school-age children that involves a real or perceived power imbalance. The behavior is repeated, or has the potential to be repeated, over time. In the context of dyslexia, the perceived power imbalance has to do with who is "normal" and who is "special," that is, the outlier. Schools that are not providing appropriate accommodations lock students with dyslexia out of the path of academic achievement, and peers pick up on this. For this reason, securing accommodations with an IEP that allows your child to stay on top of her work is not just important but a critical factor in long-term happiness.

As a child, I regularly tripped over the names of characters we were discussing in English class. This evoked snickers from my classmates and made me self-conscious about participating. Worse, I often missed key plot details or fell behind in the reading. Once when we were reading *To Kill a Mockingbird,* I stuck my hand up and talked about what Tom Robinson was doing—only to discover that the character had been killed in the next chapter, which I had not yet read even though it had been assigned. My classmates snickered, and the teacher admonished me for not paying attention. Note that this is a minor instance, but when this laughing happens every other time a student makes a comment, it can leave a serious mark. This is the sort of situation that can lead to bullying after class. If I'd had accommodations, I wouldn't have made this mistake, and I would not have had to feel embarrassed when my classmates made fun of me. When you talk to adults who are dyslexic, many have a little story like this that is still raw even twenty or thirty years later. You will not be able to prevent every stigmatizing experience, but you can give your child a voice to be able to discuss these situations and a path to change contexts if they get unmanageable.

Once your child's accommodations are in place, the next step is to work with the school to establish a context in which the accommodations can be used in a way that does not embarrass her. The most fundamental element of this is for your child to get comfortable using tools and talking about them in a positive context. Teaching your child the techniques laid out in Chapter Five on how to tell her story takes on extra importance here. If someone is going to mock your child for not being able to read, having her master how to talk about her disability or the tools she uses is both face-saving and affirming.

If bullying and harassment become a pattern in your child's school, happening week after week without attempts at intervention, the school may be in violation of a number of civil rights laws. The administrators can be investigated and penalized for creating a hostile environment that constitutes "disability harassment." It is a serious enough issue that in 2000 the Department of Education issued a letter to schools on the topic. One scenario highlighted in the letter directly addressed what could constitute disability harassment in the context of dyslexia: "Several students continually remark out loud to other students during class that a student with dyslexia is 'retarded' or 'deaf and dumb' and does not belong in the class."

This is another instance in which the law can be your bodyguard. Bringing one of these claims and seeing it through the courts is an expensive and time-consuming process, but merely raising the possibility that the school might be in violation of Section 504 or Title II of the Americans with Disabilities Act is an effective way of spurring action. Make sure to follow the guidelines I laid out earlier regarding using written communication and following up on your meetings with notes and timelines to the relevant official.

Above all, make sure that your child is in a safe environment when he goes to school. StopBullying.gov has a number of good guidelines on how to talk about bullying with school officials and how to respond on the spot if you see it happening.

COURSE CORRECTIONS

Not every problematic learning situation is so extreme that your child needs to change schools. There are many instances where the school is well-intentioned about meeting your child's needs, but the accommodations are not well implemented.

A typical default when a child is having difficulty in school is to blame the child instead of looking at teaching methods. A teacher or administrator might ask the child to work harder, or question whether she is up to intellectual standards. In the case of a dyslexic child, your first recourse should start with an investigation of the classroom and the methods being used to evaluate kids before you focus on your own child's capabilities and attitudes.

In this situation you will have to go into the school and retool the system. In general you should be monitoring your child's progress and constantly updating the IEP you have in place. The law requires that the plan be reviewed and updated every year, but I recommend checking it at least once a semester and adjusting as you go. This is because children's workloads change rapidly in elementary school. For example, your child might start coming home with worksheets that were not considered when the IEP was put in place. You'll need to find out if these worksheets are available in electronic form so that a computer can read them out loud, or if they can be emailed home to use with text-to-speech software.

Assuming you've got accommodations in place that are leveling the playing field for your child, and her attitudes are well aligned, she should be able to keep up with the other kids and be able to learn independently. Your child has a right to receive an average grade for completing an average amount of work, and a great grade for doing outstanding work. Dyslexia should not be a factor in the quality of your child's education, nor in her grades if she is well accommodated and has a positive attitude.

Even when you are happy with the accommodations you've worked out on paper, it's still important to visit the school and see the accommodations in use by your child. On-site investigation will help you discover the conditions on the ground. You want to be sure to be polite about visiting, reaching out to the school and trying to figure out a convenient time to come by and observe. Make sure that your child is the one to demonstrate all of her tools, not some technology expert within the school. I would also recommend you come in during the regular school day, not merely as part of any regularly scheduled parent-teacher conferences.

There are two factors that can influence the effectiveness of accommodations for a student even if the school has agreed to everything you asked. The first factor is how effectively these accommodations have been implemented. Perhaps the school bought Dragon NaturallySpeaking software and a good headset, but there is a virus on the designated computer and it crashes every three minutes, making its use so annoying that your child effectively does not have an accommodation. Or perhaps the school subscribes to Bookshare or Learning Ally but is not allowing your child to listen through headphones in class for fear that other students will think your child is getting special treatment. Make sure you follow the pipeline of any accommodation all the way from its purchase to its implementation, to ensure that your child is independently using it in the least restrictive environment.

The second factor, as highlighted in Chapters Three and Five, is your child's attitude toward these accommodations. When you visit the classroom, it might become clear that your son won't use the accommodation because he is embarrassed to be seen as different. In this case, you'll need to work with your child's teachers to figure out if there is a way they could reduce his anxiety so that he would be more open to using the accommodation. The answer might be that they allow him to use the software in a separate room. The best scenario would be that they set up a day on which your child will demonstrate the technology for other students so that, rather than teasing him for being different, his peers might be impressed with it and would understand why he leaves the room.

Remember that seeing the accommodations work when you visit is not the end of the story. It's extremely important to train your child to be her own best advocate, helping her learn to raise concerns as they come up. The nature of accommodations is that they are a variation for the system, and therefore the system will keep trying to reject them unless someone diligently monitors their use. You need to get your child comfortable saying to the teacher, "This isn't working for me" when he is frustrated with an accommodation. Your child may not be able to tell you exactly why specific accommodations aren't working; he might start off saying, "I'm bored with this" or "This is stupid," both of which may be his best version of "I'm having difficulty in this environment and I'm not performing up to my capacity."

You need to listen for your child's versions of such comments and then draw him out into a fuller explanation. Use role-play to develop your child's capacity to talk about his own needs. You can adapt the lessons about telling your story from Chapter Five, and have your child learn to introduce the topic of dyslexia. This doesn't have to be part of any formal IEP meeting. Rather, it can be an ongoing conversation about how the classroom is functioning, in the same way that a student might need to learn to speak up when he has to go to the bathroom, or when he needs help getting into a snowsuit to go outside. You can practice going through what he wants to communicate. If he is not able to talk to his teacher about it directly, which is quite common, it makes sense to join him for the initial meetings. In the first few instances this will be primarily you communicating information, with your child validating it. But as your child gets older, the goal is that he should be able to take over the meeting and speak up for himself.

HOW TO RECOGNIZE A TOXIC SCHOOL ENVIRONMENT

I have heard countless parents apologize for a poorly designed school system. These apologies might take the form of feeling uncomfortable asking teachers to provide audiobooks along with standard books. Or it might show up as parents acquiescing when they are told that there just aren't enough resources to support their child. The types of problems that create a toxic environment for your child are not your fault, and they are not your child's fault. As I outlined in

Chapter Seven, in a public school your child has a right to a free and appropriate education. If the school is not providing this, or will never be willing to, you need to get past the idea that the frustration you're feeling is the cost of having a dyslexic child.

Here are some warning signs that your school is not a good place for your dyslexic child:

- *The administration is inflexible about providing and assessing accommodations.*

    Does your child's general classroom teacher complain about the use of accommodations in her classroom? Is the school slow to provide the materials that your daughter requested? For whatever reason, does it turn out that an accommodation that is agreed to doesn't show up on the day of an important test? If any of these scenarios happens once or twice, and you speak up and it is corrected, then this is part of the school's adoption curve. On the other hand, if you've gotten to the third and fourth time and there doesn't appear to be a course correction, you may have a significant issue.

- *The administration is rigid about other elements of the learning environment.*

    Outside the context of accommodations, schools may emphasize outdated methods of teaching or become rigid about scheduling and other issues that affect your child's education. In one school district in San Francisco, the administration recently announced that college counseling services would not be provided to students in special education. Parents protested and the administration reversed course, but you can expect that other schools will try this sort of cost-saving or staff-saving tactic.

- *The school is bullying your child or you.*

    Some schools create a culture in which people are encouraged to exclude those who don't fit in. This can happen to parents as well as to children. Worse, some administrators and teachers still subscribe to the fear model of education, in which they threaten students with consequences for not performing well rather than provide them with the tools they need to succeed. If your child is at a school where he is asked to get up in front of the class if he gets a bad grade or is prevented from joining his peers for a fun activity because he couldn't do work that was affected by his disability (e.g., "No recess if you don't finish your spelling words"), you've got a problem.

- *The school limits activities based on grades, despite not giving accommodations.*

    This could mean that they will not allow a child to play on a sports team until he gets his grades up to a C while not providing the tools he needs to keep up. This punitive approach is a terrible one, as often the out-of-class activities are the only ones holding your child's life together. Be sure to defend the elements of the school day that keep your child engaged with peers and work with the school to create a plan that does this.

- *You don't have close friends (other parents) in the school community, or you feel that you are unable to be open about your child's disability and not feel judged.*

    This is a flag that you may be in an unsustainable situation. Your job is not to try to just please people. Rather, you need to check in about your own needs and realize that you have the ability to alter or leave your environment.

- *The school segregates your child physically or programmatically.*

    Institutions often find it easier to move students who are outliers away from mainstream students. A small amount of separation may be necessary. For example, if a student needs to go to a learning specialist for one hour a day in order to get some one-on-one attention, this makes sense. However, I have seen schools take it to an extreme even while leaving the student in the classroom. My dyslexic and ADHD friend Marcus Soutra, chief operating officer of Eye to Eye, tells the story about a teacher who decided to literally put a box around him. She found that Marcus was disturbing other children by acting out in the classroom, so she decided to place an empty refrigerator box over his desk and cut a hole in the top so that she could drop in test materials to keep him isolated from the other children for parts of the day. The most telling point about this story is that initially Marcus accepted this as a standard practice. Children tend to try to fit in, and he was trusting enough that he didn't complain. Only when he mentioned it in passing to his parents did they find out (and they promptly dealt with the school). I hope your child will never experience something this stark, but if you find that your child is not being allowed to participate with other students in regular classroom activities, you've got a problem.

WATCH YOUR CHILD'S EMOTIONAL LIFE CAREFULLY

Your child's behavior is a very good indicator of whether or not she is thriving at school. Every child is allowed a bad day now and again. However, bad days should not be the norm. One of the challenges for a parent, particularly if it's your first child and the child is dyslexic, is knowing what a reasonable baseline of happiness looks like. It's a good idea to talk to other parents in your community whom you trust to find out how their children experience school. On the one hand, you may find that your child's anxiety and frustration levels are far above those of his peers. This could be evident in her destroying things when she gets home or yelling at her siblings over minor issues regularly. On the other hand, it could be that there are particular teachers whom all students find frustrating. In one school, I spoke with four different parents who all reported anxiety about a particular middle school teacher known for giving massive amounts of homework. Each of the parents in isolation didn't realize that the other parents shared the same concern. By working together you may be able to figure out patterns in the school that are not good for dyslexic students generally, or even for all students.

If you worry that the problems your child is having are outside the experience of her peers, consider these three questions from the Revised Child Anxiety and Depression Scale (RCADS), a widely used measure of child anxiety. Ask your child how often she feels the following:

1. "I feel scared when I have to take a test."
   Never   Sometimes   Often   Always

2. "I worry that I will do badly at my school work."
   Never   Sometimes   Often   Always

3. "I have trouble going to school in the mornings because I feel nervous."
   Never   Sometimes   Often   Always

The full version of this instrument has forty-seven questions and touches on many more elements of life, so these three questions are by no means a definitive test. However, if your child replies with "often" or "always" to all three of these, that's a sign that your child is dealing with more stress in her daily school life than is appropriate.

Keep in mind that your child may not be willing to report to you his true stress levels. Look for examples in his behavior: Is he extremely sensitive to criticism, particularly around schoolwork? Do you see frequent fearfulness or sadness? Is there a major change in sleeping or eating patterns when school starts?

In general, if your child complains about school every day, this is a good indicator that something's not right. You can start by trying to unpack some of these frustrations and find out what the root causes are. While your child may initially say only, "I just don't like school," you might narrow the focus to a specific class or activity. If you find that she "hates school" because her teacher asked her to get up in front of the classroom and read from a book, this would be a great issue on which to approach the school and request an accommodation.

Other indicators that your child may be poorly served at school include:

- You see behavior problems that get your child out of certain situations (e.g., they always happen in English class or on test days). Children are very strategic. If, for example, getting into trouble gets them sent to the principal's office, they'll look for ways to get in trouble in advance of having to do an eye-reading assignment.
- Your child has few close friends at school.
- Your child is more than two grade levels behind in reading and is not catching up.

None of these indicators alone is the whole story, but if you see a cluster of them, it's likely that your child is not being well served. More important, there should be some elements in the school day that give your child joy. This might be art class, science class, or even English class. Your goal should not be merely to avoid depression but to find an environment where your child is going to experience learning as a delight.

SOCIALIZING VERSUS LEARNING

Even if your child is being damaged by the school she is in, she may want to stay to be with her friends. If the school is really failing and your child wants to stay, the first step is to talk it out with your child. In my experience, children have a great ability to rationally approach problems if you talk it through with them sufficiently. Consider a scenario where your child might say, "But my best friend in the whole world is in that class. If I leave, I'm not going to have her anymore." You can say, "That's true, but you do a great job making friends, right? Do you want to be able to have a good time at school? You enjoy learning about space and spaceships, yes? If we get you to a school that supports you, you will be able to learn more about them. Maybe we could work out a play date with Emma every Saturday."

In most cases, your child will get it. Children want to do well, to be loved, to be supported. If you frame the conversation in a way that emphasizes that your child is valuable and that this is why it's important to make a change, you are likely to see progress. You are competing with a conclusion on your child's part: "I'm stupid. I'm not working hard enough. I'll never succeed. I'm just going to be a bad kid and hang out with my friends." A superb antidote to this internalized negative message is to highlight the strengths you found for your child based on the analysis in Chapter Three and show him how the new environment will allow him to leverage these.

EXPLORING OTHER OPTIONS

If after three months of engaging your school on a particular issue you see no changes, it's important to begin exploring other options. If, for example, you have spent three months trying to get a referral for an evaluation, you definitely have a problem, given that the law requires the school to make such a referral within sixty days. On the other hand, if the school made the referral quickly, tested your child, and established an IEP, but then spent three months failing to implement any of the accommodations, you also have an issue.

I encourage you to begin exploring alternatives before you make a decision to take your child out of the existing system. It can be a healthy reality check to see what a better-functioning system looks like, and quite possibly you can identify different methods that might be incorporated in your child's current environment.

Time is one of the most precious assets we have. Most of the stuff we accumulate in life can be replaced, but once you live a moment, it's gone forever. For a young person, this is magnified. Three months isn't an arbitrary amount of time—it's giving the school enough time to act, while also making sure that your child doesn't linger in limbo for too long. A child who spends too much time behind his peers is likely to feel the effects for many years to come. This is especially true if he is in a psychologically damaging environment of the sort described above.

It is extremely important that you visit any environment you anticipate your child shifting over to and kick the proverbial tires. Talk with the staff responsible for administering IEPs and special education. Be sure to check out where the physical location is for special education classrooms and administrators. Are they in the basement in a windowless room off the library, or perhaps in a trailer at the back of the school? Or are they centrally located with easy access to the rest of the school? The relative power and influence of the special education staff within the new school will correlate highly to how well positioned they are in the physical school building.

Ask to see what the new school offers in the way of technology to support students with disabilities. Look for the use of technology in the classrooms. A school may have a shiny and new computer lab, but it is segregated from the rest of the school. This is a warning sign, because if technology is centralized and separated from daily activities, it's unlikely to be integrated into the classroom. The lessons in Chapter Five are useful in terms of approaching the issue of dyslexia in this new environment and in determining whether it has the right set of attitudes and tools.

Next, contact parents of kids with dyslexia in the school and talk with them about their experience. Use the techniques outlined in Chapter Five, such as asking the school to make the introduction or send out an email from you. It's also important to talk to students, in particular those who are receiving similar services, if you can. Again, you can ask the school if it would be possible for your child to meet some peers, and if they're unwilling to make that type of introduction, then you may be able to identify the families through informal conversations in your community or the other techniques in Chapter Five.

SMALL CHANGES CAN MAKE A BIG DIFFERENCE

Start by exploring changes within the school district you are already in. Can your child switch classrooms? If your child's teacher has been teaching for thirty-five years, she might believe that there is only one path to learning. But down the hall is Mr. Smith, a newer teacher who is open to new methods. Here you can use some of the techniques in Chapter Five to approach administrators in the middle ranks of the organization, or seek information from a trusted teacher whom your student liked in a previous year to look for a way to get your child into Mr. Smith's class.

In some school districts you can choose which school your child attends. Even if they say you can't, you often can. If you are perceived as "too demanding," your child's current school won't want you around and will miraculously find a way to pass you off to another school across town. You can use this reality to your advantage and proactively identify the school you'd like to be passed along to.

Public charter schools that pay attention to specific learning disabilities could be another great option. These charter schools may not scream "specific-learning-disability friendly" above the front door, but they often take an alternative approach, such as emphasizing the arts or offering "hands-on learning."

Another gradual step you might consider if transferring out of your current school is not an option is to get an Orton-Gillingham-certified one-on-one tutor for your child. A few hours a week with the right instruction can help your child to maximize his native reading skill. Per the discussion in Chapter Six, you're not looking for a cure, and this should be a complement to assistive technologies.

WHEN SLD SCHOOLS ARE AN OPTION

Most major metropolitan areas have at least one if not several independent schools dedicated to learning disabilities. While many of them are superb, almost all have extremely high tuition rates. At the bottom end of the range you can expect to pay $25,000 a year. There are some schools that can cost as much as $65,000 a year when you factor in boarding and other fees. In some cases these schools have scholarships available, but this financial aid is incredibly hard to secure and should not be counted on. Refer back to Chapter Seven to explore the possibility that your school district or state may be willing to pay for the cost of one of these private schools. Typically this involves an intense legal battle, but it can be worth it if you're facing tens or even hundreds of thousands of dollars of educational expense. If you do pursue this option, make sure that you take intermediate steps to effect the changes that you can along the way, including potentially changing teachers or getting assistive technology at home.

When done right, these schools are a safe haven and—in part based on their skill in adapting to highly variable students—are considered some of the best learning environments in the country, period. When you're selecting a private school, it's extremely important to visit the school and check out the physical space. Be sure to bring your child along. In a number of instances I have heard from parents that the moment their child stepped into the lobby of a dyslexia-specific school, the child immediately knew the school was a good fit for him or her. A boy I know turned to his father after seeing the art the other kids had made in the lobby and said, "The kids here are like me, Dad. I want to come here."

The physical layout of the building can also tell you a lot about the school's priorities. The Lawrence School near Cincinnati, Ohio, was built from the ground up to be a school for kids with SLD. The architect put the theater, the metal and wood shops, and the art area in the center of the school and built the classrooms around this core. Everyone who walks into the building knows that those activities are valued and are literally central to the curriculum.

Pay particular attention to the school's attitudes toward universal design. Are they supportive of multiple modalities for learning in the classroom? Do they equip students with iPads? Do they use Learning Ally or Bookshare? Make sure that you witness use of these technologies in the classroom. They might, for example, have fancy new Smart Boards in each classroom that allow a teacher to use websites or create a common learning space for digital exchange, but never actually use these features as part of their day-to-day teaching.

Before you select a school, make sure that you get to meet with the person who runs it. Private schools gain a lot of their culture from the leadership at the top. I am a fan of schools that have a person who is dyslexic and open about it running the school. It can be extremely helpful for faculty to know that their boss is someone who is "in the club." Dyslexic school heads at dyslexia-focused schools tend to have a drive that allows the school to become a truly exceptional institution.

There are, of course, a number of outstanding independent or charter schools where the school head is not dyslexic. You should, however, be able to find some members of faculty who are dyslexic and open about it. This is a good question to ask when considering schools. You want to try to meet with those faculty and see what their attitude is. I would not encourage you to try to dig into anyone's background and figure out if he or she is dyslexic. If dyslexic teachers are easily identifiable through conversation (or even their bio on the school website), they'll be proud of who they are and therefore a great role model for your child.

It's important to remember that standard private schools—that is, those not specializing in specific learning disabilities—can be a far worse environment for your child compared to public schools. They have greater legal flexibility in terms of their choice to provide accommodations or not. Given this legal flexibility, an elitist attitude can lead to even more judgmental and exclusionary practices when it comes to students who are dyslexic. In a school that is allowed to select students, if you start rocking the boat, it's likely that the school will encourage you to find another place to educate your child.

One might assume that religious schools or parochial schools would be less flexible when it comes to admitting children with dyslexia, but this is not uniformly the case. For example, the archdiocese that runs all of the Catholic schools in the San Francisco Bay Area has made a strong commitment to include students who are dyslexic. As of this writing they are the single largest bloc of schools that attends Education Revolution, the fabulous conference I mentioned in Chapter Two.

Some parents have asked me if moving to a private school would be better simply because their student would be guaranteed a smaller class size. Overall, smaller class sizes can be an indicator that a school is more attentive to individual needs. However, it still comes back to the school's attitude toward dyslexia and flexibility in methods overall.

HOME SCHOOLING

Some parents consider home schooling as an option if they're not satisfied with the support that they're getting in a public school and/or can't afford a private school. I would, however, view this as a last resort. There are many reasons that people will choose to home-school and I certainly don't challenge the decision at a fundamental level. If, however, you're doing it primarily because you want to avoid the label of special education for your child, or because the school is not willing to provide you with accommodations, you should fight the battle with the school first before taking on your child's education yourself. It's better to see if you can create change so that your child can get the resources that are associated with professional special education.

If your child is in a genuinely hostile environment, home schooling can be a good backup option for the balance of the school year. Meanwhile, I encourage you to try to identify Orton-Gillingham tutors or online training (see Chapter Six) to support yourself in the first year or two of your child's integration as well as to try to secure the accommodation technologies discussed throughout this book. Being able to socialize with other students and learn from them is a big part of the adaptive techniques that many students who are dyslexic will use later in life. Similarly, learning to negotiate with the bureaucracy and establish her own independent accommodations is a skill that she will have to learn when she goes to college or enters the workplace. Insulating your child from these challenges—even through your well-meaning protection of her via home schooling—can have a negative impact in the long term.

FRESH BEGINNINGS: ENSURING SUCCESS IN A NEW ENVIRONMENT

If and when you do enroll your child in a new school, be sure to apply the lessons in Chapter Five from the outset, navigating the new administration and telling your story. If your child had an IEP that was not properly implemented in the previous school, bring this documentation along to the new environment and see how they respond to it. Track from that first IEP baseline rather than starting from scratch. On a personal level, if bullying or uncompromising teachers made life difficult for your child in her previous school, make sure she understands that she now has a new opportunity to build an environment that will work for her, and that you will be an ally in doing so.

It's a good idea to use the summer before enrolling in a new school to role-play with your child, talking about dyslexia and getting him comfortable introducing the topic in a new environment. If you picked a school that is dedicated to students with specific learning disabilities, be sure to attend the orientations that school offers and get to know what services and support they have in place. Yet even at a new school, you will still need to monitor the environment. As I noted above, many schools have good intentions but fail to implement accommodations properly. The odds are that with appropriate attention you will be able to reap the benefits of having researched and selected an environment that is more suited for your child. In all likelihood you'll be able to look back years later and be glad that you made the leap to a new situation.

PART III

CHANGING *the* WORLD

CHAPTER NINE

Building Community

When I was growing up, I felt scared and lonely whenever I dwelled on my dyslexia. Today, I feel a sense of joy when I connect with people over it. This is in large part because I'm open about my dyslexia, so I'm recognized for who I really am. I first began to feel empowered about my dyslexia when I met other people who shared my experience. Once I began integrating my own dyslexia, I started tracking down dyslexic mentors and colleagues with whom I built a shared community. Before long, I was able to finally wash away the shame I felt.

It's heartbreaking to see your child feel unworthy. The best way to address this feeling is to find a community for him or her. One of my strongest recommendations in this book is to go find other people who share your child's experience. At www.headstrongnation.org, you will find a list of resources where you can connect online or physically participate in an educational event. Perhaps the best national organization on this issue is Eye to Eye (www.eyetoeyenational.org). Started in 1998 by a group of SLD students at Brown University, this program currently has fifty-seven chapters across the country and is growing each year. Their strength-based methodologies are simply the best. Their methodology involves getting dyslexic students and other students labeled with specific learning disabilities from a local college, or in some cases a high school, to serve as mentors for children with these profiles in primary or middle-school special education classes. Eye to Eye uses art projects to get kids talking about themselves and boost most of the attitudinal measures discussed in Chapter Three, such as resiliency and SLD integration. It will be a major win for your child if you can get him or her involved with one of these chapters or even help start one in your community. I'm also a big fan of Education Revolution, which is hosted by the Parents Education Network (PEN), and Student Advisors for Education (SAFE), community organizations focused on SLD issues (mentioned in Chapter Two). Both organizations have great videos of children and teens talking about their profiles on their websites (see Appendix C).

Another factor that allowed me to make the transition from shame to joy was the realization that I can change most systems if they are not working for me. For you and your child to be happy, you may need to change the systems you are in. If your goal is merely for your child to be "normal," you will never feel empowered. On the other hand, if you can guide your child toward the entrepreneurial thinking that so many dyslexics use, you'll be able to facilitate change and develop community for other dyslexics who follow in your family's path.

There are at least five skills involved in entrepreneurial thinking:

- An appetite for risk
- Breaking conventions
- Delegating well
- Collaborating with others
- The ability to handle failure (that is, resiliency)

These also happen to be the skills dyslexics must learn at an early age. For children who are dyslexic, walking into school each day involves taking a serious risk: their peers might mock them or the school might not provide the accommodations that they need to learn independently. And just by its nature, dyslexia means doing most things in an unconventional way (ear reading versus eye reading, for example). Delegation is a strong skill set for dyslexics because there are many things we simply can't do ourselves. For example, I'm still delegating proofreading to someone else, whether it's a colleague or a trusted friend. Dyslexics do better when we are collaborating, bringing to the table our strengths and relying on others who are strong in our areas of weakness to fill in the gaps. Finally, if you are following the path outlined in Chapter Three, measuring and improving resiliency, your child will be in good shape on this front. Small failures in third grade, such as a bad grade on a spelling test, can prepare a child to bounce back when she faces the larger challenges life gives us all.

In general, I've found that entrepreneurs and dyslexics have a common trait: we like to be the authors of the future. I'm always happiest when I'm leading a development effort, be it working on the Intel Reader, getting mentoring programs up and running, or writing this book. When you spend your entire life unsure of what will be asked of you because you have difficulty with the instructions or because institutions often throw you a curveball, you learn to step into a creative role. There's an old cliché in Silicon Valley widely attributed to legendary computer scientist Alan Kay: "The best way to predict the future is to invent it." If you're proposing something new, it's very hard for people to tell you that you're doing it wrong.

USING ENTREPRENEURIAL THINKING

As I've pointed out before, according to a series of studies performed by the Cass Business School in London, 35 percent of American entrepreneurs are dyslexic. Given that dyslexics are between 10 and 15 percent of the population, this is a threefold higher percentage than would be predicted. Conversely, the same researchers found that less than 1 percent of middle managers in large corporations were dyslexic.

Entrepreneurship refers to much more than just starting up businesses. The nonprofit organizations I mentioned above are all using entrepreneurial thinking to change the system and address the needs of dyslexics. More generally, entrepreneurship is a form of leadership that can be applied in all fields. The best definition of leadership I've heard comes from professors Jack Weber and Carol Weber at the

Darden School of Business: *leadership is either changing what people think is possible or changing what people think is appropriate.*

Entrepreneurs do this whether they work in government, nonprofits, academics, or traditional business environments, utilizing the same skill sets for risk seeking, inventiveness, delegation, and collaboration. The next section highlights a few of my favorite dyslexic people who are changing the world. You and your child can draw on their experiences, and see how you could model your path on their successes.

GAME CHANGERS

There are many well-known dyslexic entrepreneurs: Charles Schwab; Richard Branson; the founder of Kinko's, Paul Orfalea; AT&T Wireless's founder, Craig McCaw; and the current CEO of Cisco Systems, John Chambers, to name a few. I listed many more in Chapter Three. Their dyslexia is often presented as being in opposition to their success. Yet the opposite is true: these people are successful in part because of their experience with dyslexia.

Earlier I discussed how I see a direct line between Gen. George Patton's dyslexia and his perseverance and drive. Much the same way we teach the history of the general civil rights movement in our public schools, it is important to teach dyslexics the history of the disability rights movement and highlight approachable, inspirational dyslexic individuals who are living their lives today.

I know many dyslexics who are not that famous but who have integrated their dyslexia and make consistent steps toward creating a community for us all. Here are some of their stories. I have also included their unique maps from their Strengths Stars (you did one for your child in Chapter Three) to give you a sense of the ranges of their profiles.

Pete Denman

Pete is a designer at Intel, and we met when I was first developing the Intel Reader. He first called me after a workshop I ran to brainstorm ideas for the device. He explained to me, "There's something I want to tell you, but I have to ask you to keep it a secret: I'm dyslexic." Hundreds of people have shared that secret with me, but Pete was the first person who really startled me with this information. This is because Pete has another disability: he is a quadriplegic. Here was what I thought to be the poster boy for capabilities of people with disabilities in the office. He uses a power chair and has limited use of his hands, meaning he has to use uncommon tools to do the drawing and layout central to his job. Yet over his twenty-year career he had hidden the fact that he couldn't spell or read with ease. He later told me that he had failed third grade because of his dyslexia and had searing memories of being called up in front of his class and castigated for his mistakes by the priest who ran his parochial school. I respected Pete's wishes at the time, but I found it ironic that the same person who was designing the user manuals for a product for people with dyslexia wouldn't tell others that he was in the club.

When we launched the Intel Reader, Pete and I began talking about dyslexia more frequently. Over the course of a few months we had a number of conversations in which I asked him if he might be willing to talk about his dyslexia more publicly. He finally felt comfortable enough to tell his employers what was really going on with him. When that went successfully, he decided that he might reach further outside his comfort zone, and he became an official speaker for a conference held in Oregon about dyslexia. He titled his first speech "How Quadriplegia Cured My Dyslexia (Not Really)." He has since given his speech in multiple forums, and it's successful every time because he is funny while being forthright and inspiring.

In this poignant talk, Pete explained that he has been dyslexic his whole life, which led to his quitting college immediately after enrolling. Without accommodation, he could not do the work. Shortly thereafter he was injured and became a wheelchair user. At that point the school system began offering him books on tape, note takers, and other accommodations that they believed would help a person with quadriplegia succeed. What they didn't know was that they were also providing him with access to printed material and accommodating his non-obvious disability: dyslexia. With perhaps the best camouflage I've ever seen, Pete was then able to get accommodations for both of his disabilities while only publicly claiming one.

The most remarkable part of his story is how he's begun to use his experiences with disability to change the world. He recently was part of a team at Intel that helped world-renowned theoretical physicist Stephen Hawking, who has a motor neuron disease, communicate better. Combining his knowledge of speech software with his openness about his dyslexia, Pete was selected to help update the speech output interface that Dr. Hawking uses to share his ideas. Pete's role at Intel involves creating new products for the company, allowing him to apply the principles of entrepreneurship. Whether it be in creating a new interface for Dr. Hawking or taking on other cutting-edge challenges, Pete applies the entrepreneurial skills he learned in the context of his disabilities to change the world. Through his speeches he is creating community by helping people see the connection between his obvious and non-obvious disabilities.

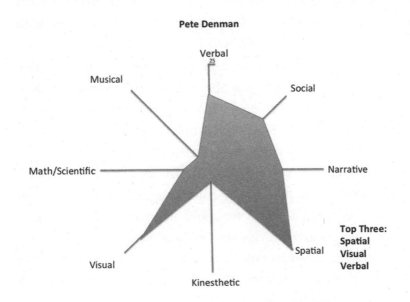

Pete Denman

Top Three:
Spatial
Visual
Verbal

Natalie Rose Traun Tamburello

Natalie was the young woman I mentioned in Chapter Three who took to singing in second grade every time she was asked to read aloud. She was identified as dyslexic in second grade and then asked to leave that school. However, she had the good fortune to have parents who got her the support she needed. As her mother, Julie Traun, told me, "We just kept asking her, 'What would make it better?' And then we would do that, whether it was making her something she particularly liked to eat before going to school, or helping her get an accommodation." By the time she was in sixth grade, Natalie had become a vocal advocate around SLD issues. She was one of the founding members of Student Advisors for Education, the organization I mentioned earlier in this chapter. For the last decade this group has sent students who are dyslexic or have other specific learning disabilities to participate in panel discussions in the Bay Area, as well as host a conference and run workshops for the community. They speak to teachers, administrators, and students as well as parents about their experiences in clear and direct ways.

Natalie has also co-authored a book entitled *Read This When You Can* with other SAFE volunteers. It highlights the voices of students who are dyslexic and who have been identified as having ADHD, adding them to the important conversation about special education and placing them at the center of the narrative. It has been assigned as reading for graduate students at the Harvard School of Education.

Natalie is currently in the Perspectives on Inclusive and Special Education Program at St. John's College, Cambridge, in the United Kingdom, where she is completing an MPhil. She recently interned at UCSF Medical Center as part of a team studying the success attributes of dyslexics. She has also worked on brain MRI studies at Stanford. Her commitment to the field also extends to starting two chapters of Eye to Eye. Natalie brings the voice of a new generation to all of these activities, putting the perspective of people who are dyslexic at the center of the conversation about how to include everyone. To do this she has spent time collaborating with others, taking risks and breaking the conventional wisdom.

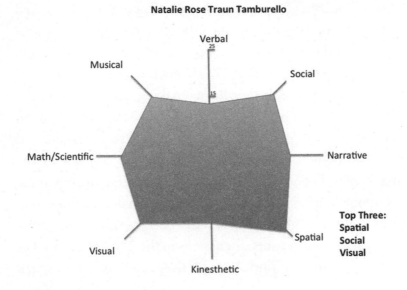

Natalie Rose Traun Tamburello

Top Three:
Spatial
Social
Visual

Sean Stevens

Sean has worked as a community intervention worker, focusing on gang prevention programs for the mayor of Columbus, Ohio. He was selected for this role because he has firsthand experience of life on the streets. Sean served twenty years in federal prison after being charged with large-scale cocaine distribution.

Sean grew up in very complicated circumstances, moving many times when he was young. When he was five, his mother was incarcerated and he was given up for adoption. He tells stories of how his foster father used to beat him when he would come home with bad grades, yelling the unthinkable at the young boy: "A nigger that don't read and write is a dead nigger!"

Sean's experience of dyslexia is unfortunately very common. A study in Texas indicated that 41 percent of the prison population could be identified as having a specific learning disability such as dyslexia. If you extrapolate this number to the national population of over 2.3 million prisoners, this means that there are more than 940,000 people with dyslexia or related specific learning disabilities in jail today.

Sean is now helping young kids avoid his mistakes, working with school administrations to address the underlying causes that can lead to gang activity in a school. When he hears of a child getting involved with a gang, he always checks if that student might be dyslexic. If the child is, as is often the case, Sean points out to the school that if the school can't provide accommodations, it's likely the student will drop out and perhaps get into more trouble.

My favorite story about Sean involves his own entrepreneurial spirit. He contacted me through an Orton-Gillingham tutor who had been volunteering time to help Sean improve his eye reading. When we spoke I asked Sean whether he used accommodation technologies. He wasn't familiar with them, so I sent him an Intel Reader. The day after he received it he called me to say, "I stayed up all night and read everything in my apartment." This included notices from his parole officer and other important information that would not have been accessible to him had he not had this technology. He explained that he was going to get the device on the local news and convince schools to start buying the technology. Two weeks later he sent me a clip of the piece a local Fox News affiliate did on Sean and the Intel Reader! He was certainly changing what people thought was appropriate and possible.

Sean is one of my favorite dyslexics because his experience highlights where a lot of the energy in dyslexia should be turned. There are some educators who want to define dyslexia primarily in terms of assisting children, not adults, and by framing the conversation in terms of the SAT or college acceptance, as opposed to access to employment and keeping kids in the classroom and off the streets. If we can support the full spectrum of people who are dyslexic, the way Sean does, we can have an even greater impact.

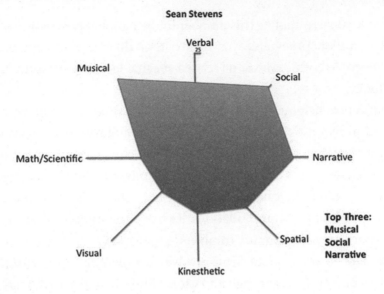

Tracy Johnson

Tracy is an enrollment counselor for Eastern College, near Philadelphia, Pennsylvania. I met her at the premiere for an HBO documentary in which we were both featured, called *Journey into Dyslexia*. In her segment, Tracy tells the story of how she was placed in special education in sixth grade but not identified as dyslexic until years later, when she saw an episode of *The Cosby Show* in which the character Theo was identified as dyslexic. At the time, Tracy was in her twenties and working as a janitor for a public school system. She then sought out tutoring based on the Orton-Gillingham method and accommodations that allowed her to go back to school. She graduated from college with a 4.0 GPA.

Tracy has since become a spokesperson for Learning Ally and was featured at the 2012 Education Revolution event as one of the keynote speakers. Through her nonprofit, Vessels of Hope, she counsels African American men and women about their career and educational paths. In this capacity, she often coaches people who have similar learning profiles to help them get back into school and find a better job.

Talking with Tracy, I've learned a tremendous amount about how to approach issues of dyslexia in the context of inner-city communities. She explained to me that expectations are often set so low that the labels of "lazy" and "stupid" associated with dyslexia land that much harder. She has dedicated herself to helping turn that tide by meeting one-on-one with people traveling the same path she did.

One of the best examples of Tracy's ability to connect with people is when I saw her give a presentation on mentoring with a successful businessman, Matthew Bickerton, an entrepreneur who set up a mentoring program in the United Kingdom. I was struck by how similar their coaching philosophies were with regard to their dyslexic mentees. Keep in mind that Tracy works in inner-city Philadelphia, while Matthew operates in London and often works with people in the technology industry. It underscored for me the tight connection there is within the dyslexia community regardless of race, gender, nationality, or wealth. The same fears and lessons could be found in both communities, and Tracy did a fabulous job of extrapolating to the larger principles involved in coaching someone who shares our profile. She is an outstanding example of how to change minds about what is possible in life, taking risks to break out of her janitorial job and into the life of an enrollment counselor. Today she uses the same entrepreneurial skills working locally to create change.

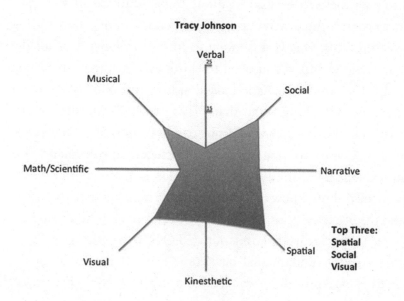

Tracy Johnson

Top Three:
Spatial
Social
Visual

Joe Stutts

Joe Stutts grew up in rural Alabama and had a terrible time in school in the 1950s. He was dyslexic and "made twenty-seven F's in second grade." The education for students with disabilities in that era consisted of him being taken out of the mainstream school and sent to a factory where he was forced to repair crates for a bottling company. He dropped out in sixth grade. When he turned eighteen he joined the military and there discovered that he was not, as he had been told, stupid and lazy. Indeed, in his class of infantry cooks, he startled everyone by getting a 97 on the final exam. This was the highest score on the base that year, earning him a trophy. As he explains, "The man read the questions and the answer [options] and I just marked them down." In that era, the military recognized that illiteracy was common among new recruits, so it provided the same accommodation for all their enlisted trainees, reading test questions aloud.

When Joe returned to Alabama, he got a job working for the Tennessee Valley Authority (TVA) shoveling coal. He dreamed of becoming a heavy-equipment operator, running the large derricks, bulldozers, and tugboats at the facility. Each year for nine years he tried to pass the written examinations to be admitted into the apprentice program, and each year he failed because of his poor reading and writing skills. One year he went in to see the supervisor for the plant and said to him, "You seem to think there's somethin' wrong with me." The boss paused and looked at him and said, "Well, Joe, I think you need to think about that." This was 1979 and the Americans with Disabilities Act would not pass for another eleven years, but as a TVA employee, Joe worked for the federal government. This meant Section 504 of the 1973 Rehabilitation Act applied to him. At the time Joe did not know this, but he had a remarkable sense of justice and the proactivity and resilience to decide to call the Equal Employment Opportunity Commission (EEOC) in Washington, D.C. He then asked a fundamental question: "I've just been told I can't drive a truck because I can't read. Is that against the law?" The beauty of this question is that it flips the source of the problem: he had come to the conclusion that perhaps the system itself was flawed.

The EEOC investigated and told him he had a case. He went to a local lawyer and filed suit against the state's largest employer. The risk taking involved in this was tremendous: everybody in his town to some degree owed his livelihood to the TVA, and Joe was a humble ditchdigger filing suit in federal court against the United States government.

In 1983, a three-judge federal appeals court panel ruled in his favor in a case called *Stutts v. Freeman*. The TVA decided to settle the case and grant him an accommodation. This case was cited in congressional testimony during the drafting of the Americans with Disabilities Act as an example of the type of case establishing that employers cannot require a screening test unrelated to the work performed while on the job. As Joe put it, you cannot tell someone he can't drive a truck simply because he can't read.

Joe is my first and greatest mentor in dyslexia. It is hard to imagine having less ideal circumstances from which to become an activist for our community than those Joe lived in. And yet he's a bona fide civil rights hero—his case opened doors for so many people with disabilities in the workplace. We can all take a lesson from his example and try to find ways to change our community through entrepreneurial skills, such as taking risks and doing things differently.

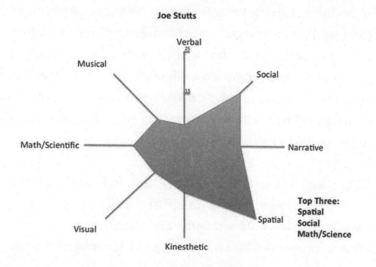

RADICAL DYSLEXIA

The people I have profiled have incredibly disparate life experiences, with only one thing in common: they are just as dyslexic now as they were when they were kids. If you asked any of them (or me) to write out two sentences by hand, not one of us could spell every word correctly. All of them have found ways to create accommodations that give them independence. And all of them have learned how to integrate the emotional experiences tied to their history. My hope is that you and your child can find something to connect to in these stories and begin applying the lessons of resiliency and openness to your own life.

Above all, I assure you that you will be happier if you begin to work on transforming your community into one that supports people who are dyslexic. It'll help heal the wounds you've incurred and enable you to find joy through connection to others. Let me be clear: this is not an easy thing to do. There are real risks involved with talking about your dyslexia publicly, whether you're a child or an adult. There will be people who have opinions that are inaccurate about dyslexia. Others will second-guess your child's ability to master her education and her life beyond the classroom. But the fear and shame you feel by hiding this part of your family's story is corrosive, and if kept out of the light, this secret can become incredibly damaging. To help you on that path, I've defined four principles that I consider to be the core of a new way to approach dyslexia. I call them the principles of Radical Dyslexia. These are principles you can teach your child, and internalize for yourself, in order to help your child integrate dyslexia and be part of a joyful community:

1. *Be proud.* To the greatest degree that feels safe for your child, coach him on how to tell the world he is dyslexic and that he has both strengths and weaknesses.
2. *Learn independently.* Use the form of learning that suits

your child best, be it eye reading, ear reading, finger reading, or any other type of reading you can think of, and ignore the methods other people try to impose on you.

3. *Build community.* Seek out other parents like you and other people who are dyslexic, forming community based on shared experiences.

4. *Leave a legacy.* Make changes in your school, workplace, or other institutions that affect both policies and culture, making it easier for other dyslexics in the future.

Start by getting your own child access to learning and accommodations that will allow him or her to be independent. But keep in mind that dyslexia is a lifetime experience. Once you have mastered the basics, and I guarantee you will, start looking for ways to go 10 percent outside your comfort zone and help other people. This could be as simple as making an announcement at a PTA meeting that you're happy to talk to other parents in the community with kids who are dyslexic. Or it could involve your child returning to a third-grade classroom once she has reached high school to talk about her experiences with dyslexia in a roomful of kids who may be uncertain about the subject. These small steps can lead to great changes in your school system. Find your own outlet for Radical Dyslexia!

CHAPTER TEN

Your Child Is Not Broken

Parents often confide in me that they are scared for their children. I always point out that the fact that they're seeking information about their child's needs shows they are on the right path. Like them, you're putting in the time and energy to find out accurate information and train your child to be independent. For this caring effort on your part, let me say "thank you."

You are doing an outstanding job for your child. It takes real dedication to sort through the uncertainties that surround dyslexia and to fight the battles that are necessary to level the playing field. It also involves a tremendous amount of trust to empower your child to handle these conversations on her own. Merely by reading this book you are ensuring that one more family will avoid some of the pitfalls I encountered. Above all, by mastering the information in this book, you're creating a world where your child will feel less lonely and will be able to be seen for who she is. Indeed, you can take a big deep breath, let it out slowly, smile, and say to yourself: "I'm doing a good job." Go on. I'll wait while you say it aloud.

You may not fully believe that statement yet. But trust me, it's true. This does not mean it's not scary or that there aren't complex questions yet to be answered. But you have an orientation now that will help you solve future problems.

THE FUTURE IS BRIGHT

Once you have a chance to put some of these lessons of this book into practice and you become comfortable with the integration of your child's SLD, some surprising things will happen. First, you will find you have much more energy because you're not carrying around as much anxiety or shame about how you child is performing as you have in the past. I've seen countless people who held this secret in their emotional Fort Knox come to have a real sense of joy once they master telling their story.

The next surprise is that you'll begin to see dyslexia everywhere. We are 10 percent of the population, and there are some who claim that the broader category of SLD encompasses as many as 20 percent of people. Even at the lower end, that means there are 30 million of us in the United States alone. I've met with dyslexics in Brazil, Britain, Spain, and Taiwan—remember, we are global! As you begin to become more public about this issue you'll find that people will seek you out and start to disclose their dyslexia. I encourage you to keep their information confidential if they ask you to do so, but to point out to them that they might be happier if they reached 10 percent outside their comfort zone and talked to a few more people about it. I expect that you'll find some of your deepest friendships will come from relationships you build via dyslexia. In Chapter Nine, I articulated the special bond among people in the Nation of Dyslexia. It is yours to enjoy the more community you build.

Another phenomenon you'll find startling is the complete lack of context most people have around dyslexia. The most interesting revelations on this front, however, will be among your close friends and family. I cannot tell you the number of instances where I have seen adults who integrated their dyslexia be startled by gaps in their own family's or friends' knowledge about their profile. Just this last week a friend who decided to begin talking about needing accommodations in the workplace found his own father asking: "Why do you need a talking computer? I see you read stuff all the time." While his father wasn't meaning to judge him, he just didn't understand the internal workings of his son's brain, or—more important—how daunting the day-to-day experience of eye reading can be. These gaps are quite common, and they underscore how complex this issue is and how helpful you can be to others by resetting the context.

One of my favorite versions of this is the conversation that goes: "You're dyslexic? You don't look dyslexic."

Really? What am I supposed to look like?

A while back a friend I went to college with came to visit me in my new home. He walked into my living room and exclaimed, "Wow, you really are dyslexic!"

I responded, "What about my living room makes you understand my dyslexia?"

"You have no books on the shelf. I am used to browsing some-one's shelves to see what they're reading and discuss it. But there's nothing here to discuss." I had told him about my profile a decade ago. He had heard stories about me getting extra time on exams, or relying on lectures alone to understand a topic. But until he saw the physical evidence, or rather the lack of something physical in my life, he did not get it. Even though I ear-read two to three books a month, those MP3s don't stack up on the shelf. In the spirit of validating ear reading, I recently had someone sign my audiobook. I read *My Dyslexia* by the Pulitzer Prize–winning poet Philip Schultz. When I met him at a conference, I had him sign the case to my smart phone, an autograph I enjoy showing off to anyone who will listen. You can see a video of him signing it at the Headstrong Nation's website.

The final surprise is that you'll find that there will be two phases to your life around this issue. This is true both for yourself and for your child. There will be the era of pre–dyslexia integration (PDI) and the time after dyslexia integration (ADI). While there may not be a specific day you can put your finger on, there will definitely be a turning point when you'll notice that neither you nor your child is holding back or hiding this issue. These are new terms I am introducing, and I encourage you to use them when you talk about your and your child's history with this profile. My hope is that your PDI will be as short as possible and that your ADI will be as long as possible.

My ADI moment came while I was a graduate student. In my second year in grad school, I participated in a brain study of adult dyslexics. Researchers were trying to establish that the same brain patterns they see in dyslexic children persisted in dyslexic adults. To be admitted to the study I had to undergo many hours of written and oral tests at Stanford Medical Center to prove that I was dyslexic.

After I completed my testing, I started to get nervous. It occurred to me that all the testing might come back and indicate that I was not really dyslexic after all. If there was no dyslexia, then all of the accommodations I had been getting in school were ill-gotten. Maybe I really was lazy and just didn't focus the way my classmates could. Maybe I was stupid and couldn't cut it at the highest level.

When I came back to get my results, the lab coat–wearing researcher looked very nervous. She couldn't make eye contact with me and fidgeted in her seat. The more anxious she looked, the more nervous I got that this would not go well. She finally looked up from her clipboard and said,

"Ben, I don't know how to tell you this . . . but you're really dyslexic."

"Really? Excellent!" I meant it. I was greatly relieved.

"Wait, that's good news?"

"Definitely. I'm thrilled!"

"Well, you're in the bottom 15 percent when it comes to reading and writing."

"Outstanding!"

"And you're in the bottom 1 percent on letter recognition—we don't even really have a number to describe how bad you are at recognizing a letter when it's shown to you."

"That's wonderful news. I thought I might have been faking these problems. It's great to know they're real!"

It was then that I realized I had turned the corner on integration. I had reached ADI. I had gone from not liking my dyslexia, and therefore not liking myself, to viewing it as an essential part of who I was. I also realized that I was going to succeed not despite my dyslexia but because of it.

When you reach your ADI period, you will begin to be able to use the lessons you have learned and the skills of entrepreneurship that you adopted to support your child to do something more than just get through the day. Eventually you'll find that you and your child take real pleasure in helping other people who are just like you. I challenge you at that point to begin looking for ways to transform the landscape. Our schools, our workplaces, and in some cases our families can do so much better on this issue. It starts with local change. Every time each one of us talks about our disability positively, or a disability we embrace in our family, it works its way into the broader conversation. Eventually we can make even the largest institutions rethink what is possible and what is appropriate. The most interesting part about dyslexia is the future of it, and you and your child can help. I am betting that you both will enjoy making that future a bright one.

APPENDIX A

What Dyslexia Looks LIke

This Appendix can be cut out of the book and brought with you when you need to discuss dyslexia.

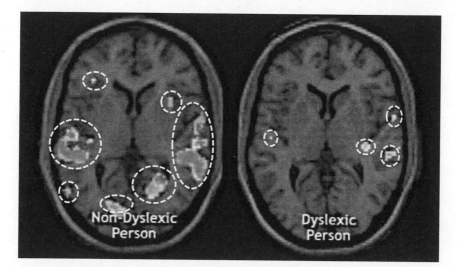

The images above show what dyslexia can look like in the brain. They are functional magnetic resonance images (fMRI) highlighting brain activity while the subjects read. Activity is seen in areas circled with dashed lines. On the left is a composite scan of a typical reader with lots of brain activity in the temporal parietal lobes. The image on the right is of a dyslexic person, Ben Foss, author of The Dyslexia Empowerment Plan: A Blueprint for Renewing Your Child's Confidence and Love of Learning *(Random House, 2013). The images were taken at Stanford University when Ben was a graduate student. They show the physical evidence of dyslexia, a specific learning disability. For more information visit www.headstrongnation.org.*

Independent Schools Focused on Dyslexia

The following is a list of exceptional independent schools that focus on dyslexia and other specific learning disabilities. In most cases I have personally visited the schools. These schools focus on the emotional health of the child as well as including training on advocacy and mastery of accommodations to allow them to lead independent lives.

Charles Armstrong School
1405 Solana Drive
Belmont, CA 94002
650-592-7570
www.charlesarmstrong.org

Churchill School and Center
301 East 29th Street
New York, NY 10016
212-722-0610
www.churchillschool.com
(Note that there are a number of other dyslexia-specific schools with "Churchill" in the name. They are not affiliated with this school.)

Eagle Hill School Southport
214 Main Street

Southport, CT 06890

203-254-2044

www.eaglehillsouthport.org

Hamilton School at Wheeler

216 Hope Street

Providence, RI 02906

(401) 421-8100

www.wheelerschool.org/hamilton

Hamilton is a "school within a school" contained within the
Wheeler School. Hamilton focuses on dyslexia. Wheeler is a
mainstream independent school.

Kildonan Boarding School

425 Morse Hill Road

Amenia, NY 12501

845-373-8111

www.kildonan.org

Lab School of Washington

4759 Reservoir Road, NW

Washington, DC 20007

410-261-5500

www.labschool.org

Lawrence School

10036 Olde Eight Road

Sagamore Hills, OH 44067

330-908-6800

www.lawrenceschool.org

There are two campuses for this school. I have listed the Upper
School campus. Both are excellent and are part of the same
overall school.

Thomas A. Edison High School
9020 SW Beaverton Hillsdale Highway
Portland, OR 97225
503-297-2336
www.taedisonhs.org

Westmark School
5461 Louise Avenue
Encino, CA 91316
818-986-5045
www.westmarkschool.org

Marburn Academy
1860 Walden Drive
Columbus, Ohio 43229
614-433-0822
www.marburnacademy.org

If you do not live near one of these schools, or even if you do and find that the cost is prohibitive, I recommend you look for a public school in your area that has an Eye to Eye chapter (www.eyetoeyenational.org).

Each chapter mentors a group of elementary school students, generally in a public school. If you can find a school in your area that has one of these mentoring programs, your child is going to get more support than she would in the standard school. This does not mean that the school will have a tailored curriculum for dyslexia, but it is a strong indication the school is open to this form of diversity and that your child specifically would be assigned a mentor who could be helpful to her.

APPENDIX C

Useful Resources

Extracurricular Activities

Inter-School Robotics Challenge. There is a list of fun robotics competitions for U.S. kids at www.usfirst.org/competition; at http://robots.net/rcfaq.html is a worldwide listing of competitions, mainly for adults, but still fun to attend.

Films

Films can be a great way to introduce the concepts of dyslexia to your child or to educate your circle of friends, your school, or even your own family. In many cases you can obtain a copy for viewing by a large audience for free, and in some cases the directors may even attend a viewing to talk about their work.

> *Journey into Dyslexia,* HBO Documentaries, 2011
> The best overall introduction to dyslexia. I am featured in this film, along with some other people mentioned throughout this book.
> Directed by Susan and Allen Raymond
> www.videoverite.tv/pages/film-JID-about.html

> *Headstrong: Inside the Hidden World of Dyslexia and Attention Deficit/Hyperactivity Disorder,* Schechter Films, 2007
> This is a film created by Headstrong Nation, a nonprofit I

founded, and it features the story of Joe Stutts.
Directed by Steve Schechter
www.headstrongnation.org

Read Me Differently
An insightful and powerful treatment of family dynamics in
relation to specific learning disabilities.
Directed by Sarah Entine
www.readmedifferently.com

Including Samuel
A great introduction to the challenges of inclusion faced within
the family and in school settings for people with disabilities.
Directed by Dan Habib
www.IncludingSamuel.com

Books

The following are excellent on dyslexia and disabilities more generally:

The Dyslexic Advantage by Brock and Fernette Eide, 2011
This book outlines the brain science pointing toward upsides to
dyslexia.

No Pity by Joseph Shapiro, 1994
This book offers the best overview of the recent history of the
disability movement.

Shame: The Power of Caring by Gershen Kaufman, 1992
A general psychological text on the phenomenon of shame.
Given that this is such a powerful underlying experience for
people who are dyslexic, this framework can be very helpful. It
is also worth checking out other books by Kaufman including:

The Psychology of Shame by Gershen Kaufman, 2004
The definitive overview of the subject in my view.

Read This When You Can by SAFE Voices, 2008
www.parentseducationnetwork.org/SAFEbook
This is a great compendium of stories about students who are
dyslexic and have other specific learning disabilities. Most
important, it is written by those students. Be sure to get an
audio version of the text for your child or simply read it
aloud.

Proust and the Squid: The Story and Science of the Reading Brain
by Maryanne Wolf, 2007
An excellent synthesis of brain science and the history of
literacy, with a focus on dyslexia.

Organizations with Useful Information on Dyslexia

Headstrong Nation
www.headstrongnation.org
Headstrong Nation is a nonprofit I founded in 2003. Its mission
is to form a community of dyslexics. We promote strength-
based models of dyslexia that lead to joy and pride in our
identity as dyslexics.

Dyslexiaville
www.dyslexiaville.com
This free web destination provides a range of videos and
activities designed for dyslexic children age 5 to 12 as well as a
community where children gain confidence, build self-esteem,
and share their strengths. As of this writing, they have executed
a successful Kickstarter campaign and plan to launch by the end
of 2013. The founder of this "virtual world for dyslexic children"
is Peggy Stern, an Oscar-winning filmmaker who is also
dyslexic. You can go to dyslexiaville.com, sign up and join the
conversation.

National Center for Learning Disabilities (NCLD)
www.ncld.org
The NCLD focuses on empowering parents, enabling young
adults, transforming schools, and creating policy and advocacy
impact to address dyslexia and other specific learning
disabilities. Their website is a good source of information about
brain science, dyslexia, and other learning issues.

Lime Connect
www.limeconnect.com
Lime Connect is a not-for-profit organization that's improving
the workplace by attracting, preparing, and connecting high-
potential students and alumni who happen to have disabilities
for scholarships and internships. College students who are
dyslexic or have other specific learning disabilities can get
fellowships working for Google, Target, Goldman Sachs,
Bloomberg, and PepsiCo, among others, through the Lime
Connect Fellowship Program.

Eye to Eye
eyetoeyenational.org
Eye to Eye is the best mentoring organization in this space. They
have fifty-seven chapters across the country and are expanding,
offering an empowering curriculum that pairs college students
and elementary school students with specific learning
disabilities.

Parents Education Network (PEN)
www.parentseducationnetwork.org
PEN offers regular conferences and events on dyslexia and other
specific learning disabilities in the San Francisco Bay Area.
Their annual conference, Education Revolution (www.edrevsf.
org/), is excellent.

Student Advisors for Education (SAFE)

www.parentseducationnetwork.org/SAFE

SAFE is the student arm of PEN. They regularly hold meetings of middle schoolers and teenagers in the San Francisco Bay Area. They also do excellent talks in schools.

Smart Kids with Learning Disabilities

www.smartkidswithld.org

This nonprofit organization is dedicated to empowering the parents of children with learning disabilities (LD) and attention deficit/hyperactivity disorder (ADHD). They offer excellent content on destigmatizing dyslexia.

Dyslexic Advantage

www.dyslexicadvantage.com

This site, managed by Fernette and Brock Eide, is based on their book of the same title. It is regularly updated with useful news and information regarding successful dyslexics.

Emily Hall Tremaine Foundation

171 Orange Street

New Haven, CT 06510

203-639-5544

www.tremainefoundation.org

This foundation focuses its grantmaking in the areas of art, the environment, and specific learning disabilities. Every five years they conduct a public poll regarding attitudes on specific learning disabilities. They also have helpful papers on public policy recommendations, as well as hosting conferences on Dyslexia and Talent. These can be useful resources in explaining the issues to your school.

Legal Resources

Disability Rights Education and Defense Fund (DREDF)
3075 Adeline Street, Suite 210
Berkeley, CA 94703
510-644-2555
510 841-8645 (fax/TTY)
www.dredf.org
This national civil rights law and policy center is directed by
individuals with disabilities and parents who have children with
disabilities. Their website is particularly useful as a place to find
sample letters to schools and information on the law regarding
individual education plans (IEPs).

Disability Rights Advocates
2001 Center Street, Fourth Floor
Berkeley, CA 94704-1204
510-665-8644
510-665-8716 (TTY)
www.dralegal.org
If you feel that your civil rights have been violated in a way that
raises systemic issues that may impact a large number of people
with disabilities, this national nonprofit legal center is a good
place to contact. They do not handle individual cases.

National Dissemination Center for Children with Disabilities
http://nichcy.org/state-organization-search-by-state
If you are seeking help with an individual education plan (IEP)
or other education issues, this website provides a list of
disability-related agencies in your state that may be helpful.

Jo Anne Simon, Attorney at Law
Jo Anne Simon, P.C.

356 Fulton Street
Brooklyn, NY 11201
718-852-3582
www.joannesimon.com
Jo Anne Simon, P.C., provides direct representation to people with disabilities, including those who are dyslexic or have other specific learning disability profiles. The firm concentrates on matters related to accommodations on tests such as the SAT, ACT, GRE, LSAT, and MCAT. The firm is based in New York City and is national in practice.

The National Center for Learning Disabilities Checklist

The National Center for Learning Disabilities (www.ncld.org) has developed a comprehensive checklist that allows you to gain insight into your child's experiences in the classroom and beyond. There are a number of other specific learning disabilities (SLD) defined under IDEA that are related to oral expression, memory, listening, writing, reading, or math that can also be identified using this checklist. There are also profiles related to attention deficit and hyperactivity, and while these are not technically SLD, I consider them to be closely related to dyslexia and many times they are part of the set of profiles this book is intended to help. Even if your child does not check a majority of these boxes, she can still have a significant specific learning disability. This is one of the complexities of this field. The NCLD material covers a broader range of issues, including those related to motor skills, attention, and social and emotional elements. Also keep in mind the following comments and advice from the director of LD Resources & Essential Information at NCLD.

> Most people have problems with learning and behavior from time to time. During the school years, parents and educators should be on the alert for consistent (and persistent) patterns of difficulty that children and adolescents may experience over time as they may signal an underlying learning disability (LD). While variations in the course of development are to be expected, unevenness or lags in the mastery of skills and

behaviors, even with children as young as 4 or 5, should not be ignored. And because LD can co-occur with other disorders, it's important to keep careful and complete records of observations and impressions so they can be shared among parents, educators and related service providers when making important decisions about needed services and supports.

Keep in mind that LD is a term that describes a heterogeneous ("mixed bag") group of disorders that impact listening, speaking, reading, writing, reasoning, math, and social skills. And remember: learning disabilities do not go away! A learning disability is not something that can be outgrown or that is "cured" by medication, therapy, or expert tutoring. So, early recognition of warning signs, well-targeted screening and assessment, effective intervention, and ongoing monitoring of progress are critical to helping individuals with LD to succeed in school, in the workplace, and in life.

The following checklist is designed as a helpful guide and not as a tool to pinpoint specific learning disabilities. The more characteristics you check, the more likely that the individual described is at risk for (or shows signs of) learning disabilities. When filling out this form, think about the person's behavior over at least the past six months. And when you're done, don't wait to seek assistance from school personnel or other professionals.

—Sheldon H. Horowitz, Ed.D.
    Director of LD Resources & Essential Information, NCLD

Learning Disabilities Checklist

Domains and Behaviors

Areas with a box (❑) indicate a characteristic is more likely to apply at that stage of life. Check all that apply.

	PRE-SCHOOL KINDERGARTEN	GRADES 1–4	GRADES 5–8	HIGH SCHOOL AND ADULT
GROSS AND FINE MOTOR SKILLS				
Appears awkward and clumsy, dropping, spilling, or knocking things over	❑	❑		
Has limited success with games and activities that demand eye-hand coordination (e.g., piano lessons, basketball, baseball)		❑	❑	❑
Has trouble with buttons, hooks, snaps, zippers, and learning to tie shoes	❑	❑		
Creates artwork that is immature for age	❑	❑		
Demonstrates poor ability to color or write "within the lines"	❑	❑		
Grasps pencil awkwardly, resulting in poor handwriting	❑	❑	❑	❑
Experiences difficulty using small objects or items that demand precision (e.g., Legos, puzzle pieces, tweezers, scissors)	❑	❑		
Dislikes and avoids writing / drawing tasks	❑	❑	❑	❑
LANGUAGE				
Demonstrates early delays in learning to speak	❑			
Has difficulty modulating voice (e.g., too soft, too loud)	❑	❑	❑	❑
Has trouble naming people or objects	❑	❑		
Has difficulty staying on topic	❑	❑		
Inserts invented words into conversation	❑	❑	❑	
Has difficulty re-telling what has just been said	❑	❑	❑	
Uses vague, imprecise language and has a limited vocabulary	❑	❑	❑	❑
Demonstrates slow and halting speech, using lots of fillers (e.g., uh, um, and, you know, so)	❑	❑	❑	❑
Uses poor grammar or misuses words in conversation		❑	❑	❑
Mispronounces words frequently	❑	❑	❑	
Confuses words with others that sound similar		❑	❑	❑
Inserts malapropisms ("slips of the tongue") into conversation (e.g., a rolling stone gathers no moths; he was a man of great statue)		❑	❑	❑

	PRE-SCHOOL KINDERGARTEN	GRADES 1–4	GRADES 5–8	HIGH SCHOOL AND ADULT
Has difficulty rhyming	❑	❑		
Has limited interest in books or stories	❑	❑	❑	
Has difficulty understanding instructions or directions	❑	❑	❑	❑
Has trouble understanding idioms, proverbs, colloquialisms, humor, and/or puns (note: take into account regional and cultural factors)		❑	❑	❑
Has difficulty with pragmatic skills (e.g., understanding the relationship between speaker and listener, staying on topic, gauging the listener's degree of knowledge, making inferences based on a speaker's verbal and non-verbal cues)		❑	❑	❑
READING				
Confuses similar-looking letters and numbers	❑	❑		
Has difficulty recognizing and remembering sight words		❑		
Frequently loses place while reading		❑	❑	❑
Confuses similar-looking words (e.g., beard/bread)		❑	❑	❑
Reverses letter order in words (e.g., saw/was)		❑	❑	
Demonstrates poor memory for printed words	❑	❑	❑	❑
Has weak comprehension of ideas / themes			❑	❑
Has significant trouble learning to read		❑	❑	❑
Has trouble naming letters	❑	❑		
Has problems associating letters and sounds, understanding the difference between sounds in words or blending sounds into words	❑	❑		
Guesses at unfamiliar words rather than using word analysis skills		❑	❑	❑
Reads slowly		❑	❑	❑
Substitutes or leaves out words while reading		❑	❑	❑
Has poor retention of new vocabulary	❑	❑	❑	
Dislikes and avoids reading or reads reluctantly	❑	❑	❑	❑
WRITTEN LANGUAGE				
Dislikes and avoids writing and copying	❑	❑	❑	❑
Demonstrates delays in learning to copy and write	❑	❑		
Has messy and incomplete writing, with many "cross outs" and erasures		❑	❑	❑
Has difficulty remembering shapes of letters and numerals	❑	❑		
Frequently reverses letters, numbers, and symbols	❑	❑		
Uses uneven spacing between letters and words, and has trouble staying "on the line"		❑	❑	❑

	PRE-SCHOOL KINDERGARTEN	GRADES 1–4	GRADES 5–8	HIGH SCHOOL AND ADULT
Copies inaccurately (e.g., confuses similar-looking letters and numbers)		❏	❏	❏
Spells poorly and inconsistently (e.g., the same word appears differently other places in the same document)		❏	❏	❏
Has difficulty proofreading and self-correcting work		❏	❏	❏
Has difficulty preparing outlines and organizing written assignments			❏	❏
Fails to develop ideas in writing so written work is incomplete and too brief			❏	❏
Expresses written ideas in a disorganized way			❏	❏
ATTENTION				
Fails to pay close attention to details or makes careless mistakes in schoolwork, work, or other activities			❏	❏
Has difficulty sustaining attention in work tasks or play activities	❏	❏	❏	❏
Does not follow through on instructions and fails to finish schoolwork, chores, or duties in the workplace		❏	❏	❏
Has difficulty organizing tasks and activities		❏	❏	❏
Avoids, dislikes, or is reluctant to engage in tasks that require sustained mental effort such as homework and organizing work tasks		❏	❏	❏
Loses things consistently that are necessary for tasks / activities (e.g., toys, school assignments, pencils, books, or tools)		❏	❏	❏
Is easily distracted by outside influences		❏	❏	❏
Is forgetful in daily/routine activities		❏	❏	❏
MATH				
Has difficulty with simple counting and one-to-one correspondence between number symbols and items / objects	❏	❏		
Has difficulty mastering number knowledge (e.g., recognition of quantities without counting)		❏	❏	❏
Has difficulty with learning and memorizing basic addition and subtraction facts		❏	❏	❏
Has difficulty learning strategic counting principles (e.g., by 2, 5, 10, 100)		❏	❏	❏
Poorly aligns numbers resulting in computation errors			❏	❏
Has difficulty estimating (e.g., quantity, value)		❏	❏	❏
Has difficulty with comparisons (e.g., less than, greater than)		❏	❏	❏
Has trouble telling time	❏	❏	❏	❏
Has trouble conceptualizing passage of time	❏	❏	❏	❏
Has difficulty counting rapidly or making calculations	❏	❏	❏	❏

	PRE-SCHOOL KINDERGARTEN	GRADES 1–4	GRADES 5–8	HIGH SCHOOL AND ADULT
Has trouble learning multiplication tables, formulas, and rules			☐	☐
Has trouble interpreting graphs and charts			☐	☐
SOCIAL/EMOTIONAL				
Does not pick up on other people's moods / feelings (e.g., may say the wrong thing at the wrong time)		☐	☐	☐
May not detect or respond appropriately to teasing		☐	☐	☐
Has difficulty "joining in" and maintaining positive social status in a peer group	☐	☐	☐	☐
Has trouble knowing how to share / express feelings			☐	
Has trouble "getting to the point" (e.g., gets bogged down in details in conversation)			☐	☐
Has difficulty with self-control when frustrated	☐	☐		
Has difficulty dealing with group pressure, embarrassment, and unexpected challenges		☐	☐	☐
Has trouble setting realistic social goals			☐	☐
Has trouble evaluating personal social strengths and challenges			☐	☐
Doubts own abilities and prone to attribute successes to luck or outside influences rather than hard work			☐	☐
OTHER				
Confuses left and right		☐	☐	☐
Has a poor sense of direction; is slow to learn the way around a new place; is easily lost or confused in unfamiliar surroundings			☐	☐
Finds it hard to judge speed and distance (e.g., hard to play certain games, drive a car)			☐	☐
Has trouble reading charts and maps			☐	☐
Is disorganized and poor at planning			☐	☐
Often loses things		☐	☐	☐
Is slow to learn new games and master puzzles		☐	☐	☐
Has difficulty listening and taking notes at the same time			☐	☐
Performs inconsistently on tasks from one day to the next		☐	☐	☐
Has difficulty generalizing (applying) skills from one situation to another		☐	☐	☐

ACKNOWLEDGMENTS

I am filled with gratitude for all the many favors, the acts of friendship, and the support and co-creation that have gone into this work. None of this would have been possible without my wonderful agent, Carol Mann, who invited me into a world few people, and even fewer dyslexics, understand: publishing. I am also indebted to Eliza Dreier at the Carol Mann Agency for her feedback and dedication to the project. Through Carol I met the fabulous Marnie Cochran at Ballantine Books, an insightful and dedicated woman of letters who dramatically improved this work with her tireless time and attention. My friend Pam Liflander, a writer, was incalculably helpful working with me to create this book. I would also like to thank my copy editor, Sue Warga, and the team that designed the cover, including Robbin Schiff, Victoria Allen, and Misa Erder, as well as book designer Donna Sinisgalli. Also at Random House, I would like to thank my speaking agents, Kelle Ruden and Jayme Boucher, and Lisa Barnes, Quinn Roger, and Laura Goldin from the publicity, marketing, and legal teams, respectively. I would also like to thank Theresa Zoro, director of publicity, who asked the best question of my pitch meeting: "What should a parent do if they have a dyslexic child?"

For all of their help in bringing this book to fruition, I would especially like to thank Brock and Fernette Eide, who helped me with the first step on the book path. They have continued their efforts to tell the story of dyslexia and talent, convening a fabulous conference with the help of the Emily Hall Tremaine Foundation on the topic in 2013. Stewart Hudson and Jon Tremaine from the Foundation deserve special credit for supporting this effort as well, as do James Wendorf and the staff at the NCLD. I'm greatly in debt to Cynthia Haan, Mike Gerber, Claudia Koochek, Susan Lang, Marshall Raskind, Susan and Alan Raymond, Lisa Schmidt, Jo Anne Simon, and Maryanne Wolf for all their insights on the book and this field. Much thanks to all my great friends at Disability Rights Advocates for teaching me so much about the community of people with disabilities. For guiding me on my path through technology, thanks to my favorite bosses at Intel, Doug Busch and Yoav Hochberg, and to my friend and favorite coach, Andy Grove.

For letting me use their stories and benefit from their wisdom as fellow movement-oriented thinkers, I thank Matthew Bickerton, Alexandra Cantel, Katie Coleman, Pete Denman, Sarah Entine, James Gandolfini, Tracy Johnson, Laura Maloney, Eric McGehearty, Heather McGehearty, Muir Meredith, Chris Ohara, Angela Maria Puccini, Ben Powers, Lou Salsa, Matt Schnepps, Sat Sing, Marcus Soutra, Peggy Stern, Sean Stevens, Vonda Stutts, and Natalie Tamburello.

David Flink is owed a special debt of gratitude from me personally and from everyone in the movement who benefits from his organizing and warmth.

On the personal front I must thank Stacey Abrams, Matt Braithwaite, Kate Brenton, Heidi Burbage, Annette Caldwell, David Carmel, Elizabeth Churchill, Meghan Cleary, Sara D'Angelo, Jonathan Daves, Darren David, and Liana Downey; Asano, Bruce, Emily, and Mei Duncan; Ame Elliot, Aimee Gilbreath, Ben Kleinman, Tracy Knapp, Nalini Kotumraju, Chris Krammer, Alan Kubler, Leah Lamb, Eliza Leighton, Eric Meyerson, Peter Sims, Chloe Sladden, Jim Twiss, Roxanne Williams and Tanya Wischerath. And special thanks to Brooks Burdette for all he did.

I would also like to thank Alexis Filippini for all the love and lessons she has brought me.

Finally, thank you for more than they'll ever know to Steve Walker and to my oldest and best friend, Walter Duncan, forever. And my deepest thanks to my family: Cal, Chris, and the two who have been there with mountains of unconditional love from the start: my dad, Perkins Foss, and my mom, Susan Moore.

NOTES

Introduction

Indeed, 35 percent of American entrepreneurs are dyslexic: J. Logan, "Dyslexic Entrepreneurs: The Incidence; Their Coping Strategies and Their Business Skills," *Dyslexia* 15, 4 (2009): 328–46.

Interestingly, in research conducted in 2003: P. E. Turkeltaub, L. Gareau, D. L. Flowers, T. A. Zeffiro, and G. F. Eden, "Development of Neural Mechanisms for Reading," *Nature Neuroscience* 6, 7 (July 2003): 767–73.

Dr. Manuel Casanova at the University of Louisville School of Medicine: Brock L. Eide and Fernette F. Eide, *The Dyslexic Advantage: Unlocking the Hidden Potential of the Dyslexic Brain* (New York: Plume, 2012), 37–41.

Gershen Kaufman, PhD, a leading psychological expert on the general: Gershen Kaufman, *Shame: The Power of Caring* (Rochester, VT: Schenkman, 1992), 199.

Chapter One: Embrace Your Child's Profile

In 2010, an eight-year-old boy: "Mom: Bullies Drove 8-Year-Old Son to Jump from Second Floor of School," Rucks Russell, KHOU, March 26, 2010, www.khou.com/news/local/Mom-Bullies-drove-8-year-old-son-to-jump-from-second-floor-of-school-89300872.html.

An updated version of the definition of SLD: 20 USC § 1401(26)(A); 34 CFR § 300.7(c)(10).

It first appeared in law as part of the: Children with Specific Learning Disabilities Act of 1969 (CSLD), Public Law 91-230, 45 CFR § 121.2.

In one recent national survey by Roper Worldwide: "Measuring Prog-

ress in Public and Parental Understanding of Learning Disabilities," Roper
Public Affairs and Corporate Communications, September 2010, 30.

I guarantee that dyslexics such as General George S. Patton: Carlo
D'Este, *Patton: A Genius for War* (New York: Harper Perennial, 1995), 85.

Carol Greider discusses her dyslexia in the HBO documentary *Journey into Dyslexia.*

Chapter Two: Discard the Myths

While we got tons of positive media coverage: "Intel Reader Reads
Books to the Lazy and Infirm," www.engadget.com/2009/11/10/intel-
reader-reads-books-to-the-lazy-and-infirm-video, January 28, 2013.

One study from the University of Pennsylvania concluded: J. Baron
and M. F. Norman, "SATs, Achievement Tests, and High-School Class Rank
as Predictors of College Performance," *Educational and Psychology Measurement* 52 (1992).

In 2012, the University of California dropped the SAT Subject Test:
University of California admission policy: http://admission.universityof
california.edu/counselors/q-and-a/policy-change/index.html.

Bates College made the SAT optional: www.bates.edu/news/2005/
10/01/sat-study.

One longitudinal study from Yale tracked: Sally E. Shaywitz, Bennett A. Shaywitz, Jack M. Fletcher, and Michael D. Escobar, "Prevalence
of Reading Disability in Boys and Girls," *Journal of the American Medical
Association* 264, 8 (1990): 998, doi:10.1001/jama.1990

As ignorant as this statement may sound: "Measuring Progress in
Public and Parental Understanding of Learning Disabilities," Roper Public Affairs and Corporate Communications, September 2010, 18.

Interestingly, dyslexia can manifest: W. T. Siok et al, "Biological Abnormality of Impaired Reading Is Constrained by Culture," *Nature* 431
(2004): 71–76.

Chapter Three: Identify Your Child's Strengths

Many of us know about the extreme examples of this thinking: Joseph Shapiro, *No Pity: People with Disabilities Forging a New Civil Rights
Movement* (New York: Three Rivers Press, 1993), 271–72.

In 1904, psychologists Alfred Binet and Theodore Simon: Stephen Jay Gould, *The Mismeasure of Man* (New York: Norton, 1996), 181, 187, 229.

Dr. Robert Brooks, a Harvard Medical School child psychologist: Robert Brooks and Sam Goldstein, *Raising Resilient Children: Fostering Strength, Hope, and Optimism in Your Child* (New York: McGraw-Hill, 2002).

A study from the late 1990s conducted at the Frostig Center: Marshall H. Raskind, Roberta J. Goldberg, Eleanor L. Higgins, and Kenneth L. Herman, "Patterns of Change and Predictors of Success in Individuals with Learning Disabilities: Results from a Twenty-Year Longitudinal Study," *Learning Disabilities Research and Practice* 14, 1 (1999): 35–49.

In a longitudinal study started in 1955 on the Hawaiian island: Emmy E. Werner, *Risk, Resilience, and Recovery: Perspectives from the Kauai Longitudinal Study* (New York: Cambridge University Press, 1993).

One of the most successful dyslexics of the twentieth century: Carlo D'Este, *Patton: A Genius for War* (New York: Harper Perennial, 1995), 84.

Chapter Four: Allow Your Child to Dream Big

However, a recent survey of the literature conducted at Brown University concluded: Lindsey Musen, "Early Reading Proficiency" (2010), Annenberg Institute for School Reform, Brown University, Providence, RI.

Chapter Five: Tell Your Story

Consider Bruce Springsteen. In his sixties: David Remnick, "We Are Alive: Bruce Springsteen at Sixty-Two," *New Yorker*, July 30, 2012.

Chapter Six: A Tool Kit of Accommodations

The research suggests quite the opposite: A. Meyer and D. H. Rose, "The Future Is in the Margins: The Role of Technology and Disability in Educational Reform," in D. H. Rose, A. Meyer, and C. Hitchcock, eds., *The Universally Designed Classroom: Accessible Curriculum and Digital Technologies* (Cambridge, MA: Harvard Education Press, 2005).

A 2006 study from the University of Massachusetts: S. G. Sireci, S. Li, and S. Scarpati, "The Effects of Test Accommodation on Test Performance: A Review of the Literature," Center for Educational Assessment, Research Report no. 485, School of Education, University of Massachusetts, Amherst, 2006.

In 2011, the National Conference of Bar Examiners lost a federal case: *Enyart v. National Conference of Bar Examiners*, 630 F.3d 1153 (2011).

Chapter Seven: Assert Your Rights

Legally, the right to a free and appropriate education that your child now enjoys: The three cases cited are *Brown v. Board of Education*, 347 U.S. 483 (1954), *Pennsylvania Association for Retarded Citizens (PARC) vs. the Commonwealth of Pennsylvania*, 334 F. Supp. 1257 (E.D. PA 1972), and *Mill v. Board of Education of the District of Columbia*, 348 F. Supp. 866 (1972).

In 1997, a seminal case taken up against Boston University: *Guckenberger v. Boston University*, 974 F. Supp. 106 (D. Mass. 1997).

U.S. Department of Education data from 2010 suggest: U.S. Department of Education, OSEP, "Data Tables for OSEP State Reported Data, Part B Child Count (2010)," found at https://www.ideadata.org/arc_toc12.asp#partbCC.

The problem has gotten bad enough that the U.S. Department of Education: Memorandum to State Directors of Special Education, from Melody Musgrove, "A Response to Intervention (RTI) Process Cannot Be Used to Delay-Deny an Evaluation for Eligibility under the Individuals with Disabilities Education Act (IDEA)," U.S. Department of Education, Office of Special Education and Rehabilitative Services, January 21, 2011.

IDEA and U.S. Department of Education regulations regarding Section 504 explain: 29 USC 705(20) (b).

If the school is not willing to identify your child: 20 USC § 1415.

The College Board, the governing body: *Breimhorst v. Educ. Testing Serv.*, No. C-99-3387 (N.D. Cal. Jan. 24, 2001).

Chapter Eight: Is It Time to Exit?

In the 1930s, Kenneth Clark and Mamie Clark: Ludy T. Benjamin Jr., *A Brief History of Modern Psychology* (Oxford: Blackwell, 2007), 193.

One scenario highlighted in the letter directly addressed: Memorandum from the Department of Education Office of Civil Rights re: Prohibited Disability Harassment Reminder of Responsibilities Under Section 504 of the Rehabilitation Act of 1973 and Title II of the Americans with Disabilities Act, July 25, 2000, http://www2.ed.gov/about/offices/list/ocr/docs/disabharassltr.html.

Chapter Nine: Building Community

according to a series of studies performed by the Cass Business School in London: J. Logan, "Dyslexic Entrepreneurs: The Incidence, Their Coping Strategies and Their Business Skills," *Dyslexia* 15, 4 (2009): 328–46.

The best definition of leadership I've heard: Course materials for "Intel—Leadership for Extraordinary Performance," Jack Weber and Carol Weber, University of Virginia, Darden School of Business, Feb. 4–8, 2008.

There are many well-known dyslexic entrepreneurs: Betsy Morris, "Overcoming Dyslexia," *Fortune*, May 13, 2002, http://money.cnn.com/magazines/fortune/fortune_archive/2002/05/13/322876/index.htm.

Combining his knowledge of speech software: Larry Greenemeier, "Chipmaker Races to Save Stephen Hawking's Speech as His Condition Deteriorates," *Scientific American*, Jan. 18, 2012, www.scientificamerican.com/article.cfm?id=intel-helps-hawking-communicate.

A study in Texas indicated that 41 percent of the prison population: Tony Fabelo, James Austin, and Angela Gunter, *The Impact of Ignoring Dyslexia and Reading Disabilities in the Criminal Justice System: What We Know and Need to Know*, report to the Dyslexia Research Foundation of Texas, April 2004, JFA Associates/The Institute.

Joe Stutts grew up in rural Alabama and had a terrible: Interview with Joe Stutts in the documentary *Headstrong: Inside the Hidden World of Dyslexia and Attention Deficit/Hyperactivity Disorder*, San Francisco, 2007, www.headstrongnation.org/documentary.

In 1983, a three-judge federal appeals court: *Stutts v. Freeman*, 694 F. 2d 666, Court of Appeals, 11th Circuit 1983.

INDEX

ABOUT THE AUTHOR

BEN FOSS is a prominent entrepreneur and activist and the founder of Headstrong Nation, a not-for-profit organization serving the dyslexic community. Foss graduated from Wesleyan University and earned a JD/MBA from Stanford Law and Business Schools. He invented the Intel® Reader, a mobile device that takes photos of text and recites it aloud on the spot. Foss is a cofounder of Integration Ventures, a venture capital firm that is looking to invest in dyslexic entrepreneurs. He has been featured in *The New York Times, The Wall Street Journal,* and on Fox Business, as well as ABC, CNN, HBO and the BBC. Represented by the Random House Speakers Bureau, he regularly speaks to Fortune 500 companies, public policy organizations, and colleges and universities across the country.

ABOUT THE TYPE

This book was set in Minion, a 1990 Adobe Originals typeface by Robert Slimbach. Minion is inspired by classical, old style typefaces of the late Renaissance, a period of elegant, beautiful, and highly readable type designs. Created primarily for text setting, Minion combines the aesthetic and functional qualities that make text type highly readable with the versatility of digital technology.